JUDGMENT IN MANAGERIAL DECISION MAKING

SIXTH EDITION

Max H. Bazerman
Harvard Business School

JOHN WILEY & SONS, INC.

Publisher *Judith Joseph*
Acquisition Editor *Jayme Heffler*
Marketing Manager *Heather King*
Editorial Assistant *Ame Esterline*
Production Manager *Pam Kennedy*
Production Editors *Kelly Tavares, Sarah Wofman-Robichaud*
Managing Editor *Kevin Dodds*
Layout Editor *Wendy Stokes Hodge*
Cover Designer *Benjamin Reece*
Cover Photo Credits © *Royalty-Free/CORBIS*

This book was set in 10/12 New Caledonia by Leyh Publishing LLC, and printed and bound by Courier Westford. The cover was printed by Phoenix Color.

This book is printed on acid-free paper. ∞

ISBN 0-471-68430-9

Printed in the United States of America

10 9 8 7 6 5 4 3 2

Dedicated to
Dolly Chugh and Mahzarin R. Banaji
My primary teachers of
the new ideas in this edition

PREFACE

Between 1981 and 1983, I served on the faculty of Boston University. At the time, I was conducting laboratory studies on decision biases in negotiation. Behavioral decision research did not exist as a topic of study in most management schools. The faculty at Boston University provided me with a number of excellent colleagues, and yet they knew very little about the emerging research on judgment. This lack of awareness in colleagues that I respected motivated me to write this book. I wanted to make the area of judgment a more central part of the management literature. I also wanted to present this information to managers, students, and researchers in an interesting manner that would improve their judgment capabilities. I wrote the first edition of this book with no vision that I would be revising it to create the sixth edition twenty years later.

Behavioral decision research has developed considerably over the past twenty-five years, and now provides important insights into managerial behavior. This book embeds behavioral decision research into the organizational realm by examining judgment in a variety of managerial contexts. The audience for this book is anyone who is interested in improving his or her judgment and decision making. The first five editions were used in economics, psychology, decision making, negotiations, and organizational behavior courses, and in a variety of executive programs as well. For the psychology audience, the book offers a systematic framework for using psychological findings to improve judgment. For the economics audience, the book offers a critique of the classic economic model of decision making. And for the consumer, management, and financial communities, this book creates opportunities to make better decisions.

In the first edition, I noted that many fine colleagues influenced my early understanding of judgment: Joel Brockner, Ed Conlon, Hank Farber, Toni Wegner, Harry Katz, Tom Kochan, Leigh McAlister, Bob McKersie, Maggie Neale, Jeff Rubin, Bill Samuelson, and David Schoorman. Four people read the entire original manuscript and provided extremely helpful feedback and support during the three years of its creation: John Carroll, Marla Felcher, Tim Hall, and Roy Lewicki. Each helped in critical ways as I was assembling my initial organization of the decision-making field.

In July 1985, just as I was finishing the first edition, I joined Northwestern University, which provided me with an exciting research and teaching environment for fifteen years. Since then, Harvard University has provided a wonderful set of new colleagues, activities, and ideas. My interactions with excellent colleagues have been the primary source of ideas that have improved later editions of this book. These colleagues include Mahzarin Banaji, Jon Baron, Yoella Bereby-Meyer, Sally Blount, Iris Bohnet, Jeanne Brett, Art Brief, Eugene Caruso, Tina Diekmann, Nick Epley, Steve Garcia, Dedre Gentner, Dan Gilbert, James Gillespie, Linda Ginzel, Brit Grosskopf, Andy Hoffman, Chris Hsee, Lorraine Idson, Don Jacobs, Boaz Keysar, Tom Kochan,

Terri Kurtzberg, George Loewenstein, Beta Mannix, Kathleen McGinn, Doug Medin, David Messick, Don Moore, Simone Moran, Keith Murnighan, Howard Raiffa, Lee Ross, Al Roth, Holly Schroth, Pri Shah, Harris Sondak, Ann Tenbrunsel, Leigh Thompson, Cathy Tinsley, Mike Tushman, Kimberly Wade-Benzoni, Michael Watkins, and Dan Wegner.

A dramatic improvement in this book occurred between the first and second editions as a result of the excellent critical review and editing of Sally Blount. Sally (when she was a graduate student at Kellogg) provided a detailed critique of each chapter, offered specific reorganizing suggestions, and drafted numerous changes that improved the book. The third edition added a new chapter (now Chapter 6) on fairness and social comparison processes. The fourth edition added a new chapter on motivational biases (now Chapter 4). The fifth edition added a new chapter that applies the book's core concepts to the domain of investing (Chapter 7). This chapter benefited from very insightful input from three dedicated and excellent readers: Don Moore, Terry Odean, and Jason Zweig.

The sixth edition now adds chapters on bounded ethicality (Chapter 8) and bounded awareness (Chapter 11). Both of these chapters are based on my recent writing with Dolly Chugh and Mahzarin Banaji. Since I joined Harvard in 2000, Dolly and Mahzarin have profoundly changed my understanding of how we make decisions, and this new understanding dominates these chapters. These chapters also incorporate recent research that I have done with Yoella Bereby-Meyer, Eugene Caruso, Nick Epley, Brit Grosskopf, Lorraine Idson, George Loewenstein, Don Moore, Simone Moran, Lloyd Tanlu, and others. Don Moore, Nick Epley, Dolly Chugh, and Tara Abbatello offered important suggestions on the revisions for the sixth edition, and Hayley Barna served as a brilliant research assistant, finding specific examples of how the field has changed and improved in the last four years. Of course, in addition to the two new chapters, I have updated the entire book with new ideas, examples, and applications.

Finally, the book has benefited from fantastic editorial help. Katie Shonk has researched, edited, or rewritten most of my work over the last fifteen years, including multiple editions of this book. My most significant skill in the writing domain is to realize that Katie is a much better writer than I am, and to value her skill sufficiently to allow it to show in my work.

In sum, this book has been enriched by my interactions with an unusually large number of people. Perhaps my most important skills are my ability to persuade excellent people to work with me and my ability to appreciate their innovative ideas. I believe that these skills have helped to create a book that will improve the decision-making skills of its readers, and I hope you agree.

Max H. Bazerman
Harvard Business School

Contents

Introduction to Manageri&
Decision Making

On October 16, 2001, energy-trading company Enron announced that it had lost $618 million in the third quarter of 2001 and overstated its earnings by $1.2 billion, or about 20 percent, over the previous three years. Through the use of off-balance-sheet partnerships engineered by former Enron Chief Financial Officer Andrew Fastow, Enron hid its debt to increase its stock price. News of Enron's scandal and the involvement of its auditor, Arthur Andersen, covered the front page of newspapers nationwide. Enron's stock plunged, and soon the company had become the largest corporate bankruptcy in U.S. history. Stockholders and former Enron employees left without pensions filed civil lawsuits against both Enron and Andersen for deceptive practices. The question "Where were the auditors?" became a common refrain in the media. In March 2002, the Department of Justice sued Andersen for obstruction of justice for the shredding of Enron documents that occurred in the auditing firm's Houston office in the face of Securities and Exchange Commission investigations.

Enron was not Andersen's only concern. In June 2001, the SEC sued Andersen for issuing false audit reports on behalf of Waste Management Inc. and covering up the misdeeds of some of the company's former top executives. Andersen also faced questions about its earlier auditing of Sunbeam and the Baptist Foundation of Arizona. In June 2002, Andersen was found guilty in its federal case of obstruction of justice. Hours later, Andersen announced the end of its auditing practice. The once-venerable company had collapsed.

The auditing partners at Andersen, like the partners of other audit firms held liable for similar negligence, are very bright people. In addition, I believe that, evidence of document shredding to the contrary, most of them are very honest people. How did a prominent auditing firm with a reputation for intelligence and integrity fail to see that so many of its clients were misrepresenting earnings by hundreds of millions of dollars? Critics of the profession suggest that auditor neglect and corruption are to blame. I argue that audit failures rarely result from deliberate collusion between the auditor and the client. Rather, most audit failures result from systematic biases in judgment.

While I write about Enron with the benefit of hindsight (see Chapter 2), I offered a similar analysis of the case of Phar-Mor and Coopers and Lybrand in the previous edition of this book. In addition, in 1997, my coauthors and I wrote an article entitled "The Impossibility of Auditor Independence" in which we argued that, when evaluating accounting scandals, it is a mistake to focus solely on auditor corruption. We believe that bias arises not only when auditors report their judgments, but long beforehand—at the unconscious stage where decisions are made. For this reason, we wrote that "audit failures are the natural product of the auditor-client relationship." Finally, we argued then, as I continue to argue now, "Under current institutional arrangements, it is psychologically impossible for auditors to maintain their objectivity; cases of audit failure are inevitable, even with the most honest auditors" (Bazerman, Morgan, and Loewenstein, 1997). In 2000, I presented these opinions on auditor independence at the SEC's hearings on the topic.

My views about the impossibility of auditor independence are based on extensive psychological research on the "self-serving bias." Research demonstrates that when professionals are asked to make impartial judgments, those judgments are likely to be unconsciously and powerfully biased according to the individual's self-interest. People tend to form a preference for a certain outcome and then justify this preference on the basis of fairness.

Chapter 8 of this book will provide substantial evidence that it is psychologically impossible for auditors to maintain their objectivity. Cases of audit failure are inevitable, even from the most honest of firms. The expectation of objective judgment from an auditor hired by the client is unrealistic. Although deliberate misreporting can occur, bias more typically becomes an unconscious, unintentional factor at the stage where judgments are made. When people are called upon to make impartial decisions, judgments are likely to be unconsciously and powerfully biased in a manner commensurate with the judge's self-interest. The self-serving bias exists because people are imperfect information processors. One of the most important subjective influences on information processing is self-interest. People tend to confuse what is personally beneficial with what is fair or moral.

Enron is not the only disaster that we can trace to failed decision making. Faulty decisions played an important role in the weakness of the U.S. aviation security system that allowed terrorists to use airplanes as weapons on September 11, 2001. The U.S. government knew terrorists were willing to become martyrs for their cause and that they hated the United States. The World Trade Center had been bombed in 1993, and in 1994 terrorists hijacked an Air France airplane and tried to turn it into a missile aimed at the Eiffel Tower. In 1995, terrorists failed in an attempt to hijack twelve U.S. commercial airplanes in Asia at the same time. In addition, the general public knew how simple it was to board an airplane with items, such as small knives, that could be used as weapons. In 1997, Vice President Al Gore's aviation security commission put all of this data together and provided comprehensive evidence that the system was full of holes. Yet despite the warning signs, the Clinton administration did little to improve airline safety.

In the summer of 2001, the new Bush administration received a variety of information of more imminent danger, including the now-famous August 6, 2001, President Daily Briefing entitled "Bin Laden Determined to Strike in U.S." President Bush later said, "Had I known there was going to be an attack on America I would have moved mountains to stop the attack" (*New York Times*, 18 April 2004, p. 1). Unfortunately, terrorists do not send their game plans in advance. Our leaders and their advisers need to do some of the thinking for themselves.

I am not claiming that anyone in the Clinton or Bush administrations or the intelligence agencies knew that four airplanes would be used to attack New York and Washington, that both World Trade towers would fall, that the Pentagon would be hit, and that thousands would die. But our leaders did have all of the data they needed to know that dangerous deficiencies in airline security existed (Bazerman and Watkins, 2004). Any reasonable analysis would have dictated that the cockpit doors of every aircraft in the United States be sealed and that knives and other weapons be prohibited on airplanes.

Why weren't these and other essential security measures taken? We now know the FBI and CIA failed to communicate effectively. We also know that the airlines and their trade organization spent millions of dollars to lobby to prevent the government from improving the aviation security system, due to the cost and expected backlash from passengers. But the problem was caused at least in part by systematic biases in the decision processes of key actors in leadership positions. My recent book with Michael Watkins, *Predictable Surprises*, argues that the human tendency to maintain positive illusions, to make self-serving interpretations, to discount research evidence, and to overlook easily available and relevant information contributed to the "predictable surprise" of September 11. In this book, I will provide details on how these biases affect the judgment of all professionals on a regular basis.

My goal in this book is to clarify the common errors that even very bright people make on a regular basis, errors that partially explain September 11 and the fall of Enron, as well as daily crises in the organizations that surround you. What advice was available to Andersen, the SEC, and ethically minded CEOs? How about to the Bush administration and the CIA? This book will introduce you to a number of cognitive biases that are predictable and likely to affect the judgment of auditors, government officials, and you as well. By identifying cognitive biases and suggesting strategies for overcoming them, this book gives executives the skills they need to improve their judgment. By understanding and limiting biases in your decision-making patterns, you can become a better decision maker and protect yourself, your family, and your organization from avoidable mistakes.

THE ANATOMY OF DECISIONS

Judgment refers to the cognitive aspects of the decision-making process. To fully understand judgment, we first need to identify the components of the decision-making process that require it. To get started, consider the following decision situations:

- You are finishing your MBA at a well-known school. Your credentials are quite good, and you expect to obtain job offers from a number of consulting firms. How are you going to select the right job?

- You are the director of the marketing division of a rapidly expanding consumer company. You need to hire a product manager for a new "secret" product that the company plans to introduce to the market in fifteen months. How will you go about hiring the appropriate individual?

- As the owner of a venture capital firm, you have a number of proposals that meet your preliminary considerations but only a limited budget with which to fund new projects. Which projects will you fund?

- You are on the corporate acquisition staff of a large conglomerate that is interested in acquiring a small-to-moderate-sized firm in the oil industry. What firm, if any, will you advise the company to acquire?

What do these scenarios have in common? Each one proposes a problem, and each problem has a number of alternative solutions. Let us look at six steps you should take, either implicitly or explicitly, when applying a "rational" decision-making process to each scenario.

1. **Define the problem.** The problem has been fairly well specified in each of the four scenarios. However, managers often act without a thorough understanding of the problem to be solved, leading them to solve the wrong problem. Accurate judgment is required to identify and define the problem. Managers often err by (a) defining the problem in terms of a proposed solution, (b) missing a bigger problem, or (c) diagnosing the problem in terms of its symptoms. Our goal should be to solve the problem, not just eliminate its temporary symptoms.

2. **Identify the criteria.** Most decisions require the decision maker to accomplish more than one objective. When buying a car, you may want to maximize fuel economy, minimize cost, maximize comfort, and so on. The rational decision maker will identify all relevant criteria in the decision-making process.

3. **Weight the criteria.** Different criteria will be of varying importance to a decision maker. Rational decision makers will know the relative value they place on each of the criteria identified (for example, the relative importance of fuel economy versus cost versus comfort).

4. **Generate alternatives.** The fourth step in the decision-making process requires identification of possible courses of action. Decision makers often spend an inappropriate amount of search time seeking alternatives, thus creating a barrier to effective decision making. An optimal search continues only until the cost of the search outweighs the value of the added information.

5. **Rate each alternative on each criterion.** How well will each of the alternative solutions achieve each of the defined criteria? This is often the most difficult stage of the decision-making process, as it typically requires us to forecast future events. The rational decision maker will be able to carefully assess the potential consequences of selecting each of the alternative solutions on each of the identified criteria.

6. **Compute the optimal decision.** Ideally, after all of the first five steps have been completed, the process of computing the optimal decision consists of (1) multiplying the ratings in step 5 by the weight of each criterion, (2) adding up the weighted ratings across all of the criteria for each alternative, and (3) choosing the solution with the highest sum of the weighted ratings.

The model of decision making just presented assumes that we follow these six steps in a fully "rational" manner. That is, decision makers are assumed to (1) perfectly define the problem, (2) identify all criteria, (3) accurately weigh all of the criteria according to their preferences, (4) know all relevant alternatives, (5) accurately assess each alternative based on each criterion, and (6) accurately calculate and choose the alternative with the highest perceived value.

There is nothing special about these six steps. Different researchers specify different steps—which typically overlap a great deal. For example, in a wonderful book on rational decision making, Hammond, Keeney, and Raiffa (1999) suggest eight steps: (1) work on the right problem, (2) specify your objectives, (3) create imaginative alternatives, (4) understand the consequences, (5) grapple with your tradeoffs, (6) clarify your uncertainties, (7) think hard about your risk tolerance, and (8) consider linked decisions. Both of these lists provide a useful order for thinking about what an optimal decision-making process might look like.

SYSTEM 1 AND SYSTEM 2 THINKING

Do people actually reason in the logical manner described above? Sometimes, but not most of the time. Stanovich and West (2000) make a useful distinction between System 1 and System 2 cognitive functioning. System 1 thinking refers to our intuitive system, which is typically fast, automatic, effortless, implicit, and emotional. We make most decisions in life using System 1 thinking. By contrast, System 2 refers to reasoning that is slower, conscious, effortful, explicit, and logical (Kahneman, 2003). Hammond, Keeney, and Raiffa's logical steps above provide a prototype of System 2 thinking. The busier and more rushed people are, the more they have on their minds, and the more likely they are to rely on System 1 thinking. The frantic pace of managerial life suggests that executives often rely on System 1 thinking (Chugh, 2004). Clearly, a complete System 2 process is not required for every decision we make. In most situations, our System 1 thinking is quite sufficient; it would be impractical, for example, to logically reason through every choice we make while shopping for groceries. But System 2 logic should preferably influence our most important decisions. One key goal for managers is to identify situations in which they should move from the intuitively compelling System 1 thinking to the more logical System 2.

Many readers have a great deal of trust in their intuition—their System 1 thinking. To prepare for the rest of the book, which is designed to challenge this confidence, consider the following diagram from Shepard (1990):

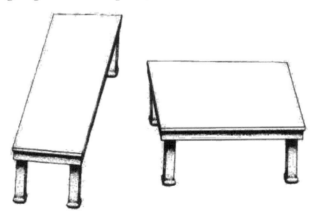

I trust that, like most people, you view the table on the right to be more of a square than the one on the left, which appears to be longer and skinnier. Well, your System 1 processing is failing you, as it fails most people in this instance. Don't believe me? Try this System 2 strategy: put a sheet of paper over the drawing and trace the top of either table. Now line up your tracing over the other table, and see how your intuition has failed you!

Throughout this book, I will provide you with plenty of other reasons to question your intuition. Even the brightest people make judgmental errors on a regular basis. These errors, or biases, are much more likely to occur in System 1 thinking than in System 2. At the same time, any System 2 process will use some System 1 (intuitive) inputs. In fact, the two systems frequently work in tandem, the quick initial response of System 1 modified after more in-depth consideration by System 2. Sometimes, however, System 2 thinking does not fully adjust. For example, people have been shown to be loath to eat sugar out of a container labeled "cyanide" even if they saw the sugar being poured into the container and wrote the label themselves (Rozin, Markwith, and Ross, 1990). System 1 thinking intuitively, but mistakenly, leads people to feel a strong aversion to tasting the sugar. Even after rational, System 2 thinking, subjects will try to avoid what they logically know and admit is completely safe. Because of this dual system, the biases we will discuss influence all decision making, but we can identify the conditions in which they are most likely to have a dysfunctional impact.

THE BOUNDS OF DECISION MAKING

In this book, the term *rationality* refers to the decision-making process that is logically expected to lead to the optimal result, given an accurate assessment of the decision maker's values and risk preferences. The rational model is based on a set of assumptions that prescribe how a decision *should* be made rather than describing how a decision *is* made. In his Nobel Prize–winning work, Simon (1957; March and Simon, 1958) suggested that individual judgment is bounded in its rationality and that we can better understand decision making by explaining actual, rather than normative ("what would rationally be done"), decision processes. While the bounded-rationality framework views individuals as attempting to make rational decisions, it acknowledges that decision makers often lack important information on the definition of the problem, the relevant criteria, and so on. Time and cost constraints limit the quantity and quality of available information. Furthermore, decision makers retain only a relatively small amount of information in their usable memory. Finally, limitations on intelligence and perceptions constrain the ability of decision makers to accurately "calculate" the optimal choice from the information that is available. Together, these limitations prevent decision makers from making the optimal decisions assumed by the rational model. The irrational decisions that result typically reflect a reliance on intuitive biases that overlook the full range of possible consequences. Decision makers will forgo the best solution in favor of one that is acceptable or reasonable. That is, decision makers *satisfice*. Rather than examining all possible alternatives, they simply search until they find a solution that meets a certain acceptable level of performance.

The field of decision making can be loosely divided into two parts: the study of prescriptive models and the study of descriptive models. Prescriptive decision scientists develop methods for making optimal decisions. For example, they might suggest a mathematical model to help a decision maker act more rationally. Descriptive decision researchers consider the bounded ways in which decisions are actually made. Why use a descriptive approach when a prescriptive approach should lead to an optimal decision? My answer is that, while there is plenty of good advice available, most people do not follow it. Why not? Because we fall victim to a variety of predictable errors that not only destroy our intuition, but also hinder our tendency to implement good advice. We need to understand these mistakes before moving on to wiser decision strategies.

Although the concepts of bounded rationality and satisficing are important in showing that judgment deviates from rationality, they do not tell us *how* judgment will be biased. These concepts help decision makers identify situations in which they may be acting on the basis of limited information, but they do not help diagnose the specific systematic, directional biases that affect our judgment. Fifteen years after the publication of Simon's work, Tversky and Kahneman (1974) continued what he had begun. They provided critical information about specific systematic biases that influence judgment. Their work, and work that followed, led to our modern understanding of judgment. Specifically, researchers have found that people rely on a number of simplifying strategies, or rules of thumb, in making decisions. These simplifying strategies are called heuristics. As the standard rules that implicitly direct our judgment, heuristics serve as a mechanism for coping with the complex environment surrounding our decisions. In general, heuristics are helpful, but their use can sometimes lead to severe errors. A central goal of this book is to identify and illustrate these heuristics and the biases that can result from them in the managerial setting. I will use examples of a variety of heuristics and biases to explain how people deviate from a fully rational decision-making process in individual and competitive situations.

Between 1957 and 2000, bounded rationality served as the integrating concept of the field of behavioral decision research. With time, we have refined and clarified this thinking. In 2000, Thaler suggested that decision making is bounded in two ways not precisely captured by the concept of bounded rationality. First, our willpower is bounded, such that we tend to give greater weight to present concerns than to future concerns. As a result, our temporary motivations are often inconsistent with our long-term interests in a variety of ways, such as the common failure to save adequately for retirement (this will be developed in Chapters 4 and 7). Second, Thaler suggests that our self-interest is bounded; unlike the stereotypic economic actor, we care about the outcomes of others (this will be developed in Chapter 6).

More recently, two other important bounds have been added to the list. First, Chugh, Bazerman, and Banaji (2005) have introduced the concept of bounded ethicality, which refers to the notion that our ethics are limited in ways we are not even aware of ourselves. Bounded ethicality will be developed in a chapter new to this edition, Chapter 8. Second, my colleague Dolly Chugh has developed the concept of bounded awareness (Bazerman and Chugh, 2005) to refer to the broad category of focusing failures, or ways in which we fail to notice obvious and important information that is available to us. Bounded awareness is also developed in a new chapter for this edition, Chapter 11. Overall, this book develops a systematic structure for understanding the bounds to our decision making, including bounded rationality, bounded willpower, bounded self-interest, bounded ethicality, and bounded awareness.

INTRODUCTION TO JUDGMENTAL HEURISTICS

Consider the following example:

> While finishing an advanced degree in computer science, Marla Bannon put together a Web-based retailing concept that many of her colleagues consider to be one of the best ever developed. While the product is great, Marla has far less skill in marketing her ideas. She decides to hire a marketing MBA with experience in Web-based environments to formalize the business plan she will use to approach venture capitalists. Marla follows the heuristic of limiting her search to new MBAs from the top six management schools. How would you evaluate her strategy?

If we evaluate this strategy in terms of the degree to which it follows the rational model outlined earlier, Marla's heuristic of limiting her search to six schools will be deficient, because her search will not be complete. Her heuristic may eliminate the best possible candidates from consideration if they do not attend one of the top schools. However, the heuristic also has some benefits. While it could eliminate the best choice, the expected time savings of focusing on only six schools may outweigh any potential loss resulting from Marla's limited search strategy. For this reason, this job search heuristic could produce more good decisions than bad ones. In fact, economists would argue that individuals use heuristics such as this because the benefit of time saved often outweighs the costs of any potential reduction in the quality of the decision.

Heuristics provide time-pressured managers and other professionals with a simple way of dealing with a complex world, usually producing correct or partially correct judgments. In addition, it may be inevitable that people will adopt some way of simplifying decisions. The only drawback of these heuristics is that individuals frequently are unaware that they rely on them. Unfortunately, the misapplication of heuristics to inappropriate situations leads people astray. When managers become aware of the potential adverse impact of using heuristics, they will be able to decide when and where to use them and, if it is to their advantage, eliminate certain heuristics from their cognitive repertoire.

People use a variety of types of heuristics. The poker player follows the heuristic "never play for an inside straight." The mortgage banker follows the heuristic "spend only 35 percent of your income on housing." Although an understanding of these specific heuristics is important to the poker player and mortgage banker, our concern in this book is with more general cognitive heuristics that affect virtually everyone. Thus, the heuristics described next are not specific to particular individuals; rather, research has shown that they can be applied across the population. The three general heuristics that we will focus on are (1) the availability heuristic, (2) the representativeness heuristic, and (3) the affect heuristic.

The Availability Heuristic

People assess the frequency, probability, or likely causes of an event by the degree to which instances or occurrences of that event are readily "available" in memory (Tversky and Kahneman, 1973). An event that evokes emotions and is vivid, easily imagined, and specific will be more available than an event that is unemotional in nature, bland, difficult to imagine, or vague. For example, a subordinate who works in close proximity to the manager's office will receive a more critical performance evaluation at year-end than a worker who sits down the hall, since the manager will be more aware of the nearby subordinate's errors. Similarly, a product manager will base her assessment of the probability of a new product's success on her recollection of the successes and failures of similar products in the recent past. Peter Lynch, the former director of Fidelity's Magellan Fund (one of the two largest mutual funds), argues in favor of buying stock in firms that are unavailable in the minds of most investors (for example, due to their blandness) because the more available the stock is, the more overvalued it will be. The availability heuristic can be a very useful managerial decision-making strategy, since instances of events of greater frequency are generally revealed more easily in our minds than less frequent events. Consequently, this heuristic will often lead to accurate judgment. This heuristic is fallible, however, because the availability of information is also affected by factors unrelated to the objective frequency of the judged event. These irrelevant factors can inappropriately influence an event's immediate perceptual salience, the vividness with which it is revealed, or the ease with which it is imagined.

The Representativeness Heuristic

When making a judgment about an individual (or object or event), people tend to look for traits an individual may have that correspond with previously formed stereotypes. "A botanist assigns a plant to one species rather than another by using this judgment strategy," wrote Nisbett and Ross (1980, p. 7). "The plant is categorized as belonging to the species that its principal features most nearly resemble." In this case, the degree to which the unknown plant is representative of a known species of plant is the best information available to the botanist. Managers also use the representativeness heuristic. They predict a person's performance based on an established category of persons that the focal individual represents for them. They predict the success of a new product based on the similarity of that product to past successful and unsuccessful product types. In some cases, the use of the heuristic is a good first-cut approximation. In other cases, it leads to behavior that many of us find irrational and morally reprehensible— like discrimination. A clear problem is that individuals tend to rely on such strategies even when information is insufficient and when better information exists with which to make an accurate judgment.

The Affect Heuristic

Most of our judgments are evoked by an affective, or emotional, evaluation that occurs even before any cognitive reasoning takes place (Kahneman, 2003). While these affective evaluations often are not conscious, Slovic, Finucane, Peters, and MacGregor (2002) provide evidence that people nonetheless use them as the basis of their decisions rather than engaging in a more complete analysis and reasoning process. A manifestation of System 1 thinking, the affect heuristic is all the more likely to be used when people are busy or under time constraints (Gilbert, 2002). Hsee (1998) has shown that people place a greater value on an overfilled small cup of ice cream than an underfilled larger cup, even when the latter has more ice cream in it. Why? The smaller cup creates a positive affect (or satisfaction) by being overfilled, while the underfilling of a larger cup creates a negative affect (dissatisfaction). Yet, when people are presented with both options, reasoning (System 2 thinking) takes place, and they assign greater value to the cup with more ice cream. Similarly, appraisals of potential employees can be affected by a wide variety of variables that influence the manager's affect, independent of applicant quality. These variables could include how a candidate compares to the previous applicant, the mood of the manager, or the degree to which the applicant reminded the manager of a recently divorced spouse. Environmental conditions that change affect can also influence decision making. It has been shown that stock prices go up on sunny days, presumably due to the good mood and optimism induced by the weather. So while affect can be a good guide, when it replaces more reflective decision making it can prevent you from making optimal choices.

In a related vein, Kahneman, Schkade, and Sunstein (1998) use the term "outrage heuristic" to describe the fact that legal awards are highly predicted by the jury's affective outrage at the defendant's behavior, rather than simply by logical reasoning about the harm created by the defendant. Like Kahneman and Frederick (2002), I see significant overlap between the affect heuristic and the outrage heuristic; in this book, I will focus on the more general affect heuristic. Chapters 3, 4, and 6 will develop the affect heuristic in more detail.

AN OUTLINE OF THINGS TO COME

The main objective of this book is to improve the reader's judgment. How can the book help improve Marla Bannon's judgment? First, we must identify the errors in her intuitive judgment, making her aware of biases that are likely to affect her decision. This awareness will improve her current decision-making process and lead to a more beneficial outcome. However, Lewin (1947) suggests that in order for change to occur and last over time, the individual must do more than simply be aware of imperfections. For change to be successful, Lewin argues, it is necessary to (1) get the individual to "unfreeze" existing decision-making processes, (2) provide the content necessary for change, and (3) create the conditions that "refreeze" new processes, thus making the change part of the manager's standard repertoire. This book will attempt to unfreeze your present decision-making processes by demonstrating how your judgment systematically deviates from rationality. You will also be given tools to allow you to change your decision-making processes. Finally, the book will discuss methods that you can use to refreeze your thinking to ensure that the changes will last.

Nisbett and Ross (1980, pp. xi–xii) write:

> One of philosophy's oldest paradoxes is the apparent contradiction between the greatest triumphs and the dramatic failures of the human mind. The same organism that routinely solves inferential problems too subtle and complex for the mightiest computers often makes errors in the simplest of judgments about everyday events. The errors, moreover, often seem traceable to violations of the same inferential rules that underlie people's most impressive successes....How can any creature skilled enough to build and maintain complex organizations, or sophisticated enough to appreciate the nuances of social intercourse, be foolish enough to mouth racist clichés or spill its lifeblood in pointless wars?

While Nisbett and Ross refer to the general population, the essence of their question defines a fascinating issue for the field of managerial effectiveness. This book views managers as intelligent employees who have been generally successful, but whose decisions are biased in ways that seriously compromise their potential. The reader will see how habit forces us into a set of hard-to-break heuristics, imposing constraints on our decision-making effectiveness.

Before individuals can change their decision-making processes, they must be convinced that elements of their cognitive repertoire could use improvement—that is, the unfreezing process must occur. "Why should I change my existing decision-making processes when I've been so successful throughout my managerial career?" the reader might ask. In response to this very appropriate question, I include a number of experiential decision-making items that encourage the reader to personally identify with the biases that are discussed. In presenting this material to MBA and executive students in a classroom setting, I have found that many individuals are initially offended by being "tricked" by an "ivory tower" academic. It might be helpful to clarify at the outset that my intention is not to insult the reader, but to help identify and communicate biases that generally affect human judgment. Perhaps one reason for my personal interest in this material lies in my discomfort with the fact that many of these "evil" biases affect my own personal judgment.

Chapters 2 through 8 focus on individual decision making. In these chapters, little attention is given to the fact that many managerial decisions are made in conjunction with other individuals. Instead, the focus is simply on how individuals approach decisions. Chapters 9 and 10 reexamine judgment in the context of negotiation. Chapter 11, new to this edition of the book, overviews research on the failure to notice critical information that would significantly change our decisions. Chapter 12 summarizes the book's arguments and focuses on how to incorporate the changes suggested throughout into the reader's decision-making processes. Specifically, the remaining chapters will focus on the following:

Chapter 2. This chapter identifies and illustrates a series of specific biases that affect the judgment of virtually all managers. These biases are caused by the three heuristics described in this chapter. Quiz items and short scenarios demonstrate these biases and emphasize their prevalence.

Chapter 3. Among the most striking biases in the decision literature are problems that lead managers to reverse their preference based on information that they would agree should not affect their behavior. This chapter will examine how the framing of information affects decisions.

Chapter 4. Are there biases that are created by the self-serving motivations of individuals, rather than by purely cognitive mistakes? This chapter complements the presentation of cognitive biases in Chapters 1, 2, 3, and 5 with an overview of "motivated biases."

Chapter 5. There is much evidence that managerial decision makers who commit themselves to a particular course of action may make subsequent nonoptimal decisions in order to justify their previous commitment. This chapter examines the research evidence and psychological explanations for this behavior. We will see how escalation has a significant effect in a variety of managerial domains, including new product development, bank loans, and performance appraisal.

Chapter 6. When do people care about fairness? When will individuals accept nonoptimal outcomes in order to maintain fairness? This chapter examines how we think about fairness and explores inconsistencies in our assessments of fairness.

Chapter 7. Perhaps the research area that has been most influenced by decision research has been behavioral finance. In the last decade, we have learned a great deal about the mistakes that investors commonly make. This chapter will explore these mistakes and apply the messages of the book to help readers become wiser investors.

Chapter 8. This chapter connects the concept of bounded ethicality to the decision-making field. We will examine how decision making provides a useful approach for understanding managerial ethics and identify specific ways in which our ethical judgments deviate from our ethical standards.

Chapter 9. This chapter outlines a framework to help the reader think about two-party negotiations. The focus is on how you can make decisions to maximize the joint gain available in a two-party decision-making situation, while simultaneously thinking about how to obtain as much of that joint gain as possible for yourself.

Chapter 10. This chapter looks at the judgmental mistakes we make in negotiations. The resulting framework shows how consumers, managers, salespersons, and society as a whole can benefit simultaneously by debiasing their negotiations.

Chapter 11. This chapter examines how the amazing ability of the human mind to focus can prevent us from seeing information that is readily available and important. We will review new research on bounded awareness that show systematic ways in which our sharp focus degrades the quality of our decisions.

Chapter 12. The final chapter evaluates six explicit strategies for improving judgment: (1) acquiring expertise, (2) debiasing, (3) analogical reasoning, (4) finding an outside view, (5) using linear models, and (6) adjusting for the biases of other decision makers. This chapter will teach you how to use the information in this book to create permanent improvements in your future decisions.

CHAPTER TWO

Common Biases

*P*eople make mistakes. More interestingly, people make a variety of systematic and predictable mistakes. The predictability of these mistakes means that once we identify them, we can learn to avoid them. As explained in Chapter 1, individuals develop rules of thumb, or heuristics, to reduce the information-processing demands of decision making. By providing managers with efficient ways of dealing with complex problems, heuristics produce good decisions a significant proportion of the time. However, heuristics also can lead managers to make systematically biased mistakes. Cognitive bias occurs in situations in which an individual inappropriately applies a heuristic when making a decision.

By highlighting a number of mistakes that even very smart people make on a regular basis, this chapter offers you the opportunity to audit your own decision-making process and identify the biases that affect you. Throughout the chapter, quiz items allow you to examine your problem-solving abilities and discover how your judgments compare to those of others. The quiz items illustrate thirteen predictable biases that frequently lead managers to judgments that systematically deviate from rationality.

To begin, answer the following two problems:

Problem 1. The following ten corporations were ranked by *Fortune* magazine to be among the largest 500 United States-based firms according to sales revenues for 2003:

Group A: Reebok International, Hilton Hotels, Starbucks, RadioShack, Hershey Foods

Group B: CoconoPhillips, American International Group, McKesson, AmerisourceBergen, The Altria Group

Which group of organizations (A or B) had the larger total sales revenues?

Problem 2 (adapted from Kahneman and Tversky, 1973). The best student in my introductory MBA class this past semester writes poetry and is rather shy and small in stature. What was the student's undergraduate major?

a. Chinese studies

b. Psychology

If you answered A for each of the two problems, you may gain comfort in knowing that the majority of respondents also choose A. If you answered B, you are in the minority. In this case, however, the minority represents the correct response. All corporations in group B were among the top twenty-five firms in terms of sales revenue, while none of the corporations in group A had sales large enough to be in the top 375 firms. In fact, the total revenue for group B was more than *sixteen times* the total revenue for group A. In the second problem, the student described was actually a psychology major, but more important, selecting psychology as the student's major represents a more rational response given the limited information.

Problem 1 illustrates the availability heuristic discussed in Chapter 1. In this problem, group A consists of consumer firms, while group B consists of conglomerates less well known to consumers. Because most of us are more familiar with consumer firms than conglomerates, we can more easily generate information in our minds about their size. If we were aware of our bias resulting from the availability heuristic, we would recognize our differential exposure to this information and adjust our judgments accordingly, or at least question them.

Problem 2 illustrates the representativeness heuristic. The reader who responds "Chinese studies" has probably overlooked relevant base-rate information—namely, the likely ratio of Chinese studies majors to psychology majors within the MBA student population. When asked to reconsider the problem in this context, most people acknowledge the relative scarcity of Chinese studies majors seeking MBAs, and change their response to "psychology." This example emphasizes that logical base-rate reasoning is often overwhelmed by qualitative judgments drawn from available descriptive information.

Problems 1 and 2 demonstrate how easy it is to draw faulty conclusions when we over-rely on cognitive heuristics. Throughout this chapter, additional quiz items are presented to further increase your awareness of the impact of heuristics on your decisions and to help you develop an appreciation for the systematic errors that emanate from overdependence on them. Some of the thirteen biases examined in this chapter are related to the availability heuristic. Another group emanates from the representativeness heuristic. A third group has causes beyond these two heuristics. The affect heuristic will appear in later chapters.

The goal of the chapter is to help you "unfreeze" your decision-making patterns by showing you how easily heuristics become biases when improperly applied. By working on numerous problems that demonstrate the failures of these heuristics, you will become more aware of the biases in your decision making. Once you are able to spot these biases, you will be able to improve the quality of your decisions.

Before reading further, please take a few minutes to respond to the problems presented in Table 2-1.

TABLE 2.1 Chapter Problems

Respond to the following problems before reading the rest of the chapter.

Problem 3. Please rank order the following causes of death in the United States between 1990 and 2000, placing a 1 next to the most common cause, 2 next to the second most common, etc.

_____ Tobacco

_____ Poor diet and physical inactivity

_____ Motor vehicle accidents

_____ Firearms (guns)

_____ Illicit drug use

Now estimate the number of deaths caused by each of these five causes between 1990 and 2000.

Problem 4a. In four pages of a novel (about 2,000 words), how many words would you expect to find that have the form _ _ _ _ *ing* (seven-letter words that end with "ing")? Indicate your best estimate by circling one of the following values:

  0   1–2   3–4   5–7   8–10   11–15   16+

Problem 4b. In four pages of a novel (about 2,000 words), how many words would you expect to find that have the form _ _ _ _ _ *n* _ (seven-letter words that have the letter "n" in the sixth position)? Indicate your best estimate by circling one of the following values:

  0   1–2   3–4   5–7   8–10   11–15   16+

Problem 5. Mark is finishing his MBA at a prestigious university. He is very interested in the arts and at one time considered a career as a musician. Where is he more likely to take a job?

  a. In arts management

  b. With a consulting firm

Problem 6 (from Tversky and Kahneman, 1974). A certain town is served by two hospitals. In the larger hospital about forty-five babies are born each day and in the smaller hospital about fifteen babies are born each day. As you know, about 50 percent of all babies are boys. However, the exact percentage varies from day to day. Sometimes it may be higher than 50 percent, sometimes lower.

For a period of one year, each hospital recorded the days in which more than 60 percent of the babies born were boys. Which hospital do you think recorded more such days?

  a. The larger hospital

  b. The smaller hospital

  c. About the same (that is, within 5 percent of each other)

(Continues)

TABLE 2.1 Chapter Problems (*Continued*)

Problem 7. You have started buying stocks on the Internet, beginning with five different stocks. Each stock goes down soon after your purchase. As you prepare to make a sixth purchase, you reason that it should be more successful, since the last five were "lemons." After all, the odds favor making at least one successful pick in six decisions. This thinking is:

   a. Correct

   b. Incorrect

Problem 8. You are the sales forecaster for a department store chain with nine locations. The chain depends on you for quality projections of future sales in order to make decisions on staffing, advertising, information system developments, purchasing, renovation, and the like. All stores are similar in size and merchandise selection. The main difference in their sales occurs because of location and random fluctuations. Sales for 2004 were as follows:

Store	2004	2006
1	$12,000,000	
2	11,500,000	
3	11,000,000	
4	10,500,000	
5	10,000,000	
6	9,500,000	
7	9,000,000	
8	8,500,000	
9	8,000,000	
TOTAL	**$90,000,000**	**$99,000,000**

Your economic forecasting service has convinced you that the best estimate of total sales increases between 2004 and 2006 is 10 percent (to $99,000,000). Your task is to predict 2006 sales for each store. Since your manager believes strongly in the economic forecasting service, it is imperative that your total sales equal $99,000,000.

Problem 9. Linda is thirty-one years old, single, outspoken, and very smart. She majored in philosophy. As a student, she was deeply concerned with issues of discrimination and social justice, and she participated in antinuclear demonstrations.

Rank the following eight descriptions in order of the probability (likelihood) that they describe Linda:

   ___ a. Linda is a teacher in an elementary school.

   ___ b. Linda works in a bookstore and takes yoga classes.

   ___ c. Linda is active in the feminist movement.

   ___ d. Linda is a psychiatric social worker.

   ___ e. Linda is a member of the League of Women Voters.

(*Continues*)

TABLE 2.1 Chapter Problems *(Continued)*

___ f. Linda is a bank teller.

___ g. Linda is an insurance salesperson.

___ h. Linda is a bank teller who is active in the feminist movement.

Problem 10. A new Internet company recently made its initial public offering, becoming publicly traded. At its opening, the stock sold for $20 per share. The company's closest competitor went public one year ago, also at a price of $20 per share. The competitor's stock is now priced at $100 per share. What will the new firm be worth one year from now?

$___ per share

Problem 11. Which of the following appears most likely? Which appears second most likely?

a. Drawing a red marble from a bag containing 50 percent red marbles and 50 percent white marbles.

b. Drawing a red marble seven times in succession, with replacement (a selected marble is put back into the bag before the next marble is selected), from a bag containing 90 percent red marbles and 10 percent white marbles.

c. Drawing at least one red marble in seven tries, with replacement, from a bag containing 10 percent red marbles and 90 percent white marbles.

Problem 12. Listed below are ten uncertain quantities. Do not look up any information on these items. For each, write down your best estimate of the quantity. Next, put a lower and upper bound around your estimate, so that you are confident that your 98 percent range surrounds the actual quantity.

Estimate	Lower	Upper	
___	___	___	a. Wal-Mart's 2003 revenue
___	___	___	b. Microsoft's 2003 revenue
___	___	___	c. Median age of U.S. citizens according to the 2000 Census
___	___	___	d. Market value of Best Buy as of March 14, 2003
___	___	___	e. Market value of Heinz as of March 14, 2003
___	___	___	f. Rank of McDonald's in the 2003 *Fortune* 500
___	___	___	g. Rank of Nike in the 2003 *Fortune* 500
___	___	___	h. The average amount of money that a family in the U.S. will spend on each child from the time he/she is born until the time he/she turns eighteen (as of 2003)
___	___	___	i. Number of endangered species listed in the United States as of February 25, 2004
___	___	___	j. Percentage of the U.S. population under five years old according to the 2000 Census

BIASES EMANATING FROM THE AVAILABILITY HEURISTIC

Bias 1: Ease of Recall (based on vividness and recency)

Problem 3. Please rank order the following causes of death in the United States between 1990 and 2000, placing a 1 next to the most common cause, 2 next to the second most common, etc.

_____ Tobacco

_____ Poor diet and physical inactivity

_____ Motor vehicle accidents

_____ Firearms (guns)

_____ Illicit drug use

Now estimate the number of deaths caused by each of these five causes between 1990 and 2000.

It may surprise you to learn that, according to the *Journal of the American Medical Association* (Mokdad, Marks, Stroup, and Gerberding, March 10, 2004, p. 1240), the causes above are listed in the order of how many deaths that they cause, with tobacco consumption causing the most deaths and illicit drug use causing the fewest. Even if you got the order right or came close, my guess is that you underestimated the magnitude of difference between the first two causes and the last three causes. The first two causes, tobacco and poor diet/physical inactivity, resulted in 435,000 and 400,000 deaths respectively, while the latter three causes resulted in far few deaths—43,000, 29,000, and 17,000 deaths respectively. Vivid deaths caused by cars, guns, and drugs tend to get a lot of press coverage. The availability of vivid stories in the media biases our perception of the frequency of events toward the last three causes over the first two. As a result, we may underestimate the likelihood of death due to tobacco and poor diet, while overestimating the hazards of cars, guns, and drugs.

Many life decisions are affected by the vividness of information. Although most people recognize that AIDS is a devastating disease, many individuals ignore clear data about how to avoid contracting AIDS. In the fall of 1991, however, sexual behavior in Dallas was dramatically affected by one vivid piece of data that may or may not have been true. In a chilling interview, a Dallas woman calling herself C.J. claimed she had AIDS and was trying to spread the disease out of revenge against the man who had infected her. After this vivid interview made the local news, attendance at Dallas AIDS seminars increased dramatically, AIDS became the main topic of Dallas talk shows, and requests for HIV tests surged citywide. Although C.J.'s possible actions were a legitimate cause for concern, it is clear that most of the health risks related to AIDS are not a result of one woman's actions. There are many more important reasons to be concerned about AIDS. However, C.J.'s vivid report had a more substantial effect on many people's behavior than the mountains of data available.

Tversky and Kahneman (1974) argue that when an individual judges the frequency with which an event occurs by the availability of its instances, an event whose instances are more easily recalled will appear to be more frequent than an event of equal frequency whose instances are less easily recalled. They cite evidence of this bias in a lab study in which individuals were read lists of names of well-known personalities of both genders. Different lists were presented to two groups. One group was read a list in which the women listed were relatively more famous than the listed men, but the list included more men's names overall. The other group was read a list in which the men listed were relatively more famous than the listed women, but the list included more women's names overall. After hearing their group's list, participants in both groups were asked if the list contained the names of more women or men. In both groups, participants incorrectly guessed that the gender that included the relatively more famous personalities was the more numerous. Participants apparently paid more attention to vivid household names than to less well-known figures, leading to inaccurate judgments.

While this example of vividness may seem fairly benign, it is not difficult to see how the availability bias could lead managers to make potentially destructive workplace decisions. The following came from the experience of one of my MBA students: As a purchasing agent, he had to select one of several possible suppliers. He chose the firm whose name was the most familiar to him. He later found out that the salience of the name resulted from recent adverse publicity concerning the firm's extortion of funds from client companies!

Managers conducting performance appraisals often fall victim to the availability heuristic. Working from memory, vivid instances of an employee's behavior (either positive or negative) will be most easily recalled from memory, will appear more numerous than commonplace incidents, and will therefore be weighted more heavily in the performance appraisal. The recency of events is also a factor: Managers give more weight to performance during the three months prior to the evaluation than to the previous nine months of the evaluation period.

Because of our susceptibility to vividness and recency, Kahneman and Tversky suggest that we are particularly prone to overestimating unlikely events. For instance, if we actually witness a burning house, our assessment of the probability of such accidents is likely to be greater than if we had merely read about the fire in the local newspaper; our direct observation of the event makes it more salient to us. Similarly, Slovic and Fischhoff (1977) discuss the implications of the misuse of the availability heuristic in debates about the perceived risks of nuclear power. They point out that any discussion of potential hazards, regardless of their likelihood, will increase the salience of these hazards and increase their perceived risks.

Bias 2: Retrievability (based on memory structures)

Problem 4a. In four pages of a novel (about 2,000 words), how many words would you expect to find that have the form _ _ _ _ ing (seven-letter words that end with "ing")? Indicate your best estimate by circling one of the following values:

0   1–2   3–4   5–7   8–10   11–15   16+

Problem 4b. In four pages of a novel (about 2,000 words), how many words would you expect to find that have the form _ _ _ _ _ n _ (seven-letter words that have the letter "n" in the sixth position)? Indicate your best estimate by circling one of the following values:

0   1–2   3–4   5–7   8–10   11–15   16+

Tversky and Kahneman (1983) found that most people respond with a higher number for Problem 4a than for Problem 4b. However, this response pattern must be incorrect. Since all words with seven letters that end in "ing" also have an "n" as their sixth letter, the frequency of words that end in "ing" cannot be larger than the number of words with "n" as the sixth letter. Tversky and Kahneman (1983) argue that "ing" words are more retrievable from memory because of the commonality of the "ing" suffix, whereas the search for words that have an "n" as the sixth letter does not easily generate this group of words.

Just as retrievability affects our vocabulary-search behavior, organizational modes affect information-search behavior within our work lives. We structure organizations to provide order, but this same structure can lead to confusion if the presumed order is not exactly as suggested. For example, many organizations have an information systems division that has generalized expertise in computer applications. Assume that you are a manager in a product division and need computer expertise. If that expertise exists within the information systems group, the organizational hierarchy will lead you to the correct resource. If, however, the information systems group lacks expertise in a specific application, but this expertise exists elsewhere in the organization, the hierarchy is likely to bias the effectiveness of your search. I am not arguing for the overthrow of organizational hierarchies; I am merely identifying the dysfunctional role of hierarchies in potentially biasing search behavior. If we are aware of the potential bias, we need not be affected by this limitation.

Retail store location is influenced by the way in which consumers search their minds when seeking a particular commodity. Why are multiple gas stations at the same intersection? Why do "upscale" retailers want to be in the same mall? Why are the biggest bookstores in a city often located within a couple blocks of each other? An important reason for this pattern is that consumers learn the "location" for a particular type of product or store and organize their minds accordingly. To maximize traffic, the retailer needs to be in the location that consumers associate with this type of product or store.

Bias 3: Presumed Associations

People frequently fall victim to the availability bias in their assessment of the likelihood of two events occurring together. For example, consider your response to the following two questions: Is marijuana use related to delinquency? Are couples who get married under the age of twenty-five more likely to have bigger families? In assessing the marijuana question, most people typically try to remember several delinquent marijuana users and either assume or do not assume a correlation based on the availability of this mental data. However, a proper analysis would require you to recall *four* groups of people: marijuana users who are delinquents, marijuana users who are not delinquents, delinquents who do not use marijuana, and nondelinquents who do not use marijuana.

The same analysis applies to the marriage question. Proper analysis would include four groups: couples who married young and have large families, couples who married young and have small families, couples who married older and have large families, and couples who married older and have small families.

Indeed, there are always at least four separate situations to consider when assessing the association between two dichotomous events. However, our everyday decision making commonly ignores this scientifically valid fact. Chapman and Chapman (1967) have noted that when the probability of two events co-occurring is judged by the availability of perceived co-occurring instances in our minds, we usually assign an inappropriately high probability that the two events will co-occur again. Thus, if we know a lot of marijuana users who are delinquents, we assume that marijuana use is related to delinquency. Similarly, if we know of a lot of couples who married young and have had large families, we assume that this trend is more prevalent than it may actually be. In testing for this bias, Chapman and Chapman provided participants with information about hypothetical psychiatric patients. The information included a written clinical diagnosis of a "patient" and a drawing of a person made by the "patient." The participants were asked to estimate the frequency with which each diagnosis (for example, suspiciousness or paranoia) was accompanied by various facial and body features in the drawings (for example, peculiar eyes). Throughout the study, participants markedly overestimated the frequency of pairs commonly associated together by social lore. For example, diagnoses of suspiciousness were overwhelmingly associated with peculiar eyes.

To summarize, a lifetime of experience has led us to believe that, in general, we recall frequent events more easily than infrequent events and recall likely events more easily than unlikely events. In response to this learning, we have adopted the availability heuristic to help us estimate the likelihood of events. This simplifying heuristic often leads us to accurate, efficient judgments. However, as these first three biases (ease of recall, retrievability, and presumed associations) indicate, the misuse of the availability heuristic can lead to systematic errors in managerial judgment. We too easily assume that our available recollections are truly representative of the larger pool of events that exists outside of our range of experience.

BIASES EMANATING FROM THE REPRESENTATIVENESS HEURISTIC

Bias 4: Insensitivity to Base Rates

> **Problem 5.** Mark is finishing his MBA at a prestigious university. He is very interested in the arts and at one time considered a career as a musician. Where is he more likely to take a job?
>
> a. In arts management
>
> b. With a consulting firm

How did you decide on your answer? Odds are, you responded like most people. Using the representativeness heuristic discussed in Chapter 1, most people approach this problem by analyzing the degree to which Mark is representative of their image of individuals who take jobs in each of the two areas. Consequently, they usually conclude that Mark took the arts management job. However, as we discussed in our analysis of Problem 2 earlier in this chapter, this response overlooks relevant base-rate information. Reconsider the problem in light of the fact that a much larger number of MBAs take jobs with consulting firms than in arts management—relevant information that should enter into any reasonable prediction of Mark's career path. With this base-rate data, it is only reasonable to predict that he will be more likely to work for a consulting firm.

Judgmental biases of this type frequently occur when individuals cognitively ask the wrong question. If you answered "arts management," you probably wondered, "How likely is it that a person working in the management of the arts would fit Mark's description?" In fact, the problem requires you to ask the question, "How likely is it that someone fitting Mark's description will choose arts management?" By itself, the representativeness heuristic incorrectly results in a similar answer to both questions, since this heuristic leads individuals to compare the resemblance of the personal description and the career path. However, when base-rate data are considered, they are irrelevant to the first question listed, but crucial to a reasonable prediction based on the second question. While a large percentage of individuals in arts management may fit Mark's description, there are undoubtedly a larger absolute number of management consultants fitting Mark's description because of the relative preponderance of MBAs in consulting.

Participants do use base-rate data correctly when no other information is provided (Kahneman and Tversky, 1972). In the absence of a personal description of Mark in Problem 5, people will choose "consulting firm" based on the past frequency of this career path for MBAs. Thus, people understand the relevance of base-rate information, but tend to disregard such data when descriptive data are also available. Ignoring base rates has many unfortunate implications. Prospective entrepreneurs typically spend far too much time imagining their success and far too little time considering the base rate for business failures. Entrepreneurs think that the base rate for failure is not relevant to their situation, and many individuals lose their life savings as a result. Similarly, unnecessary emotional distress is caused in the divorce process because of the failure of couples to create prenuptial agreements that facilitate the peaceful resolution of a marriage. The suggestion of a prenuptial agreement is often viewed as a sign of bad faith. However, in far too many cases, the failure to create prenuptial agreements occurs when individuals approach marriage with the false belief that the very high base rate for divorce does not apply to them.

Bias 5: Insensitivity to Sample Size

Problem 6 (from Tversky and Kahneman, 1974). A certain town is served by two hospitals. In the larger hospital about forty-five babies are born each day and in the smaller hospital about fifteen babies are born each day. As you know, about 50 percent of all babies are boys. However, the exact percentage varies from day to day. Sometimes it may be higher than 50 percent, sometimes lower.

For a period of one year, each hospital recorded the days in which more than 60 percent of the babies born were boys. Which hospital do you think recorded more such days?

a. The larger hospital

b. The smaller hospital

c. About the same (that is, within 5 percent of each other)

Most individuals choose C, expecting the two hospitals to record a similar number of days in which 60 percent or more of the babies born are boys. People seem to have some basic idea of how unusual it is to have 60 percent of a random event occurring in a specific direction. By contrast, simple statistics tell us that it is much more likely to observe 60 percent of male babies in a smaller sample than in a larger sample. The interested reader can verify this fact with an introductory statistics book. However, anecdotally, this effect is easy to understand. Think about which is more likely: getting six heads in ten flips of a coin or getting 6,000 heads in 10,000 flips of a coin. Our intuition correctly tells us that six out of ten is not that unusual, but 6,000 in 10,000 is very unusual. Sampling theory tells us that the expected number of days in which more than 60 percent of the babies are boys is three times greater in the small hospital, since a large sample is less likely to deviate from the mean. However, most people judge the probability to be the same in each hospital, effectively ignoring sample size.

Although the importance of sample size is fundamental in statistics, Tversky and Kahneman (1974) argue that sample size is rarely a part of our intuition. Why not? When responding to problems dealing with sampling, people often use the representativeness heuristic. For instance, they think about how representative it would be for 60 percent of babies born to be boys in a random event. As a result, people ignore the issue of sample size—which is critical to an accurate assessment of the problem.

Consider the implications of this bias for advertising strategies. Market research experts understand that a sizable sample will be more accurate than a small one, but use consumers' bias to the advantage of their clients: "Four out of five dentists surveyed recommend sugarless gum for their patients who chew gum." Without mention of the exact number of dentists involved in the survey, the results of the survey are meaningless. If only five or ten dentists were surveyed, the size of the sample would not be generalizable to the overall population of dentists.

Bias 6: Misconceptions of Chance

> **Problem 7.** You have started buying stocks on the Internet, beginning with five different stocks. Each stock goes down soon after your purchase. As you prepare to make a sixth purchase, you reason that it should be more successful, since the last five were "lemons." After all, the odds favor making at least one successful pick in six decisions. This thinking is:
>
> a. Correct
>
> b. Incorrect

Most people are comfortable with the preceding logic, or at least have used similar logic in the past. However, the logic in Problem 7 is incorrect. In fact, the performance of the first five stocks will not directly affect the performance of the sixth stock. Relying on their intuition and the representativeness heuristic, most individuals incorrectly conclude that a sixth poor performance is unlikely because the probability of getting six "lemons" in a row is extremely low. Unfortunately, this logic ignores the fact that we have already witnessed five "lemons" (in itself an unlikely occurrence), and the performance of the sixth stock is independent of the performance of the first five. Before you make similar mistakes in the stock market, be sure to read Chapter 7.

This question parallels research by Kahneman and Tversky (1972) showing that people expect a sequence of random events to "look" random. Specifically, participants routinely judged the sequence of coin flips H–T–H–T–T–H to be more likely than H–H–H–T–T–T, which does not "appear" random, and more likely than the sequence H–H–H–H–T–H, which does not represent the equal likelihood of heads and tails. Simple statistics, of course, tell us that each of these sequences is equally likely because of the independence of multiple random events.

Problem 7 moves beyond dealing with random events in recognizing our inappropriate tendency to assume that random and nonrandom events will balance out. Will the sixth stock perform well? Maybe! But your earlier failures are completely irrelevant to its potential for success.

The logic concerning misconceptions of chance provides a process explanation of the gambler's fallacy. After holding bad cards on ten hands of poker, the poker player believes he is "due" for a good hand. After winning $1,000 in the Pennsylvania State Lottery, a woman changes her regular number—after all, how likely is it that the same number will come up twice? Tversky and Kahneman (1974) note: "Chance is commonly viewed as a self-correcting process in which a deviation in one direction induces a deviation in the opposite direction to restore the equilibrium. In fact, deviations are not corrected as a chance process unfolds, they are merely diluted."

In the preceding examples, individuals expected probabilities to even out. In some situations, our minds misconstrue chance in exactly the opposite way. In sports such as basketball, we often think of a particular player as having a "hot hand" or "being on a good streak." If your favorite player has made his last four shots, is the probability of his making his next shot higher, lower, or the same as the probability of his making a shot without the preceding four hits? Most sports fans, sports commentators, and players believe that the answer is "higher." In fact, there are many biological, emotional, and physical reasons that this answer could be correct. However, it is wrong! In an extensive analysis of the shooting of the Philadelphia 76ers and the Boston Celtics, Gilovich, Vallone, and Tversky (1985) found that immediately prior shot performance did not change the likelihood of success on the upcoming shot. Out of all of the findings in this book, this is the effect that my managerial students have the hardest time accepting. We can all remember sequences of five hits in a row; streaks are part of our conception of chance in athletic competition. However, our minds do not think of a string of "four in a row" shots as a situation in which "he missed his fifth shot." As a result, we have a misconception of connectedness when, in fact, chance (or the player's normal probability of success) is really in effect.

The belief in the hot hand has interesting implications for how players compete. Passing the ball to the player who is "hot" is commonly endorsed as a good strategy. Similarly, the opposing team often will concentrate on guarding the "hot" player. Another player, who is less hot but is equally skilled, may have a better chance of scoring. Thus the belief in the "hot hand" is not just erroneous, but could also be costly if you make decisions under this illusion.

The mythical perception of a "hot hand" is not limited to basketball. Imagine that you receive a free copy of an investor newsletter that advises you to sell stock because the market will fall during the next six months. You ignore this newsletter, and then it happens to be correct. At the end of the six months, another free copy of this newsletter tells you the market will rise during the next six months. Again, you ignore the advice, and again the newsletter is correct. A third free copy of the newsletter advises you to buy stocks for the next six-month period. Once again, you ignore the newsletter, and once again it is correct. After these eighteen months, you receive a direct-mail solicitation for this newsletter, pointing out that they have been giving you great free advice for the past eighteen months. If you want this excellent advice in the future, you must pay a small subscription fee. Are you tempted to subscribe to this publication? Many people would be impressed by its consistent past performance and would sign up, expecting more sound advice.

Now consider what this advice may look like from the other side. Suppose a publisher creates eight financial newsletters, each managed by a different expert. In their first issues, each of the eight makes a six-month recommendation about the general direction of the market; four predict a rise in the market, and four predict a fall in the market. The four who predicted a fall in the market were correct, and the four who predicted a rise go out of business. Of the remaining four newsletters, two predict a rise for the second six-month period and two predict a fall. The market rises, and the two that predicted a fall in the second six-month period go out of business. Of the two remaining in business after twelve months, one predicts a rise in the market for the third six-month period, and the other predicts a fall. The market rises, and the newsletter that was correct all three times advertises this fact. It seems they have some important insight into financial markets. Yet, we can see that if there are many "experts" making predictions, some will be consistently correct simply by chance, though we will be biased to give credit to the one that got lucky.

Tversky and Kahneman's (1971) work also shows that misconceptions of chance are not limited to gamblers, sports fans, or laypersons. Research psychologists also fall victim to the "law of small numbers." They believe that sample events should be far more representative of the population from which they were drawn than simple statistics would dictate. Putting too much faith in the results of initial samples, scientists often grossly overestimate the replicability of empirical findings. The representativeness heuristic may be so well institutionalized in our decision processes that even scientific training and its emphasis on the proper use of statistics may not eliminate its biasing influence.

Bias 7: Regression to the Mean

Problem 8. You are the sales forecaster for a department store chain with nine locations. The chain depends on you for quality projections of future sales in order to make decisions on staffing, advertising, information system developments, purchasing, renovation, and the like. All stores are similar in size and merchandise selection. The main difference in their sales occurs because of location and random fluctuations. Sales for 2004 were as follows:

Store	2004	2006
1	$12,000,000	
2	11,500,000	
3	11,000,000	
4	10,500,000	
5	10,000,000	
6	9,500,000	
7	9,000,000	
8	8,500,000	
9	8,000,000	
TOTAL	**$90,000,000**	**$99,000,000**

Your economic forecasting service has convinced you that the best estimate of total sales increases between 2004 and 2006 is 10 percent (to $99,000,000). Your task is to predict 2006 sales for each store. Since your manager believes strongly in the economic forecasting service, it is imperative that your total sales equal $99,000,000.

Think about the processes you might use to answer this problem. Consider the following logical pattern of thought: "The overall increase in sales is predicted to be 10 percent ([$99,000,000 – $90,000,000]/$90,000,000). Lacking any other specific information on the stores, it makes sense simply to add 10 percent to each 2004 sales figure to predict 2006 sales. This means that I predict sales of $13,200,000 for store 1, sales of $12,650,000 for store 2, and so on." This logic, in fact, is the most common approach people use in response to this item.

Unfortunately, this logic is faulty. Why? Statistical analysis would dictate that we first assess the predicted relationship between 2004 and 2006 sales. This relationship, formally known as a correlation, can vary from total independence (that is, 2004 sales do not predict 2006 sales) to perfect correlation (2004 sales are a perfect predictor of 2006 sales). In the former case, the lack of a relationship between 2004 and 2006 sales would mean that 2004 sales would provide absolutely no information about 2006 sales, and your best estimates of 2006 sales would be equal to total sales divided by the number of stores ($99,000,000 divided by 9 equals $11,000,000). However, in the latter case of perfect predictability between 2004 and 2006 sales, our initial logic of simply extrapolating from 2004 performance by adding 10 percent to each store's performance would be completely accurate. Obviously, 2004 sales are likely to be partially predictive of 2006 sales—falling somewhere between independence and perfect correlation. Thus, the best prediction for store 1 should lie between $11,000,000 and $13,200,000, depending on how predictive you think 2004 sales will be of 2006 sales. The key point is that in virtually all such predictions, you should expect the naive $13,200,000 estimate to regress toward the overall mean ($11,000,000).

In a study of sales forecasting, Cox and Summers (1987) examined the judgments of professional retail buyers. They examined sales data, during a two-week period, from two department stores for six different apparel styles for a total of twelve different sales forecasts. The task was for professional buyers to forecast the sales in week 2 based on week 1 data. The sales from week 1, in fact, regressed to the mean in week 2. However, the forecasts of thirty-one professional buyers failed to reflect the tendency for regression to the mean.

Many effects regress to the mean. Brilliant students frequently have less successful siblings. Short parents tend to have taller children. Great rookies have mediocre second years (the "sophomore jinx"). Firms that achieve outstanding profits one year tend to perform less well the next year. In each case, individuals are often surprised when made aware of these predictable patterns of regression to the mean.

Why is the regression-to-the-mean concept, while statistically valid, counterintuitive? Kahneman and Tversky (1973) suggest that the representativeness heuristic accounts for this systematic bias in judgment. They argue that individuals typically assume that future outcomes (for example, 2002 sales) will be directly predictable from past outcomes (2000 sales). Thus, we tend to naively develop predictions based on the assumption of perfect correlation with past data.

In some unusual situations, individuals do intuitively expect a regression-to-the-mean effect. In 2001, when Barry Bonds hit seventy-three home runs, few expected him to repeat this performance the following year. When Wilt Chamberlain scored 100 points in a single game, most people did not expect him to score 100 points in his next game. When a historically 3.0 student got a 4.0 one semester, her parents did not expect a repeat performance the following semester. When a real estate agent sold five houses in one month (an abnormally high performance), his coagents did not expect equally high sales from him the following month. Why is regression to the mean more intuitive in these cases? Because, when a performance is extreme, we know it cannot last. Thus, under very unusual circumstances, we expect performance to regress. However, we generally do not recognize the regression effect in less extreme cases.

Consider Kahneman and Tversky's (1973) classic example in which misconceptions about regression led to overestimation of the effectiveness of punishment and the underestimation of the power of reward. In a discussion about flight training, experienced instructors noted that praise for an exceptionally smooth landing was typically followed by a poorer landing on the next try, while harsh criticism after a rough landing was usually followed by an improvement on the next try. The instructors concluded that verbal rewards were detrimental to learning, while verbal punishments were beneficial. Obviously, the tendency of performance to regress to the mean can account for the results; verbal feedback may have had absolutely no effect. However, to the extent that the instructors were prone to biased decision making, they were liable to reach the false conclusion that punishment is more effective than positive reinforcement in shaping behavior.

What happens when managers fail to acknowledge the regression principle? Consider an employee who performs extremely well during one evaluation period. He (and his boss) may inappropriately expect similar performance in the next period. What happens when the employee's performance regresses toward the mean? He (and his boss) will begin to make excuses for not meeting expectations. Managers who fail to recognize the tendency of events to regress to the mean are likely to develop false assumptions about future results and, as a result, make inappropriate plans.

Bias 8: The Conjunction Fallacy

> **Problem 9.** Linda is thirty-one years old, single, outspoken, and very smart. She majored in philosophy. As a student, she was deeply concerned with issues of discrimination and social justice, and she participated in antinuclear demonstrations.
>
> Rank the following eight descriptions in order of the probability (likelihood) that they describe Linda:
>
> a. Linda is a teacher in an elementary school.

    b. Linda works in a bookstore and takes yoga classes.

    c. Linda is active in the feminist movement.

    d. Linda is a psychiatric social worker.

    e. Linda is a member of the League of Women Voters.

    f. Linda is a bank teller.

    g. Linda is an insurance salesperson.

    h. Linda is a bank teller who is active in the feminist movement.

Examine your rank orderings of descriptions C, F, and H. Most people rank order C as more likely than H and H as more likely than F. Their rationale for this ordering is that C–H–F reflects the degree to which the descriptions are representative of the short profile of Linda. Linda's profile was constructed by Tversky and Kahneman to be representative of an active feminist and unrepresentative of a bank teller. Recall from the representativeness heuristic that people make judgments according to the degree to which a specific description corresponds to a broader category within their minds. Linda's profile is more representative of a feminist than of a feminist bank teller, and is more representative of a feminist bank teller than of a bank teller. Thus, the representativeness heuristic accurately predicts that most individuals will rank order the items C–H–F.

Although the representativeness heuristic accurately predicts how individuals will respond, it also leads to another common, systematic distortion of human judgment—the conjunction fallacy (Tversky and Kahneman, 1983). This is illustrated by a reexamination of the potential descriptions of Linda. One of the simplest and most fundamental qualitative laws of probability is that a subset (for example, being a bank teller and a feminist) cannot be more likely than a larger set that completely includes the subset (for example, being a bank teller). Statistically speaking, the broad set "Linda is a bank teller" must be rated at least as likely, if not more so, than the subset "Linda is a bank teller who is active in the feminist movement." After all, there is some chance (although it may be small) that Linda is a bank teller but not a feminist. Based on this logic, a rational assessment of the eight descriptions will result in F being ranked more likely than H.

Simple statistics demonstrate that a conjunction (a combination of two or more descriptors) cannot be more probable than any one of its descriptors. By contrast, the conjunction fallacy predicts that a conjunction will be judged more probable than a single component descriptor when the conjunction appears more representative than the component descriptor. Intuitively, thinking of Linda as a feminist bank teller "feels" more correct than thinking of her as only a bank teller.

The conjunction fallacy can also be triggered by a greater availability of the conjunction than of one of its unique descriptors (Yates and Carlson, 1986). That is, if the conjunction creates more intuitive matches with vivid events, acts, or people than a component of the conjunction, the conjunction is likely to be perceived falsely as more probable than the component. Participants in a study by Tversky and Kahneman (1983) judged the chances of a massive flood somewhere in North America, in 1989, in which one thousand people drown, to be less likely than the chances of an earthquake in

California, sometime in 1989, causing a flood in which more than a thousand people drown. Yet, the latter possibility (California earthquake leading to flood) is a subset of the former; many other events could cause a flood in North America. Tversky and Kahneman (1983) have shown that the conjunction fallacy is likely to lead to deviations from rationality in judgments of sporting events, criminal behavior, international relations, and medical decisions. The obvious concern arising from the conjunction fallacy is that it leads us to poor predictions of future outcomes, causing us to be ill-prepared to cope with unanticipated events.

We have examined five biases that emanate from the use of the representativeness heuristic: insensitivity to base rates, insensitivity to sample size, misconceptions of chance, regression to the mean, and the conjunction fallacy. Experience has taught us that the likelihood of a specific occurrence is related to the likelihood of a group of occurrences which that specific occurrence represents. Unfortunately, we tend to overuse this information in making decisions. The five biases we have just explored illustrate the systematic irrationalities that can occur in our judgments when we are unaware of this tendency.

BIASES BEYOND AVAILABILITY AND REPRESENTATIVENESS

Bias 9: Anchoring

> **Problem 10.** A new Internet company recently made its initial public offering, becoming publicly traded. At its opening, the stock sold for $20 per share. The company's closest competitor went public one year ago, also at a price of $20 per share. The competitor's stock is now priced at $100 per share. What will the new firm be worth one year from now?

Was your answer affected by the other firm's appreciation? Most people are influenced by this fairly irrelevant information. Reconsider how you would have responded if the other firm was now worth only $10/share. On average, individuals give higher estimates of the new firm's future value when the other firm is currently worth $100 per share, rather than $10 per share.

Why do we pay attention to such irrelevant anchors? There are at least two reasons that anchors affect decisions. First, people often develop estimates by starting from an initial anchor, based on whatever information is provided, and adjusting from the anchor to yield a final answer (Epley and Gilovich, 2001; Epley, 2004). Adjustments away from anchors are usually not sufficient (Tversky and Kahneman, 1974). Second, Mussweiler and Strack (1999) show that the existence of an anchor leads people to access information that is consistent with that anchor (the commonalities between the two competitors) and not access information that is inconsistent with the anchor (differences between the two firms).

Tversky and Kahneman (1974) have provided systematic, empirical evidence of the effect of anchors—even when an anchor is known to be irrelevant. In one study, participants were asked to estimate the percentage of African countries in the United Nations. For each participant, a random number (obtained by a spin of a roulette wheel, observed by the participant) was given as a starting point. From there, participants were asked to state whether the actual quantity was higher or lower than this random value and then develop their best estimate. It was found that the arbitrary values from the roulette wheel had a substantial impact on estimates. For example, for those who received ten countries and sixty-five countries as starting points, median estimates were twenty-five and forty-five, respectively. Thus, even though the participants were aware that the anchor was random and unrelated to the judgment task, the anchor had a dramatic effect on their judgment. Interestingly, paying participants according to their accuracy did not reduce the magnitude of the anchoring effect.

Salary negotiations represent a very common context for observing the influence of an anchor in the managerial world. For example, pay increases often come in the form of a percentage increase. A firm may have an average increase of 8 percent, with increases for specific employees varying from 3 percent to 13 percent. While society has led us to accept such systems as equitable, I believe that such a system overweights the anchor (last year's salary) and leads to substantial inequities. What happens if an employee has been substantially underpaid? The raise system described does not rectify past inequities, since a pay increase of 11 percent may leave that employee still underpaid. Conversely, the system would work in the employee's favor had she been overpaid. Employers often ask job applicants to reveal their current salaries. Why? Employers are searching for a value from which they can anchor an adjustment. If the employee is worth far more than his current salary, the anchoring bias predicts that the firm will make an offer below the employee's true value. Does an employee's current salary provide fully accurate information about his or her true worth? I think not. Thus, the use of such compensation systems accepts past inequities as an anchor and makes inadequate adjustments from that point. Furthermore, these findings suggest that when an employer is deciding what offer to make to a potential employee, any anchor that creeps into the discussion is likely to have an inappropriate effect on the eventual offer, even if the anchor is "ignored" as being ridiculous.

There are numerous examples of the anchoring phenomenon in everyday life. For example:

- In education, children are tracked by a school system that may categorize them into a certain level of performance at an early age. For example, a child who is anchored in the C group may be expected to achieve a mediocre level of performance. Conversely, a child of similar abilities who is anchored in the A group may be perceived as being a better student than the student in group C merely because assignment to the A group confers high-performer status.

- We have all fallen victim to the first-impression syndrome when meeting someone for the first time. We often place so much emphasis on first impressions that we fail to adjust our opinion appropriately at a later date.

Joyce and Biddle (1981) have provided empirical support for the presence of the anchoring effect among practicing auditors of Big Four accounting firms. Auditors participating in one condition were asked the following (adapted from original to keep the problem current):

It is well known that many cases of management fraud go undetected even when competent annual audits are performed. The reason, of course, is that Generally

Accepted Auditing Standards are not designed specifically to detect executive-level management fraud. We are interested in obtaining an estimate from practicing auditors of the prevalence of executive-level management fraud as a first step in ascertaining the scope of the problem.

1.   Based on your audit experience, is the incidence of significant executive-level management fraud more than 10 in each 1,000 firms (that is, 1 percent) audited by Big Four accounting firms?

     a.   Yes, more than 10 in each 1,000 Big Four clients have significant executive-level management fraud.

     b.   No, fewer than 10 in each 1,000 Big Four clients have significant executive-level management fraud.

2.   What is your estimate of the number of Big Four clients per 1,000 that have significant executive-level management fraud? (Fill in the blank below with the appropriate number.)

     _____ in each 1,000 Big Four clients have significant executive-level management fraud.

The second condition differed only in that participants were asked whether the fraud incidence was more or less than 200 in each 1,000 firms audited, rather than 10 in 1,000. Prior to the auditing scandals that started to emerge in 2001, participants in the first condition estimated a fraud incidence of 16.52 per 1,000 on average, compared with an estimated fraud incidence of 43.11 per 1,000 in the second condition! In my own use of these problems with executive classes, answers to both versions have roughly doubled since the fall of Enron, but the differences between the two versions of the problem remain large. Seasoned executives, including professional auditors, are affected by anchors.

Epley (2004) provides evidence that we can predict when each of two different processes will be used to create the anchoring bias. Specifically, he shows that when an anchor is externally set (not set by the decision maker), the anchor leads to a biased search for information compatible with the anchor (Mussweiler and Strack, 1999, 2000a, 2000b). In contrast, when someone develops her own anchor, she will start with that anchor and insufficiently adjust away from it (Epley and Gilovich, 2001).

Nisbett and Ross (1980) note that the anchoring bias itself dictates that it will be very difficult to get you to change your decision-making strategies as a result of reading this book. They argue that the heuristics we identify are currently serving as your cognitive anchors and are central to your judgment processes. Thus, any cognitive strategy that I suggest must be presented and understood in a manner that will force you to break your existing cognitive anchors. Based on the evidence in this section, this should be a difficult challenge—but one that is important enough to be worth the effort!

Bias 10: Conjunctive and Disjunctive Events Bias

Problem 11. Which of the following appears most likely? Which appears second most likely?

a.   Drawing a red marble from a bag containing 50 percent red marbles and 50 percent white marbles.

b. Drawing a red marble seven times in succession, with replacement (a selected marble is put back into the bag before the next marble is selected), from a bag containing 90 percent red marbles and 10 percent white marbles.

c. Drawing at least one red marble in seven tries, with replacement, from a bag containing 10 percent red marbles and 90 percent white marbles.

The most common ordering of preferences is B–A–C. Interestingly, the correct order of likelihood is C (52 percent), A (50 percent), B (48 percent)—the exact opposite of the most common intuitive pattern! This result illustrates a general bias to overestimate the probability of conjunctive events, or events that must occur in conjunction with one another (Bar-Hillel, 1973), and to underestimate the probability of disjunctive events, or events that occur independently (Tversky and Kahneman, 1974). Thus, when multiple events all need to occur (choice B), we overestimate the true likelihood, while if only one of many events needs to occur (choice C), we underestimate the true likelihood.

The overestimation of conjunctive events is a powerful explanation of the timing problems that typically occur with projects that require multistage planning. Individuals, businesses, and governments frequently fall victim to the conjunctive-events bias in terms of timing and budgets. Home remodeling, new product ventures, and public works projects seldom finish on time or on budget.

Consider the following real-life scenarios:

- After three years of study, doctoral students typically dramatically overestimate the likelihood of completing their dissertations within a year. This occurs even when they plan how long each component of the project will take. Why do they not finish in one year?

- A partner managed a consulting project in which five teams were each analyzing a different strategy for a client. The alternatives could not be compared until all teams completed their analysis. As the client's deadline approached, three of the five teams were behind schedule, but the partner assured the client that all five would be ready on time. In the end, the manager presented only three of the five alternatives to the client (two were still missing). Unimpressed, the client dropped the consulting firm. Whose fault was it that the project failed?

- The City of Boston undertook a massive construction project to move Interstate Highway 93 below ground as it passes through the city (The Big Dig). City officials developed a very clear budget based on each subcontractor's estimate. Nevertheless, as of late 2003, the Big Dig was $12 billion over budget. What went wrong?

Why are we so optimistic in our assessments of a project's cost and time frame? Why are we so surprised when a seemingly unlikely setback occurs? Because of the human tendency to underestimate disjunctive events. "A complex system, such as a nuclear reactor or the human body, will malfunction if any of its essential components fails," argue Tversky and Kahneman (1974). "Even when the likelihood of failure in each component is slight, the probability of an overall failure can be high if many components are involved."

An awareness of our underestimation of disjunctive events also has its positive side. Consider the following:

It's Monday evening (10:00 P.M.). Your boss calls to tell you that you must be at the Chicago office by 9:30 A.M. the next morning. You call all five airlines that have flights that get into Chicago by 9:00 A.M. Each has one flight, and all the flights are booked. When you ask the probability of getting on each of the flights if you show up at the airport in the morning, you are disappointed to hear probabilities of 30 percent, 25 percent, 15 percent, 20 percent, and 25 percent. Consequently, you do not expect to get to Chicago in time.

In this case, the disjunctive bias leads you to expect the worst. In fact, if the probabilities given by the airlines are unbiased and independent, you have a 73 percent chance of getting on one of the flights (assuming that you can arrange to be at the right ticket counter at the right time)!

Bias 11: Overconfidence

Problem 12. Listed below are ten uncertain quantities. Do not look up any information on these items. For each, write down your best estimate of the quantity. Next, put a lower and upper bound around your estimate, so that you are confident that your 98 percent range surrounds the actual quantity.

Estimate	Lower	Upper	
————	————	————	a. Wal-Mart's 2003 revenue
————	————	————	b. Microsoft's 2003 revenue
————	————	————	c. Median age of U.S. citizens according to the 2000 Census
————	————	————	d. Market value of Best Buy as of March 14, 2003
————	————	————	e. Market value of Heinz as of March 14, 2003
————	————	————	f. Rank of McDonald's in the 2003 *Fortune* 500
————	————	————	g. Rank of Nike in the 2003 *Fortune* 500
————	————	————	h. The average amount of money that a family in the U.S. will spend on each child from the time he/she is born until the time he/she turns eighteen (as of 2003)
————	————	————	i. Number of endangered species listed in the United States as of February 25, 2004
————	————	————	j. Percentage of the U.S. population under five years old according to the 2000 Census

How many of your ten ranges will actually surround the true quantities? If you set your ranges so that you were 98 percent confident, you should expect to correctly bound approximately 9.8, or nine to ten, of the quantities. Let's look at the correct answers: (a) $246,525,000,000, (b) $28,365,000,000, (c) 35.5, (d) $9,124,100,000, (e) $10,628,900,000, f) 124, (g) 188, (h) $250,000, (i) 514, (j) 6.8%.

How many of your ranges actually surrounded the true quantities? If you surround nine or ten, we can conclude that you were appropriately confident in your estimation ability. Most people surround only between three (30 percent) and seven (70 percent), despite claiming a 98 percent confidence that each range will surround the true value. Why? Most of us are overconfident in our estimation abilities and do not acknowledge our true uncertainty.

In Alpert and Raiffa's (1969) initial demonstration of overconfidence based on 1,000 observations (100 participants on 10 items), 42.6 percent of quantities fell outside 90 percent confidence ranges. Since then, overconfidence has been identified as a common judgmental pattern and demonstrated in a wide variety of settings. For example, Fischhoff, Slovic, and Lichtenstein (1977) found that participants who assigned odds of 1,000:1 of being correct were correct only 81 to 88 percent of the time. For odds of 1,000,000:1, their answers were correct only 90 to 96 percent of the time! This effect is in part due to the fact that people are imperfect at gauging their own level of accuracy. Given this lack of self-awareness about one's knowledge, overconfidence will increase as people become more sure of themselves (Erev, Wallsten, and Budescu, 1994).

People also fail to account for the difficulty of questions; we tend to be more overconfident when asked to respond to questions of moderate to extreme difficulty than to easy questions (Fischhoff, Slovic, and Lichtenstein, 1977). As participants' knowledge of a question decreases, they do not correspondingly decrease their level of confidence. This may be another result of the fact that people imperfectly estimate their own performance. Specifically, we are most likely to overestimate our performance when it is at its lowest (Erev et al., 1994). So, participants typically demonstrate no overconfidence, and often some underconfidence, when asked questions with which they are familiar. Thus, we should be most alert to the potential for overconfidence when considering areas outside of our expertise.

Are groups as overconfident as individuals? Sniezek and Henry (1989) investigated the accuracy and confidence of groups decisions about unknown situations. They found that, in general, groups make more accurate judgments than individuals about uncertain events. This is particularly true in groups in which there is a broad variance in individual judgments and a relatively high level of disagreement. However, groups are just as susceptible as individuals to unreasonably high levels of confidence in their judgments. Some 98 percent of participants believed that their group's judgments were in the top half of all group judgments with respect to accuracy. This finding suggests that overconfidence is a significant pitfall for groups as well as for individuals.

Lichtenstein, Fischhoff, and colleagues suggest two viable strategies for eliminating overconfidence. First, Lichtenstein, Fischhoff, and Phillips (1982) found that giving people feedback about their overconfident judgments has been moderately successful at reducing this bias. Second, Koriat, Lichtenstein, and Fischhoff (1980) found that asking people to explain why their answers might be wrong (or far off the mark) can decrease overconfidence by enabling them to recognize contradictions in their judgment.

Why should you be concerned about overconfidence? After all, it has probably given you the courage to attempt endeavors that have stretched your abilities. Unwarranted confidence can indeed be beneficial in some situations. However, consider the potential adverse effects of excess confidence in the following situations:

- You are a surgeon and are trying to persuade a patient's family to agree to a difficult operation. When the family asks you to estimate the likelihood that the patient will survive the operation, you respond, "95 percent." If the patient dies on the operating table, was he one of the unlucky 5 percent, or are you guilty of malpractice for an overconfident projection?

- You are the chief legal counsel for a firm that has been threatened with a multi-million dollar lawsuit. You are 98 percent confident that the firm will not lose in court. Is this degree of certainty sufficient for you to recommend rejecting an out-of-court settlement? Suppose you learn that, if you lose the case, your firm will go bankrupt. Based on what you know now, are you still comfortable with your 98 percent estimate?

- You have developed a marketing plan for a new product. You are so confident in your plan that you have not developed any contingencies for early market failure. When the first stage of your plan falters, will you expedite changes in the marketing strategy, or will your overconfidence blind you to its flaws?

These examples demonstrate the serious problems that can result from the tendency to be overconfident. While confidence in your abilities is necessary for achievement in life, and can inspire respect and confidence in others, overconfidence can be a barrier to effective professional decision making.

Bias 12: The Confirmation Trap

Imagine that the sequence of three numbers below follows a rule, and your task is to diagnose that rule (Wason, 1960). When you write down other sequences of three numbers, an instructor will tell you whether or not your sequence follows the rule.

2–4–6

What sequences would you write down? How would you know when you had enough evidence to guess the rule? Wason's study participants tended to offer fairly few sequences, and the sequences tended to be consistent with the rule that they eventually guessed. Commonly proposed rules included "numbers that go up by two" and "the difference between the first two numbers equals the difference between the last two numbers." In fact, Wason's rule was much broader: "any three ascending numbers." This solution requires participants to accumulate disconfirming, rather than confirming, evidence. For example, if you think the rule is "numbers that go up by two," you must try sequences that do not conform to this rule to find the actual rule. Trying the sequences 1–3–5, 10–12–14, 122–124–126, and so on, will only lead you into the confirmation trap. Similarly, if you think the rule is "the difference between the first two numbers equals the difference between the last two numbers," you must try sequences that do not conform to this rule to find the actual rule. Trying the sequences 1–2–3, 10–15–20, 122–126–130, again, would only bring you feedback that strengthens your hypothesis. Only six out of Wason's twenty-nine participants found the correct rule on their first guess. Wason concluded that obtaining the correct solution necessitates "a willingness to attempt to falsify hypotheses, and thus to test those intuitive ideas that so often carry the feeling of certitude" (p. 139).

I have used this task hundreds of times in classes. My first volunteer typically guesses "numbers going up by two" and is quickly eliminated. My second volunteer is often just as quick with a wrong answer. Interestingly, at this stage, it is rare that I will have answered "no" to a sequence proposed by either volunteer. Why? Because people tend to seek confirmatory information, even when disconfirming information is more powerful and important.

Once you become aware of the confirmation trap, you are likely to find that it pervades your decision-making processes. When you make a tentative decision (to buy a new car, to hire a particular employee, to start research and development on a new product line), do you search for data that supports your decision before making the final commitment? Most of us do. However, the existence of the confirmation trap implies that the search for challenging, or disconfirming, evidence will provide the most useful insights. For example, when you are seeking to confirm your decision to hire a particular employee, you will probably have no trouble finding positive information on the individual, such as recommendations from past employers. In fact, it may be more important for you to determine whether negative information on this individual, such as a criminal record, as well as positive information on another potential applicant, also exists. Now consider the last car you purchased. Imagine that the day after you drove your new car home, your local newspaper printed two lists ranking cars by performance—one by fuel efficiency and one by crash test results. Which list would you pay more attention to? Most of us would pay more attention to whichever list confirms that we made a good purchase.

I recently watched my friend Dick Thaler engage a group of financial executives in the 2–4–6 task. After the basic demonstration, Thaler told the audience that he was forming two new consulting firms. One of them, called "Yes Person," would respond to all requests for advice by telling the clients that all their ideas are great. In fact, to speed service and ensure satisfaction, Yes Person would allow the clients to write the consulting report themselves if they liked. The other consulting firm, called "Devil's Advocate," would disapprove of any plans currently being considered by a client. Reports by Devil's Advocate would consist of a list of the top ten reasons a plan should not be undertaken.

Which consulting style would be more useful to the client? Thaler insisted to his audience that Devil's Advocate would provide a much more important service than Yes Person, and I agree. However, real-world consulting engagements often bear a closer resemblance to the Yes Person format than to that of Devil's Advocate, in part because consulting firms know that clients like to hear how good their ideas are. Our desire to confirm our initial ideas is so strong that we will pay people to back us up! When pressed, Thaler conceded that his two firms don't really exist, and could never succeed. After all, he pointed out, no firm would ever hire Devil's Advocate, and Yes Person already had too much competition from established consulting firms.

Bias 13: Hindsight and the Curse of Knowledge

Imagine yourself in the following scenarios:

- You are an avid football fan, and you are watching a critical game in which your team is behind 35–31. With three seconds left and the ball on the opponent's three-yard line, the quarterback calls a pass play into the corner of the end zone. When the play fails, you shout, "I *knew* that was a bad play."

- You are riding in an unfamiliar area, and your spouse is driving. When you approach an unmarked fork in the road, your spouse decides to go to the right. Four miles and fifteen minutes later, it is clear that you are lost. You blurt out, "I knew you should have turned left at the fork."

- A manager who works for you hired a new supervisor last year. You were well aware of the choices she had at the time and allowed her to choose the new employee on her own. You have just received production data on every supervisor. The data on the new supervisor are terrible. You call in the manager and claim, "There was plenty of evidence that he was the wrong man for the job."

- As director of marketing in a consumer-goods organization, you have just presented the results of an extensive six-month study on current consumer preferences for the products manufactured by your company. At the conclusion of your presentation, a senior vice president responds, "I don't know why we spent so much time and money collecting these data. I could have told you what the results were going to be."

Do you recognize any of your own behaviors in these scenarios? Do you recognize someone else's remarks? Each scenario exemplifies "the hindsight bias" (Fischhoff, 1975). People typically are not very good at recalling or reconstructing the way an uncertain situation appeared to them before finding out the results of the decision. What play would *you* have called? Did you really know that your spouse should have turned left? Was there really evidence that the selected supervisor was a bad choice? Could the senior vice president really have predicted your study's results? While our intuition is occasionally accurate, we tend to overestimate what we knew beforehand based upon what we later learned. The hindsight bias occurs when people look back on their own judgments, as well as those of others.

Fischhoff (1975) examined the differences between hindsight and foresight in the context of judging the outcome of historical events. In one study, participants were divided into five groups and asked to read a passage about the war between the British and Gurka forces in 1814. One group was not told the result of the war. The remaining four groups of participants were told either that: (1) the British won, (2) the Gurkas won, (3) a military stalemate was reached with no peace settlement, or (4) a military stalemate was reached with a peace settlement. Obviously, only one group was told the truthful outcome—in this case, (1). Each participant was then asked what his or her subjective assessments of the probability of each of the outcomes would have been without the benefit of knowing the reported outcome. Participants tended to believe that even if they had not been told the outcome, they would have judged the outcome that they were told happened as being most likely. Based on this and other varied examples, it becomes clear that knowledge of an outcome increases an individual's belief about the degree to which he or she would have predicted that outcome without the benefit of that knowledge.

Anchoring is often used to explain the hindsight bias. According to this view, knowledge of an event's outcome becomes an anchor by which individuals interpret their prior judgments of the event's likelihood. Since adjustments to anchors are known to be inadequate, hindsight knowledge can be expected to bias perceptions of what one thinks one knew in foresight. Furthermore, to the extent that various pieces of data about the event vary in support of the actual outcome, evidence that is consistent with the known outcome may become cognitively more salient and thus more available in memory (Slovic and Fischhoff, 1977). This tendency will lead an individual to justify a claimed foresight in view of "the facts provided." Finally, the relevance of a particular piece of data may later be judged important to the extent to which it is representative of the final observed outcome.

In the short run, hindsight has a number of advantages. For instance, it is flattering to believe that your judgment is far better than it actually is! In addition, hindsight allows us to criticize other people's apparent lack of foresight. However, the hindsight bias reduces our ability to learn from the past and to evaluate decisions objectively. In general, individuals should be judged by the process and logic of their decisions, not on their results. A decision maker who makes a high-quality decision that does not work out should be rewarded, not punished. Why? Because results are affected by a variety of factors outside the direct control of the decision maker. When we rely on hindsight offered by results, we will inappropriately evaluate the decision makers' logic, judging their outcomes rather than their methods.

Closely related to the hindsight bias is the "curse of knowledge," which argues that when assessing others' knowledge, people are unable to ignore knowledge that they have that others do not have (Camerer, Loewenstein, and Weber, 1989). Knowledge that is psychologically available is hard to forget when a person is imagining how much others know; sophistication stands in the way of a fair assessment. This "curse" explains the difficulty teachers often have adjusting their lessons according to what students already know, and the tendency of product designers to overestimate the average person's ability to master high-tech devices. Similarly, Hoch (1988) found that marketing experts (who are also consumers) are generally worse at predicting the beliefs, values, and tastes of other consumers than nonexpert consumers are. This results from the marketing experts acting as if the non-expert consumer understood as much about the products as they did.

Have you ever given someone what you believed were very clear directions to your home, only to find that they got lost? Keysar (1994) argues that an individual often assumes that when she sends an ambiguous message (which is clear to her) to another individual, based on information that the receiver does not possess, her intent will be magically understood by the other party. Keysar (1994) had people read scenarios that provided them with privileged information about "David." They read that David had dinner at a particular restaurant based on a friend's recommendation. Half the participants in the experiment learned that he really enjoyed his meal, and the other half learned that he disliked it very much. All the participants read that David wrote his friend the following note: "About the restaurant, it was marvelous, just marvelous." The participants who knew that David enjoyed the restaurant had a strong tendency to believe that the friend would take the comment as sincere. In contrast, participants who knew that David disliked the restaurant had a strong tendency to believe that the friend would take the comment as sarcastic. This result occurred despite the fact that both groups of participants knew that the friend had access to the same note and no additional information about David's dining experience. A great deal of disappointment occurs as a result of the failure to communicate clearly in organizations. Part of this disappointment results from our false belief that people understand our ambiguous messages.

INTEGRATION AND COMMENTARY

Heuristics, or rules of thumb, are the cognitive tools we use to simplify decision making. The preceding pages have described thirteen of the most common biases that result when we over-rely on these judgmental heuristics. These biases, along with their associated heuristics, are summarized in Table 2.2. Again, I must emphasize that more than one heuristic can operate on our decision-making processes at any given time. Overall, the use of heuristic "shortcuts" results far more often in adequate decisions than inadequate ones. The logic of heuristics is that, on average, any loss in decision quality will be outweighed by time saved. However, as I have demonstrated in this chapter, a blanket acceptance of heuristics is unwise. First, as illustrated by the quiz items, there are many instances in which the loss in decision quality far outweighs the time saved by heuristics. Second, the foregoing logic suggests that we have voluntarily accepted the quality tradeoffs associated with heuristics. In reality, we have not: Most of us are unaware of their existence and their ongoing impact upon our decision making. Consequently, we fail to distinguish between situations in which they are beneficial and situations in which they are potentially harmful.

To emphasize the distinction between legitimate and illegitimate uses of heuristics, let's reconsider Problem 5. Participants tended to predict that Mark would be more likely to take a job in arts management, despite the fact that the contextual data overwhelmingly favored his choice of a position with a consulting firm. In this case, the representativeness heuristic prevents us from appropriately incorporating relevant base-rate data. However, if the choice of "consulting firm" were replaced with a less common career path for an MBA from a prestigious university (such as steel-industry management), then the representativeness heuristic is likely to lead to an accurate prediction. That is, when base-rate data are unavailable or irrelevant (that is, when the choices have the same base rate), the representativeness heuristic provides a reasonably good cognitive tool for matching Mark to his most likely career path. The key to improved judgment, therefore, lies in learning to distinguish between appropriate and inappropriate uses of heuristics. This chapter gives you the foundation you need to learn to make this distinction.

TABLE 2.2 Summary of the Thirteen Biases Presented in Chapter 2

Bias	Description
Biases Emanating from the Availability Heuristic	
1. Ease of recall	Individuals judge events that are more easily recalled from memory, based on vividness or recency, to be more numerous than events of equal frequency whose instances are less easily recalled.

(Continues)

TABLE 2.2 Summary of the Thirteen Biases Presented in Chapter 2 *(Continued)*

Bias	Description
2. Retrievability	Individuals are biased in their assessments of the frequency of events based on how their memory structures affect the search process.
3. Presumed associations	Individuals tend to overestimate the probability of two events co-occurring based on the number of similar associations they can easily recall, whether from experience or social influence.

Biases Emanating from the Representativeness Heuristic

4. Insensitivity to base rates	When assessing the likelihood of events, individuals tend to ignore base rates if any other descriptive information is provided—even if it is irrelevant.
5. Insensitivity to sample size	When assessing the reliability of sample information, individuals frequently fail to appreciate the role of sample size.
6. Misconceptions of chance	Individuals expect that a sequence of data generated by a random process will look "random," even when the sequence is too short for those expectations to be statistically valid.
7. Regression to the mean	Individuals tend to ignore the fact that extreme events tend to regress to the mean on subsequent trials.
8. The conjunction fallacy	Individuals falsely judge that conjunctions (two events co-occurring) are more probable than a more global set of occurrences of which the conjunction is a subset.

Biases Beyond Availability and Representativeness

9. Anchoring	Individuals make estimates for values based upon an initial value (derived from past events, random assignment, or whatever information is available) and typically make insufficient adjustments from that anchor when establishing a final value.
10. Conjunctive and disjunctive events bias	Individuals exhibit a bias toward overestimating the probability of conjunctive events and underestimating the probability of disjunctive events.
11. Overconfidence	Individuals tend to be overconfident of the infallibility of their judgments when answering moderately to extremely difficult questions.
12. The confirmation trap	Individuals tend to seek confirmatory information for what they think is true and fail to search for disconfirmatory evidence.
13. Hindsight and the curse of knowledge	After finding out whether or not an event occurred, individuals tend to overestimate the degree to which they would have predicted the correct outcome. Furthermore, individuals fail to ignore information they possess that others do not when predicting others' behavior.

CHAPTER THREE

Framing and the Reversal of Preferences

*T*he following is one of the most famous problems in the decision-making literature. Please make the best choice possible (adapted from Tversky and Kahneman, 1981):

Problem 1. Imagine that the United States is preparing for the outbreak of an unusual Asian disease that is expected to kill 600 people. Two alternative programs to combat the disease have been proposed. Assume that the exact scientific estimates of the consequences of the programs are as follows.

Program A: If Program A is adopted, 200 people will be saved.

Program B: If Program B is adopted, there is a one-third probability that 600 people will be saved and a two-thirds probability that no people will be saved.

Which of the two programs would you favor?

There are a number of factors you might consider when evaluating these options. For example, what will be the impact of each program on the broader society? Who is most at risk for the disease? Which option would provide the greatest benefit? There are many other questions you might ask. But if you had to pick Plan A or Plan B based only on the information given in the problem, which program would you choose?

Most people choose Program A—more on this preference in a few paragraphs. For now, let's consider how you might think through this decision. One simple rule for making decisions is to always select the alternative with the highest expected value— the strategy that provides the best overall outcome. But, as you can see, the expected values of the two programs are equal. Program A will definitely save 200 lives. Program B has a one-third chance of saving 600 lives or, on average, 200 lives.

The simple argument for an expected-value decision rule is that decisions made according to this rule will, in the aggregate, be optimal. But consider the following scenarios:

Big positive gamble: You can (a) receive $10 million for sure (expected value = $10 million) or (b) flip a coin and receive $22 million for heads but nothing for tails (expected value = $11 million). An expected-value decision rule would require you to pick (b). What would you do?

Lawsuit: You are being sued for $500,000 and estimate that you have a 50 percent chance of losing the case (expected value = –$250,000). However, the other side is willing to accept an out-of-court settlement of $240,000 (expected value = –$240,000). An expected-value decision rule would lead you to settle out of court. Ignoring attorney's fees, court costs, aggravation, and so on, would you (a) fight the case, or (b) settle out of court?

Most people would choose (a) in both cases, demonstrating that situations exist in which people do not follow an expected-value decision rule. Understanding when and how people deviate from expected value leads to the concept of risk preference. To explain departures from the expected-value decision rule, Daniel Bernoulli (1738) first suggested replacing the criterion of expected monetary value with the criterion of expected utility. Expected-utility theory suggests that each level of an outcome is associated with an expected degree of pleasure or net benefit, called utility. The expected utility of an uncertain choice is the weighted sum of the utilities of the possible outcomes, each multiplied by its probability. While an expected-value approach to decision making would treat $1 million as being worth twice as much as $500,000, a gain of $1 million does not always create twice as much expected utility as a gain of $500,000. Most individuals do not obtain as much utility from the second $500,000 as they did from the first $500,000.

When we prefer a certain $480,000 over a 50 percent chance of $1 million, we are described as risk averse, since we are giving up expected value to reduce risk. Similarly, in the Big Positive Gamble problem above, taking the $10 million is a risk-averse choice, since it has a lower expected value and lower risk. In contrast, fighting the lawsuit would be a risk-seeking choice, since it has a lower expected value and a higher risk. Essentially, expected utility refers to the maximization of utility, or experienced benefit, rather than simply a maximization of the arithmetic average of the possible courses of action. While expected utility departs from the logic of expected value, it provides a useful and consistent logical structure—and decision researchers see following the logic of expected utility as rational behavior.

Now consider a second version of the Asian Disease Problem (from Tversky and Kahneman, 1981):

Problem 2. Imagine that the United States is preparing for the outbreak of an unusual Asian disease that is expected to kill 600 people. Two alternative programs to combat the disease have been proposed. Assume that the scientific estimates of the consequences of the programs are as follows.

Program C: If Program C is adopted, 400 people will die.

Program D: If Program D is adopted, there is a one-third probability that no one will die and a two-thirds probability that 600 people will die.

Which of the two programs would you favor?

Close examination of the two sets of programs in Problems 1 and 2 shows that they are objectively the same. Saving two hundred people (Program A) offers the same objective outcome as losing four hundred people (Program C), and programs B and D are also objectively identical. However, informal empirical investigation demonstrates that most individuals choose Program A in the first set (72 percent in Tversky and Kahneman's 1981 sample) and Program D in the second set (78 percent in Tversky and Kahneman's 1981 sample). While the two sets of choices are objectively identical, changing the description of outcomes from lives saved to lives lost is sufficient to shift prototypic choice from risk-averse to risk-seeking behavior.

Individuals treat risks concerning perceived gains (for example, saving lives—Programs A and B) differently from risks concerning perceived losses (losing lives—Programs C and D). Kahneman and Tversky's (1979) prospect theory describes the fact that even perceived differences based on a change in the "framing" of choices—from losses to gains—can dramatically affect how people answer the question. In the decision literature, and in this chapter, the term framing refers to alternative wordings of the same objective information that significantly alter the model decision, though differences between frames should have no effect on the rational decision. Problems 1 and 2 are objectively the same. Problem 1 is framed in terms of saving lives. Most of us, when we make decisions about gains, are risk averse; thus, our tendency to take the sure $10 million in the Big Gamble problem. In contrast, Problem 2 is framed in terms of losses. Most of us, when we make decisions regarding losses, are risk seeking. Thus, many would fight the law suit in the example above, despite the lower expected value relative to Problem 1. Kahneman and Tversky's amazing insight is that you can take the same objective problem, change the frame, and get predictably different results.

The typical decision maker evaluates outcomes relative to a neutral reference point. Consequently, the location of the reference point is critical to whether the decision is positively or negatively framed and affects the resulting risk preference of the decision maker. The Asian Disease Problem illustrates the importance of reference points. In the positively framed case, the question is, how many lives can be saved? Saved from what? Saved from the possible loss of all 600 lives. Thus, the loss of 600 lives is the neutral reference point. In contrast, in the negatively framed case, the question is, how many lives will be lost? Lost from what? Lost from the existing state of having all 600 people alive.

For another example of the importance of this reference point shift, consider the following scenario:

> **Problem 3.** You were given 100 shares of stock in XYZ Corporation two years ago, when the value of the stock was $20 per share. Unfortunately, the stock has dropped to $10 per share during the two years that you have held the asset. The corporation is currently drilling for oil in an area that may turn out to be a big "hit." On the other hand, they may find nothing. Geological analysis suggests that if they hit, the stock is expected to go back up to $20 per share. If the well is dry, however, the value of the stock will fall to $0 per share. Do you want to sell your stock now for $10 per share?

What is your reference point in this problem? Is it the amount you can gain (the amount that you receive for the stock above $0 per share), or is it the amount you can lose (the amount that the stock has fallen from $20 per share when you sell it)? If you cognitively adopt $0 per share as your reference point, you will be risk averse and will likely to take the sure "gain" by selling the stock now. If your reference point is $20 per share, however, you will likely to be risk seeking and will hold onto the stock rather than accept a sure "loss."

How should this knowledge of the impact of reference points affect your decisions? First, when facing a risky decision, you should identify your reference point. Next, consider whether other reference points exist, and whether they are just as reasonable. If the answer is yes, think about your decision from multiple perspectives and examine any contradictions that emerge. At this point, you will be prepared to make your decision with a full awareness of the alternative frames in which the problem could have been presented.

Rational decision makers should be immune to the framing of choices, yet we now know that frames can have amazingly strong effects on decisions. Over the past twenty-five years, framing has generated a great deal of excitement in the fields of decision theory, psychology, marketing, law, medicine, finance, organizational behavior, and economics. The concept has been responsible for helping researchers develop a more thorough understanding of errors and inconsistencies in human judgment. In the early editions of this book, we focused simply on gain/loss frames. In recent years, there have been amazing discoveries in the way in which frames that should have no effect on our decisions exhibit profound effects. This broader definition of framing is the topic of the current chapter. In this chapter, we will examine dramatic preference reversals in the following contexts: (1) how framing can lead to a portfolio of decisions that few of us would want, yet are likely to choose; (2) how the perception of "pseudocertainty" can affect judgment; (3) how framing causes us to purchase more insurance than we need; (4) how we evaluate the quality of a transaction; (5) how ownership creates a different frame for valuation; (6) how our mental accounts affect how we frame decisions; (7) how we overvalue acts of commission versus acts of omission; (8) the differences between calling something a "bonus" versus calling it a "rebate"; and (9) whether we evaluate options separately or simultaneously.

FRAMING AND THE IRRATIONALITY OF THE SUM OF OUR CHOICES

Tversky and Kahneman (1981) asked 150 subjects the following questions.

> **Problem 4.** Imagine that you face the following pair of concurrent decisions. First, examine both decisions, and then indicate the options you prefer.
>
> *Decision A*
>
> Choose between:
>
>   a. a sure gain of $240
>
>   b. a 25 percent chance to gain $1,000, and a 75 percent chance to gain nothing
>
> *Decision B*
>
> Choose between:

c. a sure loss of $750

d. a 75 percent chance to lose $1,000, and a 25 percent chance to lose nothing

In Decision A, 84 percent of subjects chose (a) and only 16 percent chose (b). In Decision B, 87 percent of subjects chose (d) and only 13 percent chose (c). The majority chose "a sure gain of $240" in Decision A because of our tendency to be risk averse concerning gains and positively framed questions. By contrast, the majority chose "a 75 percent chance to lose $1,000" in Decision B because of our tendency to be risk seeking concerning losses and negatively framed questions. Combining the responses to the two problems, 73 percent of respondents chose (a) and (d), while only 3 percent chose (b) and (c).

Now consider the following problems presented by Tversky and Kahneman (1981) to eighty-six subjects (who were not previously exposed to Problem 4):

Problem 5. Choose between:

e. a 25 percent chance to win $240, and a 75 percent chance to lose $760

f. a 25 percent chance to win $250, and a 75 percent chance to lose $750

Not surprisingly, all eighty-six subjects chose (f) over (e). In fact, (f) dominates (e) in all respects. Why is this problem interesting? When you combine (a) and (d) (the preferred choices) in Problem 4, (e) results, whereas when you combine choices (b) and (c) (the choices not preferred), (f) results.

Adding choices (a) and (d) = (e):
$$(100\%)(\$240) + [(75\%)(-\$1,000) + (25\%)(\$0)] = (25\%)(\$240) + (75\%)(-\$760)$$

Adding choices (b) and (c) = (f):
$$[(25\%)(\$1,000) + (75\%)(\$0)] + (100\%)(-\$750) = (25\%)(\$250) + (75\%)(-\$750)$$

The sum of the undesirable choices *dominates* the sum of the desirable choices! Thus, the framing of the combined problem in two parts results in a reversal of preferences.

Why should this finding interest managers? Many interconnected decisions in the real world, such as portfolio selection, budgeting, and funding for new projects, can occur one decision at a time or in groups of decisions. The findings suggest that the natural sequential nature of the decision-making process in organizations is likely to enhance the potential for inconsistency and nonrational choice. Sales departments are encouraged to think in terms of the acquisition of corporate gains, while credit offices are encouraged to frame decisions in terms of avoiding corporate losses. To arrive at a coherent strategy for making judgments under uncertainty, individuals and organizations need to become more aware of this bias and develop procedures for identifying and integrating risky decisions across organizations.

By being risk averse some of the time and risk seeking at other times, we are likely to adopt a decision portfolio that is just as inferior as selecting the preceding choices (a) and (d). To override our intuitive tendency for our risk preferences to be highly affected by the problem frame, Kahneman and Lovallo (1993, see also Rabin and Thaler, 2000) have argued that we would generally be better off following an expected-value rule for most decisions. This can be seen in the famous story of Nobel

Prize–winning economist Paul Samuelson (1963), who offered a colleague a coin-toss gamble. If the colleague won the toss, he would receive $200, but if he lost, he would lose $100. Samuelson was offering his colleague a positive expected value with risk. The colleague, being risk averse, refused the single bet, but said that he would be happy to toss the coin one hundred times! The colleague understood that the bet had a positive expected value, and that across lots of bets, the odds virtually guaranteed a profit. Yet with only one trial, he had a 50 percent chance of regretting taking the bet. Yet the colleague doubtless faced many gambles in life (such as whether to invest extra money from this month's pay in stocks, bonds, or money markets), and would have faired better in the long run by maximizing his expected value on each decision, as his preference for running the bet one hundred times suggests. Each of us also encounters "small gambles" in life, and we should try to follow the same strategy. Though risk aversion may make us want to turn down each individual opportunity for gain, the aggregated risk of all of the positive expected-value gambles we came across would become infinitesimal and the potential profit quite large. Deviations from risk neutrality in the real world should probably be reserved for critically important decisions such as job acceptances, house buying, acquisitions, etc., after careful consideration of the problem from multiple frames. In contrast, most of us tend to be risk averse toward some choices and risk seeking toward others, enacting a suboptimal portfolio of decisions. Unless the decision is very important, a simple and effective strategy is to use expected value as the basis for decision making.

WE LIKE CERTAINTY, EVEN PSEUDOCERTAINTY

People underweight high-probability events but appropriately weight events that are certain (Kahneman and Tversky, 1979). Thus, if an event has a probability of 1.0 or zero, we tend to accurately evaluate the event's probability. However, if the event has a probability of .99, we tend to respond as the expected-utility framework would expect us to respond to a probability of less than .99. As a result, Slovic, Lichtenstein, and Fischhoff (1982) observe that "any protective action that reduces the probability of harm from, say, .01 to zero will be valued more highly than an action that reduces the probability of the same harm from .02 to .01" (p. 24). In other words, people value the creation of certainty over an equally valued shift in the level of uncertainty.

Interestingly, the perception of certainty (that is, the perception that the probability of an event is zero or 1.0) can be easily manipulated. Slovic et al. (1982) consider the best way to advertise a disaster insurance policy that covers fire but not flood. The policy can be accurately advertised either as "full protection" against fire or as a reduction in the overall probability of loss from natural disasters. The full-protection advertisement will make the policy most attractive to potential buyers. This is because the full-protection option reduces perceived uncertainty for loss from fire to zero, whereas the overall disaster policy reduces uncertainty some incremental amount to a value still above zero. The perceived certainty that results from the full-protection framing of this advertisement has been labeled "pseudocertainty" (Slovic et al., 1982).

Slovic et al. (1982) provided empirical evidence of the strength of the pseudocertainty effect in the context of disease vaccination. Two forms of a questionnaire were created. Form 1 described a disease that was expected to afflict 20 percent of the population. Subjects in this condition were asked if they would receive a vaccine that protected half of the individuals vaccinated. Form 2 described two mutually exclusive and equally probable strains of the disease, each of which was expected to afflict 10 percent of the population. In this case, vaccination was said to give complete protection (certainty) against one strain and no protection against the other. Would you take the vaccine described in Form 1? What about the vaccine described in Form 2? In either case, the vaccine would objectively reduce one's overall risk from 20 percent to 10 percent. Slovic et al. found that Form 2 (pseudocertainty) was more appealing than Form 1 (probabilistic). Some 57 percent of subjects who were given Form 2 said that they would get the vaccination, compared with only 40 percent of the subjects who received Form 1.

In the following problems, Tversky and Kahneman (1981) simultaneously investigated the impact of certainty and pseudocertainty:

Problem 6. Which of the following options do you prefer?

a. a sure win of $30

b. an 80 percent chance to win $45

Problem 7. Consider the following two-stage game. In the first stage, there is a 75 percent chance to end the game without winning anything, and a 25 percent chance to move into the second stage. If you reach the second stage you have a choice between:

c. a sure win of $30

d. an 80 percent chance to win $45

Decide whether you prefer (c) or (d). Your choice must be made before the game starts—that is, before the outcome of the first stage is known.

Problem 8. Which of the following options do you prefer?

e. a 25 percent chance to win $30

f. a 20 percent chance to win $45

Tversky and Kahneman (1981) presented each of these problems to a different group of subjects. In Problem 6, 78 percent of the subjects chose (a) and 22 percent chose (b). In Problem 7, 74 percent of the subjects chose (c) and 26 percent chose (d). In Problem 8, 42 percent of the subjects chose (e) and 58 percent chose (f). Some interesting contrasts result. Consider Problem 7: By combining the first and second part of the problem, it becomes evident that (c) offers a .25 chance to win $30 and (d) offers a .25 × .80 = .20 chance to win $45. This is the same choice offered in Problem 8! Yet the modal choice has shifted. In Problem 7, if you lose in the first stage, it does not matter what choice you made. If you win in the first stage, Problem 7 reduces to Problem 6. Consequently, there seems to be no reason to respond differently to Problems 6 and 7. Since Problem 7 is equivalent to Problems 6 and 8, it can be inferred that Problems 6 and 8 should also be treated similarly. However, subjects responded similarly to Problems 6 and 7, but differently to Problem 8. Why this discrepancy in response to Problem 8?

The difference between Problems 6 and 8 illustrates a phenomenon that Tversky and Kahneman (1981) call the *certainty effect*: "A reduction of the probability of an outcome has more importance when the outcome was initially certain than when it was merely probable" (p. 455). The discrepancy, in response to objectively identical Problems 7 and 8, illustrates the *pseudocertainty effect* (Slovic et al., 1982; Tversky and Kahneman, 1981). The prospect of winning $30 is more attractive in Problem 7 than in Problem 8 because of the perceived certainty ("a sure win") associated with choice (c). However, this potential "certainty" is contingent upon reaching the second stage of the game, which still makes the outcome uncertain.

The certainty and pseudocertainty effects lead to judgmental inconsistencies. The certainty effect makes us more apt to be interested in reducing the likelihood of certain events than uncertain events. Under the pseudocertainty effect, we are more likely to favor options that assure us certainty than those that only reduce uncertainty. Rationally, any constant reduction of risk in an uncertain situation should have the same value for the decision maker. For example, reducing the risk of cancer from 20 percent to 10 percent should have the same value as a reduction from 10 percent to 0 percent. But perceived certainty, or "pseudocertainty," has a special value to most people. Manipulations of pseudocertainty have important implications for the design of communications about medical treatments, personal insurance, corporate liability protection, and a variety of other forms of protection. The data suggest that individuals may buy insurance not only to protect against risk, but also to eliminate the worry caused by any amount of uncertainty (Tversky and Kahneman, 1981).

THE FRAMING AND THE OVERSELLING OF INSURANCE

What is an insurance premium? It is a certain loss (the premium) that you accept in exchange for the reduction of a small probability of a large loss. Virtually all insurance provides customers with negative expected value—that's how insurance companies make a profit. Interestingly, Schoemaker and associates (Hershey and Schoemaker, 1980; Schoemaker and Kunreuther, 1979) and Slovic et al. (1982) have found that framing a sure loss as an insurance premium makes the loss more attractive—even when the objective amount of loss is the same. Slovic et al. (1982) asked study participants to pick between a sure loss (insurance premium) versus a risky option that had a small probability of a significant loss. For half of the participants, the risk-free option was called a certain loss. For the other half, the risk-free option was called an insurance premium. Study participants were much more likely to choose the risk-free loss when it was called an insurance premium than when it was called a certain loss.

Kahneman and Tversky (1979) and Hershey and Schoemaker (1980) argue that the word "insurance" triggers pervasive social norms: "How can you not carry insurance?" and "All good citizens carry insurance." Buying insurance is something most of us do without considering an alternative strategy. When was the last time you considered dropping your car insurance (assuming that you live in a state where it is legal to be uninsured)?

The framing of insurance and warranties may explain a very strange set of consumer decisions. After agreeing to buy a new automobile, consumers are typically offered the option of purchasing an extended warranty. The salesperson typically notes that, "For just a few dollars more per month, you'll never have to worry about repairs." Why do nearly half of new car buyers purchase extended warranties? It could be because they are a good deal. But this does not appear to be the case. Car dealers make a great deal of money on warranties. Documents in a recent lawsuit filed against Nissan show that the typical extended warranty cost $795. A mere $131 went toward covering repairs, $109 went to Nissan for administrative costs, and the remaining $555 was straight dealer profit. It seems that the vividness of a costly repair, coupled with a social norm favoring insurance and warranties, leads many consumers to make a risk-averse choice that they would probably not make if they considered their options more carefully. As we have seen, people are more likely to accept a certain loss if they view it as insurance rather than as a sure monetary loss. Consumers would be better off if they just said "no" to all extended warranties, put the money saved in the bank, and used it to pay for necessary repairs. Across their life span, they will be making a far better set of decisions.

WHAT'S IT WORTH TO YOU?

The term *transactional utility* was introduced by Thaler (1985) and can be seen in the following scenario. Read this scenario twice—first with the words in parentheses and excluding the words in brackets, and second with the words in brackets and excluding the words in parentheses.

> You are lying on the beach on a hot day. All you have to drink is ice water. For the last hour you have been thinking about how much you would enjoy a nice cold bottle of your favorite brand of beer. A companion gets up to go make a phone call and offers to bring back a beer from the only nearby place where beer is sold (a fancy resort hotel) [a small, rundown grocery store]. He says that the beer might be expensive and asks how much you are willing to pay for it. He says that he will buy the beer if it costs as much as or less than the price you state. But if it costs more than the price you state, he will not buy it. You trust your friend, and there is no possibility of bargaining with the (bartender) [store owner]. What price do you tell him?

Notice some of the features of this dual problem. First, in both the hotel and the grocery store versions, you get the same product. Second, there is no possible negotiation on price. Third, there will be no advantage to the resort hotel "atmosphere," since you are going to drink the beer on the beach. According to expected-utility theory, people should be willing to pay the same amount in both versions of the scenario. In fact, Thaler found that participants in an executive development program were willing to pay significantly more if the beer was purchased from the "fancy resort hotel." Twenty years ago, the results were medians of $2.65 for a beer bought at the resort and $1.50 for a beer bought at the store.

Why does this contradiction occur? Thaler suggests the reason is that while "paying $2.50 for a beer at a fancy hotel would be an expected annoyance, paying $2.50 at a grocery store would be an outrageous 'rip-off.'" This leads to the conclusion that something else matters besides the value you place on the commodity acquired. Did you ever buy something because it was "too good a deal to pass up," despite the fact that you had no need for the product? Thaler explains this phenomenon by suggesting that purchases are affected by both acquisition utility and transactional utility. *Acquisition utility* describes the value you place on a commodity (in this case, the beer). *Transactional utility* refers to the quality of the deal that you receive, evaluated in reference to "what the item should cost." Obviously, paying $2.50 for a beer at a grocery store leads to a greater negative transactional utility than paying $2.50 at the fancy resort hotel. One can argue that the inclusion of transactional utility in decision making is not rational, but it does describe our behavior.

Now, consider the following two problems, adapted from Tversky and Kahneman (1981):

> **Problem 9.** Imagine that you are about to purchase a high-tech mouse for $50. The computer salesperson informs you that the mouse you wish to buy is on sale at the store's other branch, located a twenty-minute drive away. You have decided to buy the mouse today, and will either buy it at the current store or drive twenty minutes to the other store. What is the highest price that the mouse could cost at the other store such that you would be willing to travel there for the discount?

> **Problem 10.** Imagine that you are about to purchase a laptop computer for $2,000. The computer salesperson informs you that this computer is on sale at the store's other branch, located a twenty-minute drive from where you are now. You have decided to buy the computer today, and will either buy it at the current store or drive to the store a twenty-minute drive away. What is the highest price that you would be willing to pay at the other store to make the discount worth the trip?

What is a rational way of deciding whether to buy the mouse or the laptop in the current store or to drive twenty minutes to the other store? Most people quickly conclude that you should compare the value of twenty minutes of your time plus the cost of travel versus the expected savings. This would mean that the minimum discount demanded for each of the two products should be similar. In contrast, most people demand a greater discount in absolute dollars to make the computer trip than to make the mouse trip. Why? The issue of transactional utility enters into our assessments of the value of our time. Most people will be willing to travel the twenty minutes only to get a "very good deal." A $40 (2 percent) savings is not a big discount on the computer, but it is an outstanding deal on the mouse (you would be saving 80 percent). Normatively, however, the difference in percentage reduction is irrelevant. One should simply compare the savings obtained to the value of the time spent, and this value should remain consistent across decisions.

Personally, I find Tversky, Kahneman, and Thaler's insights very informative regarding how I use my own time. The items described in this section forced me to think about how I, having grown up in a family that taught me to clip coupons, trade off time and money. I learned that, due to System 1 thinking, even a decision researcher can develop patterns of behavior that are inconsistent with his preferred values. These problems clarify the importance of spending more time on search when significant amounts of money are at stake and spending less time on search for items of small value. Far too many people have mastered the skill of saving $10 or $12 by going to three grocery stores on Saturday, while failing to be thorough in their search for large purchases—like which house to buy.

THE VALUE WE PLACE ON WHAT WE OWN

Imagine that you purchased a painting from an up-and-coming artist five years ago for $50. The artist has since become very famous, and the painting is now worth about $1,000. Imagine the minimum amount that you believe would lead you to sell this painting. Now, also think about how much you would be willing to pay for a similar-quality painting.

Most people would demand far more to sell the painting than the amount they would be willing to pay for a similar painting, or the amount that they would pay for that exact same painting if they did not own it. This pattern is called the *endowment effect* (Thaler, 1980).

In any exchange, a buyer must be willing to pay at least the minimum amount that a seller is willing to accept—otherwise no agreement takes place. Objectively, the valuation of a commodity should be based on its true value. However, the value that a seller places on a commodity often includes not only its intrinsic worth, but also value based on his or her attachment to the item.

In a very clever experiment, Kahneman, Knetsch, and Thaler (1990) placed mugs in front of one-third of the participants in their study. These "sellers" were told that they owned the mug and had the option of selling it if a price, to be determined later, was acceptable to them. They were then given a list of possible selling prices, ranging from $0.50 to $9.50 (in 50-cent increments), and were told to indicate for each possible price whether they would sell the mug for that amount or keep it.

Another third of the participants—the "buyers"—were told that they would be given a sum of money which they could keep or use it to buy a mug. They were also asked their preferences between a mug and sums of money ranging from $0.50 to $9.50. The remaining third of the participants—the "choosers"—were given a questionnaire indicating that they would be given a choice between either a mug or a sum of money. They also marked their preferences between the mug and sums of money ranging from $0.50 to $9.50. All three groups were assured that their answers would not influence either the predetermined price of the mug or the amount of money to be received in lieu of the mug.

The results reveal a great deal about how our role in a buyer-seller relationship affects our value assessments. Sellers required a median value of $7.12 for the mug, the buyers $2.87, and the choosers $3.12. The buyers and choosers had very similar evaluations of the worth of the mug. In contrast, ownership made the mug much more valuable for the sellers; differences of 2:1 are common in such endowment experiments. The implication of this endowment effect is that people tend to overvalue what they own. The frame of ownership creates value that is inconsistent with a rational analysis of the worth that the commodity brings to the individual. This inconsistent valuation partially explains why so many home sellers set an inappropriately high value on their homes and find themselves without any bidders for extended periods of time. An understanding of the endowment effect is critical to making wise assessments of the value of your commodities.

Dick Thaler gave his University of Chicago MBA students the following pair of hypothetical problems, which were very realistic and easy to imagine at the time:

> **Problem 11.** It is 1998, and Michael Jordan and the Bulls are about to play their final championship game. You would very much like to attend. The game is sold out, and you won't have another opportunity to see Michael Jordan play for a long time, if ever. You know someone who has a ticket for sale. What is the most you would be willing to pay for it?

> **Problem 12.** It is 1998, and Michael Jordan and the Bulls are about to play their final championship game. You have a ticket to the game and would very much like to attend. The game is sold out, and you won't have another opportunity to see Michael Jordan play for a long time, if ever. What is the least that you would accept for a ticket?

Thaler reports that while his students were willing to pay only $330, on average, in Problem 11, they demanded $1,920, on average, in Problem 12. I can identify with this behavior, yet am also bothered by it. How much is the ticket worth? Without knowing the answer, it is far too likely that you will hold onto it long after it makes sense to give it up for a great price. The same holds true for anything you or your company owns—cars, houses, stocks, divisions of a firm, and so on.

MENTAL ACCOUNTING

The previous two sections are consistent with Thaler's (1999) work on mental accounting, which shows that people have a variety of "mental accounts" that they use to organize, evaluate, and keep track of a variety of financial activities, such as money for vacation, a renovation, this month's budget, etc. Interestingly, we apply strikingly different decisions rules to different mental accounts. The previous two sections highlighted specific aspects of mental accounting in action. This section adds other interesting components of our mental accounts.

Thaler (1999) relates a story of traveling to Switzerland to give a paid talk to a group of executives. After the talk, Thaler and his spouse traveled around the country, at a time when the dollar was weak and travel costs were high. Thaler notes that, knowing that the travel expenses would still total far less than his speaking fee, he had no trouble spending money on the trip. He then offers a mental comparison between this story and a similar story in which he earns the same speaking fee in New York, then travels with his spouse to Switzerland. In the latter story, the high costs of Swiss travel would be more bothersome. Essentially, when costs come out of the same account (the Swiss trip account), they seem less important than when they come out of a different account (the New York talk account). I can relate to the Swiss travel story, and I expect that that readers can as well.

Shafir and Thaler (1998; Thaler, 1999) asked a group of subscribers to a wine newsletter to consider the following problem:

> **Problem 13.** Suppose you bought a case of a good 1982 Bordeaux in the futures market for $20 a bottle. The wine now sells at auction for about $75 a bottle. You have decided to drink a bottle.

Which of the following best captures your sense of the cost of your drinking this bottle?

a. $0

b. $20

c. $20 plus interest

d. $75

e. –$55 (you're drinking a $75 bottle for which you paid only $20)

Shafir and Thaler (1998; Thaler, 1999) report that the percentages for each of the answers were (a) 30 percent, (b) 18 percent, (c) 7 percent, (d) 20 percent, and (e) 25 percent. The authors note that the newsletter was published by an economist, Orley Ashenfelter, and that most of respondents who answered "d" were also economists—the answer consistent with economic analysis. The rest of us do not think about the value of our assets based on what they are currently worth. Rather, we either treat costs as something that we have already expensed away (option a), as the cost that we paid (option b), or in terms of the value of the transaction (option e—you made money by making a good purchase).

Your mental accounts can also affect your satisfaction with outcomes that you did not choose. Consider the following two outcomes (adapted from Thaler, 1985):

> You receive a letter from the IRS saying that you made a minor arithmetic mistake in your tax return and must send them $100. You receive a similar letter the same day from your state tax authority saying you owe them $100 for a similar mistake. There are no other repercussions from either mistake.

> You receive a letter from the IRS saying that you made a minor arithmetic mistake in your tax return and must send them $200. There are no other repercussions from the mistake.

Which situation would be more upsetting? Most people are more upset by (a), the two small losses, than by (b), the one larger loss, despite the fact that the two sets of outcomes are equal. This emotional reaction is consistent with the nature of our reactions to losses; specifically, in assessing each loss that hits us, the first dollars lost hurt more than additional dollars lost. So, just as you learned earlier that most people do not perceive losing $200 to be twice as bad as losing $100, two losses from two different mental accounts for $100 each feels worse than one larger loss for $200. The reverse occurs with gains. The benefit of a given amount of money would be perceived as greater if it were given in smaller discrete payments rather than all at once, since we value $100 as more than half of what we value $200. So, do not give your significant other many gifts at once. Separating them will create more total joy!

Finally, Thaler (1999) tells an interesting story about how a colleague uses mental accounting to avoid becoming annoyed by the small losses that he, like all of us, incurs on a moderately regular basis. At the beginning of each year, this colleague sets up a fund that he will use to pay for annoying losses, such as speeding tickets and library fines. When those minor annoyances occur, he simply pays the cost from the account. At the end of the year, he gives the balance in the account to the United Way.

Apparently, this form of mental accounting reduces the man's annoyance about unexpected and petty expenditures. I am not sure what the net impact of the story is on charitable giving, but I like the idea. Once you set aside an amount of money into an account, the details of how you spend it become less bothersome.

DO NO HARM, THE OMISSION BIAS, AND THE STATUS QUO

Bazerman, Baron, and Shonk (2001) posed the following question:

> **Problem 14.** Which option do you prefer:
>
> If you die in an accident, your heart will be used to save another person's life. In addition, if you ever need a heart transplant, there will be a 90 percent chance that you will get a heart.
>
> If you die in an accident, you will be buried with your heart in your body. In addition, if you ever need a heart transplant, there will be a 45 percent chance that you will get a heart.

In this problem, most people chose (a). So why does the United States maintain an organ donation policy that resembles (b)? In the United States, about 50,000 people are on waiting list for organs at any given time. More than a third of them will die before an organ is found. The number of organ donors has declined in recent decades, due to increased use of seatbelts and motorcycle helmets, and only 4,500 of the 11,000 eligible donors actually donate their organs. If we could double this figure, we could save an additional one-quarter of the approximately 15,000 people who die each year in the United States because of the lack of organs.

This situation exists despite the fact that we know how to increase the number of organs available for donation. Bazerman et al. (2001) argue that either of two changes could at least double the number of lives saved. First, we could provide preferential access to organs for those who have previously signed up to be donors. We believe that this system would provide the necessary incentives to dramatically increase enrollment in organ-donation programs. Second, and alternatively, like many other countries (including Austria, Belgium, France, and Sweden), we could presume consent to organ donation (an opt-out program), rather than presuming nonconsent (an opt-in program). That is, we could change the default in the United States to assume that eligible people are organ donors upon death unless they specifically opt out of the organ-donation system. Johnson and Goldstein (2003) document that European countries with an opt-in program similar to that of the United States have donations rates that fall only between 4 and 28 percent. In contrast, European countries with opt-out programs have rates ranging from 86 to 100 percent.

When so many lives could be saved through an opt-out program, why would any country settle for an opt-in program, as the United States does? The answer lies in the psychology of the evaluation of losses and gains. Tversky and Kahneman (1991) have documented that losses loom larger in our minds than gains. This explains why Paul Samuelson's colleague, as discussed earlier in the chapter, might pass on betting on one flip of the coin. Along these lines, consider that virtually any change in government policy will create benefits and costs. Moving to an opt-out program would save lives (an important gain), but would also have costs salient to some individuals, such as the prospect of being buried without all of their organs (a comparatively less important issue). Policy makers often display an irrational preference for harms of omission (e.g., letting people die) over harms of commission (e.g., the dead losing their organs), even when the harms of inaction are much larger than the harms of action. Ritov and Baron (1990) have labeled this the omission bias.

When contemplating risky choices, many people follow the rule of thumb, "Do no harm." Implicit in this advice is the notion that "do" means "do through action," making harms of omission easy to ignore (Ritov and Baron, 1990). Interestingly, psychologists have found that on the personal level, while actions generate more regret in the short run, omissions produce more regret over time (Gilovich and Medvec, 1995). Many potential trades exist that require society to cause small harms as a means to a greater benefit. In a study of hypothetical vaccination decisions, Ritov and Baron (1990) found that many people expressed an unwillingness to vaccinate children against a disease that was expected to kill ten out of 10,000 children when the vaccine itself would kill five out of 10,000 through side effects. These people would not tolerate any deaths from the "commission" of vaccinating—even when their decision would cause five additional deaths. Thus, too often we maintain the status quo rather than acting to improve our outcomes.

When a person gets an offer for a new job that is much better than their old job on some dimensions and marginally worse on others, they often turn down the offer. For many decision makers, these losses will be more salient than any gain, even when the losses are much smaller. Why? One feature of the omission bias is that it usually supports the status quo, an irrational barrier to change. Risky decisions usually require action. Therefore, when contemplating a change, people are more likely to attend to the risk of change than to the risk of failing to change. Taking losses more seriously than gains, they will be motivated to preserve the status quo.

Now consider a problem adapted from Kahneman and Tversky (1982):

> **Problem 15.** Please read about Paul and George and assess who would feel worse:
>
> Paul owns shares in Company A. During the past year he considered switching to stock in Company B, but he decided against it. He now finds that he would have been better off by $1,200 if he had switched to the stock of Company B.
>
> George owned shares in Company B. During the past year he switched to stock in Company A. He now finds that he would have been better off by $1,200 if he had kept his stock in Company B.

Kahneman and Tversky found, as you would probably predict, that most people think that George will feel much worse than Paul. We feel worse about bad events that we caused by action than we do about bad events caused by inaction. These feelings not only affect our own choices in life, but are incorporated into the U.S. legal system, which holds pharmaceutical firms liable for harms produced unintentionally from generally well-researched and well-produced vaccines, but not for the harm caused by the decision to not produce new vaccines due to the threat of lawsuits (Baron and Ritov, 1993). As a result, far too many people become sick or die from the failure to bring beneficial drugs and vaccines to market. Similarly, the same countries that strongly punish those who participate in crimes that lead to death have no "bystander" laws that would punish those who could rescue someone from a deadly situation, but fail to do so.

REBATE/BONUS FRAMING

In September 2001, the United States government paid $38 billion to tax-paying U.S. citizens—$300, $500, or $600 per individual, depending on annual income. Government officials and the media used the term "rebate" to describe these payments, which the Bush administration argued would fuel spending and energize the flagging economy. Epley, Idson, and Mak (2005) have conducted a trio of studies that shows that the way the government framed the program—specifically, through the use of the term "rebate"—dramatically limited its effectiveness. These researchers provide fascinating evidence that if the government had described the payments as "bonuses" instead of "rebates," more citizens would have immediately spent the money instead of saving it, creating a greater stimulus to the economy.

In their first study, Epley et al. showed that the terms "rebate" and "bonus" create very different mental states within taxpayers concerning how they feel the money should be used. The researchers reminded participants, all of whom were taxpayers, that the federal government had issued checks to all taxpayers approximately six months earlier. One group of participants, the "rebate" participants, read this statement: "proponents of this tax cut argued that the government collected more tax revenue than was needed to cover its expenses, resulting in a tax surplus" that should be returned to taxpayers "as withheld income." In contrast, the "bonus" participants read: "proponents of this tax cut argued that the costs of running the government were lower than expected, resulting in a budget surplus" that should be returned to taxpayers "as bonus income." Both groups of participants were then asked to recall what percentage of their checks they spent and what percentage they saved. "Rebate" participants remembered spending 25 percent and saving 75 percent, while "bonus" participants remembered spending 87 percent and saving 13 percent. Due to random assignment, there is no reason to believe that participants in the two conditions actually spent substantially different amounts. Rather, the data suggest that people associate "bonus" with spending and "rebate" with saving. Epley et al. argue that the word "bonus" creates the image of surplus cash, while "rebate" conveys the image of money that simply returns you to the appropriate status quo.

In their second study, Epley et al. gave Harvard undergraduate student participants $50, described as either a tuition rebate or a bonus. In a follow-up a week later, the researchers asked the students how much of the $50 they saved and how much they spent. On average, "rebate" participants reported spending $10 and saving $40, while "bonus" participants reported spending $22 and saving $28; bonus participants spent more than twice as much as rebate participants. Because the students' reports could have been inaccurate, the researchers conduced a third study in which they gave Harvard undergraduates a $25 windfall framed either as "bonus money" or "rebate money." Epley et al. then set up a "lab store" and offered products for sale at about 20 percent off standard prices. On average, rebate participants spent only $2.43, while bonus participants spent $11.16, or more than four times as much.

These studies show the amazing power of framing, the importance of knowing how you can be affected by framing, and the relevance of framing to important decisions. Clearly, the U.S. government could have stimulated the economy far more with a bonus campaign instead of a rebate plan.

JOINT VERSUS SEPARATE PREFERENCE REVERSALS

Imagine that you independently assess two options and place a higher value on Option A than on Option B. You might then logically infer that if you then chose between the two options, you would select Option A over Option B. But in Chapter 1, you read about Hsee's (1998) study, in which participants evaluating two options individually placed greater value on an overfilled small cup of ice cream than on an underfilled larger cup, even when the latter contained more ice cream. When they compared the two servings side by side, they reversed their assessment. This section focuses on a similar set of preference reversals that violate the very simple condition of logical consistency.

An extensive literature on separate versus joint preference reversals now exists. Here, I examine a selective set of examples in which people place a higher value on one option than another when looking at them individually, but reverse their preference when considering two or more options at the same time (Bazerman, Loewenstein, and White, 1992). I will provide at least two explanations for these reversals, which can help clarify when we can expect them to occur.

Consider two salary packages: Package A pays $27,000 in year 1, $26,000 in year 2, $25,000 in year 3, and $24,000 in year 4. Package B pays $23,000 in year 1, $24,000 in year 2, $25,000 in year 3, and $26,000 in year 4. Hsee (1996) found that when undergraduate participants were asked to report how likely they would be to accept each of the offers, Package B was more likely than Package A to be acceptable when participants evaluated just one of the two options. But when they consider the two options together, Package A was much more acceptable. When assessing one option at a time, participants did not like to see pay go down over time. But when assessing both simultaneously, it was easy for them to see that Package A provides more money, and more quickly.

In a very different context, Hsee (1998) asked participants to imagine that they were in the market for a music dictionary and then to evaluate either one or two music dictionaries. The Large Dictionary had 20,000 words and a torn cover. The Intact Dictionary had 10,000 words and an intact cover. Participants examined either one dictionary or both and reported the highest amount they were willing to pay for each. When participants assessed their willingness to pay for both, they valued the Large Dictionary more than the Intact Dictionary ($27 versus $19, on average). By contrast, participants who assessed only one of the two dictionaries valued the Intact Dictionary more than the Large Dictionary ($24 versus $20, on average). The torn cover mattered more when participants assessed only one option, but the number of words mattered more when they assessed the dictionaries jointly.

Kahneman and Ritov (1994) showed similar inconsistencies for different types of environmental or social issues. Participants were presented with headlines that highlighted specific problems and asked to either report their level of support for government intervention in one particular cause (separate condition), or to choose between two causes by stating which one they would support more (joint condition). In separate evaluations, consistent with the affect heuristic (Slovic et al., 2002), people leaned toward "affectively arousing" environmental causes (those that triggered strong emotions), such as spotted owls, coral reefs, and toxic spills. When choosing between causes, however, participants tended to prefer causes directly relevant to people, such as skin cancer, multiple myeloma, and lead-based paint. For example, while the cause of improving the plight of a "threatened Australian mammal species" was slightly more important to people than "skin cancer in farm workers" when participants assessed them one at a time, "skin cancer in farm workers" won by more than a 2-to-1 margin when participants selected between the two causes.

In some political opinion polls, citizens are asked whether or not they approve of a particular candidate. In other polls, citizens are asked which of two candidates they would vote for. Sometimes the inferences that pollsters might make from approval polls do not match up with voting intentions. Lowenthal (1996) provides some clarity on how this can occur. She found that separate evaluations of individual candidates reversed themselves in pair evaluations and voting behavior. Specifically, she examined voter preference for two hypothetical candidates. One candidate was expected to deliver 10,000 new jobs, but was rumored to have evaded paying personal taxes. The other candidate would probably deliver 5,000 new jobs, and had no rumors of misconduct. When participants assessed the candidates individually in an approval poll, the clean candidate received much more favorable assessments. But when asked to vote between them, the candidate expected to deliver more jobs won by almost a 2-to-1 margin.

These examples document a growing body of evidence that demonstrates inconsistencies in preferences across joint versus separate evaluations (Bazerman, Moore, Tenbrunsel, Wade-Benzoni, and Blount, 1999; Hsee, Loewenstein, Blount, and Bazerman, 1999). In interpreting these examples, note that they all involve outcome pairs distinguished along two attributes. One attribute is preferred in separate evaluation, and the other attribute is preferred in joint evaluation. There are at least two explanations for these effects: the "want/should" explanation and the "evaluability" explanation.

Bazerman, Tenbrunsel, and Wade-Benzoni's (1998) want/should explanation views a tension between what an individual wants to do versus what the individual thinks he or she should do. Consistent with the affect heuristic (Slovic et al., 2002), Bazerman et al. (1998) essentially argue that the more affectively arousing option, or the "want" option, will be valued more highly in separate evaluations, while the more logical and reasoned option, or the "should" option, will be valued more highly in joint evaluations. Supporting the face validity of the want/should distinction, O'Connor, De Dreu, Schroth, Barry, Lituchy, and Bazerman (2002) show that people think of the affectively arousing option as the option that they want, and the more logical option as the option they believe they should choose. Essentially, Bazerman et al. (1998) argue that we often act on our affective preferences when assessing one option at a time, but that joint assessment triggers more reasoned analysis. In other words, System 1 thinking will be comparatively more prevalent in separate evaluations, while System 2 thinking will be comparatively more prevalent in joint evaluations.

The evaluability hypothesis (Bazerman et al., 1992; Hsee, 1996; Hsee et al., 1999) offers a more cognitive explanation of separate versus joint preference reversals. This argument suggests that separate versus joint reversals are driven by differences in the ability of attributes to be evaluated, or their "evaluability." When two options require a tradeoff between a hard-to-evaluate attribute (such as the number of words in the dictionary) and an easy-to-evaluate attribute (such as the cover torn), the hard-to-evaluate attribute will have less impact in separate evaluation than in joint evaluation. In separate evaluation, people often have difficulty assessing the desirability of an option based on a hard-to-evaluate attribute (is 10,000 words a good amount?); as a result, the hard-to-evaluate attribute has little influence on decision making. In joint evaluation, having comparison data on the hard-to-evaluate attribute for both options provides additional information and increases the attribute's evaluability. Thus, the number of words in a dictionary has much more meaning when you can compare the number of words to the number in another dictionary. In contrast, you do not need to have comparative information to know that a torn cover is bad.

The task of separate evaluation is complex. In this section, we have highlighted two processes that can lead to changes in the weight that attributes receive between joint and separate evaluations. First, based on the affect heuristic, people will go with their gut response, paying primary attention to the attribute that creates emotional arousal. Second, attributes that are hard to evaluate will be underweighted in separate evaluations. Clearly, both processes are at work in creating separate versus joint preference reversals. We will return to these reversals in Chapter 6, when we explore the conditions under which people obsess about social comparison processes.

CONCLUSION AND INTEGRATION

The categories of framing effects and reversals of preference covered in this chapter demonstrate some of the key findings in the field of behavioral decision research. The Asian disease problem that opened the chapter is a particularly important finding in the history of the field. Prior to this result, and the development of Kahneman and Tversky's (1979) prospect theory, the behavioral decision literature was largely ignored by economists. Simon's concept of bounded rationality, discussed in Chapter 1, was explained away as a rational strategy, adapting for the costs of search. The heuristics and biases explored in Chapter 2 were discounted for similar reasons. But the framing effects described in this chapter showed large effects on how people make decisions based on what even economists would agree was normatively irrelevant information. This problem, which challenged the dominant economic paradigm more than twenty-five years ago, has become an exemplar of the kind of data that is most convincing in creating a productive dialogue between psychologists and economists. The numerous other framing effects that have been documented continue this tradition, and partially account for the growth of the fields of behavioral economics and behavior finance.

One question that often emerges from these studies is whether or not these effects generalize to the real world. Three editions ago, I was optimistic about this question, but did not have the data to be convincing. Since then, numerous excellent studies have used framing effects to explain why taxi drivers drive more hours on slow days than on busy ones (Camerer, Babcock, Loewenstein, and Thaler, 1997), why so many people pay for line insurance on their telephones (Thaler and Ziemba, 1988), the conditions under which negotiators are most likely to reach an impasse (see Chapter 10), and a wide variety of investment mistakes (the topic of Chapter 7). Camerer (2000) also does an excellent job of summarizing the very positive evidence of the relevance of framing effects in the real world.

CHAPTER FOUR

Motivational and Affective Influences on Decision Making

The holiday season has come and gone, leaving you with seven extra pounds. In an attempt to lose weight, you decide to reduce the fat in your diet. Upon arriving at a party, you sit in front of a bowl of your favorite high-fat treat (cashews, potato chips, caramel popcorn, etc.). One piece goes into your mouth, and soon the bowl is empty. You have consumed over sixty grams of fat. The next day you regret your decision and wonder how you could have so easily ignored your resolution to lose weight.

*T*he day after the party, it appears as if your eating was inconsistent with your long-term preferences. Yet the preceding chapters tell us little about the mistake that you made. Until recently, most behavioral decision research, like the field of economics that it so often criticizes, viewed decision making as a cognitive process. The core focus of behavioral decision research (as exemplified in Chapters 2 and 3) has been on cognitive errors, or errors that have their root in how our minds process information. In contrast, many of the errors we make are the result of motivational and affective influences. This does not mean that cognition is irrelevant. Rather, in this chapter, we will explore systematic effects where motivation and affect also play a role.

This chapter considers situations in which we make decisions that are inconsistent with our long-term interests, because of a temporary motivation to pursue some alternative goal or affective state. I view such decisions as biased when preoccupation with the transient goal or affective state lowers the overall benefit to the decision maker and is inconsistent with what the individual would prefer for him- or herself when acting more reflectively (System 2 thinking). This chapter focuses on four categories of motivational or affective influences on decision making. The first section describes common tensions we all face between doing what we want to do and doing what we think we should do, as illustrated by the party dilemma above. The second section examines the effects of positive illusions, or the general tendency to view oneself and the world more positively than reality suggests. In the third section I discuss self-serving ways in which people interpret fairness. The fourth section explores affective influences on our judgment.

WHEN AFFECT AND COGNITION COLLIDE

In Homer's *The Odyssey,* Ulysses was confronted with a classic negotiation problem during his long voyage at sea. He knew that he would soon encounter the Sirens, mythical female "enchanters" who lured seafaring men to their island—and to their subsequent death—by singing sweetly to them from their flowering meadow. No man had ever been able to resist the Sirens, and their beach was "piled with boneheaps of men now rotted away." Ulysses was advised to put wax in his men's ears to block out the tempting voices of the Sirens. To protect himself, Ulysses told his men to bind him with ropes to the ship's mast and ordered them in advance not to release him, no matter how much he begged, until after they sailed safely by the Sirens. This way, Ulysses would have the pleasure of listening to the Sirens without falling into their trap. As his ship set sail, he warned his men: "If I supplicate you and implore you to set me free, then you must tie me fast with even more lashings." Ulysses' plan worked, and he and his men survived their latest adventure.

This section explores the internal inconsistencies that exist when what we want to do clashes with what we think we should do. Ulysses faced competing preferences: He knew that he would want to go to the Sirens, but he also knew that succumbing to this desire would be a fatal mistake. Grappling with such internal contradictions is part of the human condition:

- Ulysses wanted to visit the Sirens, but knew that he should not because they would kill him.

- The alcoholic craves a drink, but knows that he should abstain because of the negative consequences that will inevitably result.

- The gambler wants to win big in Las Vegas, but knows that she should avoid all gambling because she has difficulty knowing when to stop.

- The student wants to relax and socialize over the weekend, but knows she should stay in to study for exams.

- The author does not want to exercise regularly, but knows that he should to improve his cardiovascular health.

In our daily lives, we constantly make choices between what we want to do and what we should do. A job hunter might have to choose between an enjoyable, low-status position and one that he thinks he should take for financial or practical reasons. Consumers must often decide whether to buy the product they want or a product they think they should purchase for health, environmental, or budgetary reasons. People often want to engage in an action that will fulfill their short-term desires, while believing they should act differently to maximize their long-term goals (Bazerman, Tenbrunsel, and Wade-Benzoni, 1998).

In Chapter 1, we introduced the affect heuristic (Slovic et al., 2002), which argues that decision makers have an automatic affective, or emotional, reaction to most options. Bazerman et al. (1998) argue that this affective response is often in disagreement with the decision that an individual would make after more thoughtful reasoning. The terms "want" and "should" describe how people categorize these two types of preferences. How do individuals come to have preferences that put them in disagreement with themselves? When does affect win, and when do we follow what we "should" do instead?

Schelling argues that each individual behaves like two people: "one who wants clear lungs and long life and another who adores tobacco, or one who wants a lean body and another who wants dessert" (1984, p. 58). Economists and other social scientists have struggled to understand this multiple-selves problem for at least fifty years (Strotz, 1956), while others have devoted substantial effort and religious rhetoric to denying its existence (Stigler and Becker, 1977). Taking a more extreme view than most, Elster (1979), a philosopher and political theorist, regards the multiple-selves phenomenon as a collective action problem. According to Elster's conceptualization, the key goal for an individual should be to keep each self from defecting on a cooperative choice that will be in the best interest of the collectivity of selves.

The multiple-selves problem has been used to account for a variety of dysfunctional clinical behaviors such as alcohol, drug, and spousal abuse (Ainslie, 1975), as well as common consumer and investment errors that stem from the inappropriately high discounting that people apply to the future (Loewenstein, 1996). In almost all of these cases, one of our "selves" is in favor of a decision that provides immediate benefit rather than an alternative that would provide greater future rewards. I argue that the psychological basis for these identified internal inconsistencies is in fact widespread, covering a variety of decisions that are limited neither to clinically dysfunctional populations nor to temporal problems.

Schelling (1984) connected the multiple-selves problem to a broad range of economic behaviors, including saving money in non-interest-bearing Christmas clubs, giving free loans to the government by overpaying taxes in order to get a refund, and gambling. Schelling also connects his arguments to a variety of social phenomena such as smoking, drinking, drugs, scratching, overeating, procrastinating, exercising, and sexual behavior. By distinguishing the long-term self from the short-term self, Schelling clarifies the magnitude of the multiple-selves problem in everyday behavior. A key conceptual contribution of this work is its specification of control tactics that the long-term thinker can use to manage the short-term thinker. For example, joining the Christmas club is a commitment device by which your "should" self places money out of reach of your "want" self's whims. People are willing to forgo the interest they could have earned on that money in return for the service of preservation of their long-term goals. It is clear that in Schelling's view, as in most economic writing on this problem, self-control is viewed as a valuable asset and the long-term thinker is considered to be wiser than the short-term thinker.

Some economists, trying to maintain a full rational model despite all of the evidence to the contrary, explain inconsistencies in our behavior by claiming that a different set of information is available to the two different selves. Therefore, it is rational to eat a brownie despite the fact you vowed to go on a diet the night before because, when actually confronted with the treat, you have new information. You know how large the brownie is and what you had for lunch, allowing for a more informed (and therefore not internally inconsistent) decision about ingesting it. Most dieters, however, would not agree with this interpretation. Although rationalization often does occur after the want self contradicts the should self ("It was a quart of frozen yogurt, not a quart of ice cream"), the guilt that kicks in is difficult to reconcile with the economic argument. The full rational model also cannot account for the existence of Christmas clubs and fat farms.

Thaler (1980) agrees with Schelling that the key to resolving our internal conflicts is to recognize them and create means of self-control. Thaler identifies two selves, the *planner* and the *doer,* and describes the actions that the planner can take to control the doer, particularly through the multitude of self-help programs that have emerged in contemporary society, including Alcoholics Anonymous, drug abuse centers, diet clubs, and smoking clinics. Shefrin and Thaler (1988) argue that effective control techniques include:

- **Changing the doer's preferences.** For example, the planner can seek out a type of exercise that the doer will enjoy.

- **Monitoring the doer's behavior.** Participating in a diet club's weekly "weigh-ins" can deter eating.

- **Altering incentives.** Alcoholics can take the drug Antabuse, which will make them ill if they drink.

- **Altering rules.** Students might forbid themselves from turning on the television until they've finished their homework.

Loewenstein (1996) questions the use of a metaphor that we all know does not describe reality—the idea of two selves existing within the same person. Rather, he identifies the conditions under which visceral responses lead to an overemphasis on transient concerns. According to Loewenstein, manifestations of physiological states, such as cravings induced by withdrawal, drive states such as hunger, thirst, and sexual desire, and moods and emotions create inconsistencies between deliberation and action. Loewenstein (1996) also notes that in many professions, success is measured by one's ability to manipulate the transient concerns of other people. Automobile and electronics salespeople and real-estate agents often try to orient the customer toward a transient concern, for example, by encouraging you to imagine yourself driving your new BMW home for the first time. Con men play on transient feelings of greed, while police interrogators use hunger, thirst, and sleep deprivation to extract confessions. Cults indoctrinate new members through food deprivation, forced incontinence, and social pressures to conform, all of which cause transient concerns to overwhelm long-term self-interest (Loewenstein, 1996). By contrast, many states try to protect consumers from short-term impulses by legislating revocability periods for high-priced items (e.g., condominium share purchases). Loewenstein (1996) connects his ideas on transient concerns to behavioral decision research on vividness described in Chapter 2, which argues that decision makers overweight proximal (temporal, physical, or sensory) attributes.

Internal inconsistencies between transient concerns and long-term self-interest reflect natural tensions between what people want to do and what they think they should do. In Chapter 3, we used this distinction of "want" and "should" to explain preference reversals between separate and joint modes of evaluation. In this chapter, we again use this distinction, this time to explain when each of the multiple selves is most likely to prevail. People often hold conflicting preferences, and the basis of this conflict is the difference between "want" and "should." The want/should distinction (Bazerman et al., 1998) is broadly compatible with Loewenstein's (1996) argument; the "want" self is similar to the visceral response, while the "should" self tends to be more long-term focused. Using the two-selves description metaphorically, we develop a model that describes the contexts in which "want" and "should" dominate. We argue that the "want" self will tend to dominate in real-world decisions in which one option is salient at a time. When we assess options one at a time, we tend to place greater weight on affective, visceral criteria. In contrast, the more reasoned, reflective "should" self will tend to dominate when we confront multiple options at the same time. Thus, when we are given the option of a short-term reward (a day off, drugs, etc.) with long-term costs, the want self is salient, and the option seems attractive. But, when we consider the short-term desire versus passing on that desire in an explicit comparison, the should self becomes stronger. This pattern can be illustrated by the should self who makes New Year's resolutions, and the want self who breaks those resolutions.

Self-control problems such as procrastination, laziness, and addiction can also be explained with a different framework: *hyperbolic discounting*. The intuition behind this theory, first formally employed by Laibson (1994), is quite simple. Relative to the present time period, we view all gains and losses in the future to be worth less. For example, a free soda is worth subjectively more to you today than it would be tomorrow or 100 days from now. The difference between getting it in 100 days or 101 days is miniscule, but the same one-day delay between today or tomorrow will seem to matter much more. As O'Donoghue and Rabin (1999) put it, we are biased towards the present.

To see how this theory applies to our current discussion, consider the decision of when to clean off your desk. The cost of doing the task increases the later you start, since the piles get higher and messier as you continue to neglect it. However, because of the tendency to discount the future, it always seems more prudent to put off the clean-up until tomorrow rather than to do it right now. Unfortunately, once tomorrow comes, this illusion repeats itself and the desk gets even messier. Of course, at some point you'll get around to it, but it will be a much harder job than it would have been if you had not procrastinated. Similar patterns play out with the morning alarm clock ("I'll wake up in another five minutes") and with quitting addictive habits ("I know I said I'd quit smoking today, but work is just too stressful, it'll have to wait").

Just like the multiple selves concept, this dynamic inconsistency—contradictions between decisions made at different time periods—can be attributed to affect. The difference in the discounting factor between "right now" and "later" has to do with the vividness of the present. If you're craving a drink, you want it now, not later, and certainly not in a couple of days. Quite obviously, people are prone to caring more about what is happening to them in the present, since that is what they are actually experiencing. Therefore, imagining the future carries less weight than living in the present; as a consequence, unpleasant tasks often get delayed. This discounting logic is related to the emotionally charged concept of instant gratification.

No matter how you frame the problem of internal inconsistency, the important practical question arising from this research is: What advice can we give to internally inconsistent decision makers? Stigler and Becker (1977) would tell us to leave them alone, since their behavior will naturally follow a rational course of action. However, this recommendation fails the market test of good advice: Virtually no reasonable human being would prescribe it for someone they cared about. As outlined earlier in this chapter, Schelling (1984) and Thaler (1980) would concentrate on controlling the destructive impulses of the short-term decision maker. Kahneman and Ritov (1994) would argue that a choice between options captures our long-term interests more effectively, implying that the transient, want criteria should be suppressed if possible. I certainly believe that the advice of Schelling, Thaler, and Kahneman et al. would do far more good than harm. However, complete reliance on their advice would assume that the should self always optimizes self-interest.

Loewenstein (1996) is much friendlier to the want self, noting that transient responses are often adaptive to natural environments. That is, visceral reactions may make individuals aware of issues that they care a great deal about, but that they may have suppressed because of the desire to be responsible, mature, or otherwise to conform to society. In contrast to the tactics of self-control advocated by Thaler and Schelling, Loewenstein argues, "Hunger signals the need for nutritional input, pain indicates the impingement of some type of potentially harmful environmental factors, and emotions serve a range of interrupting, prioritizing, and energizing functions." A natural extension of this argument is that if individuals take the time to carefully consider what they should do, an important opportunity could be lost. The feelings of regret that might follow are described in folk singer Christine Lavin's song "The Moment Slipped Away":

> He works the ward at the Bellevue Hospital
> The mail delivery
> For two years every weekday mornin'
> He said hello to me
> We joke about the local team
> The weather of the day
> Though there were many other things
> I really wanted to say
> You see he wasn't like the rest of us
> It was a struggle for him to walk
> And you had to concentrate really hard
> Just to understand his talk
> I wanted to ask him,
> Where do you get the courage
> To come to work each day
> But I quit that job
> I moved along
> And the moment slipped away

As Lavin conveys, at times the should self may be too conservative, risk averse, or timid to do the right thing. The want self may serve a valuable purpose by signaling the value of emotional criteria to the should self. How do we give voice to the want self with the goal of improving the decisions of the should self? I offer advice on this issue from two areas of rational thought: Raiffa's decision-analysis perspective and the steps of rational decision making outlined in Chapter 1, and a negotiation framework for providing rational advice to negotiators that I will present in greater detail in Chapter 8.

Decision Theory Advises the Multiple Selves

Howard Raiffa has made important contributions to the fields of decision making and negotiations. In his book *Decision Analysis* (1968), Raiffa suggests prescriptive advice for decision makers, including recommendations for formalizing the identification and weighting of multiple criteria. In an apocryphal, ever-changing story, Raiffa was on the faculty at Columbia and received an offer from Harvard. According to the story, he visited his dean at Columbia, who was also his friend, and asked for help with his decision. Sarcastically, the dean, borrowing from Raiffa's writings, told Raiffa to identify the relevant criteria, weight each criterion, rate each school on each criterion, do the arithmetic, see which school had the best overall score, and go there. Supposedly, Raiffa's response was, "No, this is a serious decision."

While he enjoys this story, Raiffa says it simply isn't true. However, the story, which describes a potential tension between the want self (who would make the decision based on gut instinct) and the should self (who would accept the higher score from a formal decision-theoretic analysis), led Raiffa to clarify what he would do in a situation where conflict existed between the two selves. He advocates an approach that entails questioning each self to find out which one is making the error. Perhaps the should self can confront the want self with its limited perspective—for example, the danger of ignoring long-term implications of the decision. Alternatively, it could be that the want self can elucidate for the should self some of the more elusive feelings that have been neglected by its formal analysis. Raiffa suggests that this communication should take place until reconciliation occurs.

When the two selves are in disagreement about an important decision, I would argue that this conflict signals the need to think more carefully about the information provided by each of the two selves. The best choice might become more clear after the "umpire" self realizes that the want or should self was neglecting some part of the problem. This decision-theoretic approach to the multiple-selves problem would most likely favor the should self, but give voice, opportunity, and input to the want self.

Negotiation Research Advises the Multiple Selves

One likely result of following the decision-theoretic advice adapted from Raiffa (1968) is that the want self may rebel against the decision. For example, a diet or exercise regime could be sabotaged by an individual's failure to reconcile the want self to the should self's new agenda. By creating a rational negotiation between the two parties (the want self and the should self), my modification of Raiffa's advice grants the want self more autonomy and a stronger voice in the decision-making process. This suggestion is inspired by, but more optimistic than, Schelling's view that "the possibility of bargains and compromises is limited, if not precluded, by the absence of any internal mediator. It is hard for the different selves to negotiate if they cannot be simultaneously present. Not impossible, perhaps, but hard" (1984, p. 94). We can all think of instances in which our should self made a decision with the logic of self-interest only to be later overruled by the impulsive behavior of the want self.

I recommend the development of a rational negotiation strategy for dealing with the want self. By treating the want self as a negotiator who has the power to declare an impasse, and allowing the parties to negotiate, I aim to bypass both the domination of the should self in the decision-making stage and the want self in the implementation stage. One could easily argue that this is what occurs naturally. However, I would counter that, just as outcomes to disputes between two different individuals or groups are often suboptimal, outcomes to disputes within the self are similarly suboptimal. Once we empower the want self in the decision-making process, what criteria should we impose on the negotiation between selves? First, we should require the parties to reach an agreement, since the independent and conflicting actions of the two selves will be worse than the result of their negotiated agreement. Ongoing conflict would lead the should self to continue to make a variety of decisions that the want self sabotages. Second, the agreement should be Pareto efficient (Chapter 9); that is, there should be no other agreement that the want self and the should self both prefer over the created agreement. This agreement might be reached through "discussions" and compromises between the two selves about key issues—for example, how often the want self will get to eat ice cream, how many days a week the should self will exercise, and so on. By agreeing to reasonable times and limits, the want self is likely to be more willing to follow the agreement. Third, the should self must not push for an agreement that is outside the bargaining zone; that is, the terms must not be unacceptable to the want self, either currently or in the future. The should self must remember that there is no court of law for suing yourself for a contract violation—the want self can void the contract at any time.

Now that two different prescriptive perspectives have been proposed, we must decide when each should be used. Intuition tells us that the decision-theoretic perspective is preferable as long as the want self doesn't veto its use. However, if there is a danger that the want self will rebel against the decision, I believe that it is probably in the interest of the individual to switch to the negotiation model.

POSITIVE ILLUSIONS

Taylor (1989) argues that most people view themselves, the world, and the future in a considerably more positive light than is objectively likely or than reality can sustain. Taylor and Brown (1988) suggest that positive illusions enhance and protect self-esteem, increase personal contentment, help individuals to persist at difficult tasks, and facilitate coping with aversive and uncontrollable events. Taylor (1989) even argues that positive illusions are beneficial to physical and mental health.

Other research, however, shows that there are significant limits to beneficial self-enhancement. The extent to which people can maintain unrealistically positive beliefs about themselves may be constrained to some degree by the objectivity of these beliefs, their credibility, and the potential to disconfirm them (Allison, Messick, and Goethals, 1989). For example, it is easier for individuals to maintain the view that they are more honest than others than to maintain the belief that they are better tennis players or wittier cocktail party conversationalists. Allison et al. (1989) reason that it is harder to have optimistic illusions when they are inconsistent with easily available, objective data. In the same way, it may be easier for negotiators to maintain the belief that they are fairer than other negotiators than to believe that they are more skillful at reaching profitable agreements.

In this section, I highlight four of the most important positive illusions: (1) unrealistically positive views of the self, (2) unrealistic optimism, (3) the illusion of control, and (4) self-serving attributions. After reviewing these illusions, I explore their application to group behavior, negotiator behavior, and potential effects on society. Finally, I close the section with some commentary on the costs and benefits of positive illusions.

Unrealistically Positive Views of the Self

Individuals tend to perceive themselves as being better than others on a variety of desirable attributes (Messick, Bloom, Boldizer, and Samuelson, 1985), causing them to have unrealistically positive self-evaluations across a wide range of social contexts (Brown, 1986). For example, people have been found to perceive themselves as being superior to others across traits such as honesty, cooperativeness, rationality, driving skill, health, and intelligence (Babcock and Loewenstein, 1997; Kramer, 1994).

Epley and Dunning (2000) conducted a set of sobering experiments that look into moral superiority, or the tendency for many people to believe they are "holier than thou." It was found that people tend to overestimate their own generosity. For example, a group of subjects were asked how much of a $5 experimental participation fee they would donate if asked to do so at the end of an experimental session. Students said they would give about half the amount, or $2.50, but when another group of similar students was actually given a chance to donate, the average contribution was only $1.53. Despite this inaccuracy in self-prediction, the same people are surprisingly accurate when it comes to predicting the actions of others. The students guessed in the right range when asked how much other people would contribute, predicting $1.80 on average.

I have given my MBA and executive students lists of a variety of attributes (including decision making, negotiation, and driving ability; earning potential; likelihood of leading a long life, etc.), and asked them to assess where they stand in comparison to other members of the class. On a scale in which zero means that they believe themselves to be worse than all members, 25 percent indicates that they consider themselves better than one-fourth of the students, etc., my students average between 60 and 70 percent. While this could be true in comparison to the overall population, the problem is that the same people doing the rating are also the comparison group. Since the correct mean must be 50 percent, many of my students are not as good negotiators, drivers, and so on, as they believe themselves to be.

Unrealistic Optimism

Unrealistic optimism is a judgmental bias that leads people to believe that their futures will be better and brighter than those of other people (Kramer, 1994; Taylor, 1989). Taylor reports that students expect that they are far more likely to graduate at the top of the class, to get a good job, to obtain a high salary, to enjoy their first job, to get written up in the newspaper, and to give birth to a gifted child than reality suggests. They also assume that they are less likely than their classmates to have a drinking problem, to get fired, to get divorced, to become depressed, or to suffer physical problems. Similar patterns emerge for individuals in other age groups.

This optimism about future outcomes is fed by overly optimistic views of our abilities. Kruger and Dunning (1999) have shown that people tend to overestimate their skill in both social and intellectual domains. Those who are most incompetent are also the most deluded. As Figures 4.1 and 4.2 show, subjects, especially those in the lowest percentiles, can be drastically overoptimistic about their performance on grammar and logic tests. Those in the bottom quartile estimated that their performance put them in the sixty-second percentile, when in fact they were actually in the twelfth. The authors concluded that the same cognitive miscalibration that was causing the poor performance was also preventing the incompetent from recognizing their errors.

In a similar vein, Taylor notes that we persist in believing that we can accomplish more in a day than is humanly possible, yet we seem immune to the continual feedback that the world provides on our limitations. Brinthaupt, Moreland, and Levine (1991)

FIGURE 4.1 Perceived versus Objective Grammar Ability

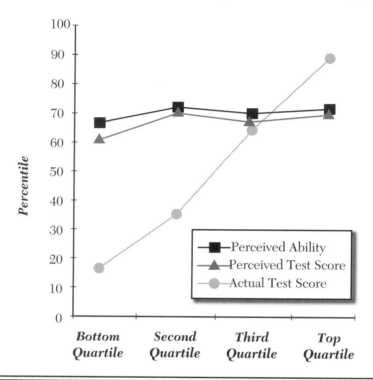

SOURCE: Kruger and Dunning (1999).

find that prospective group members are unrealistically positive about the outcomes that they will obtain from group membership. Specifically, individuals expect to receive more rewards than the average group member, expect their own rewards to be higher than the average group member's, and expect that the costs that they will incur as group members will be lower than average. Kramer (1991) found that 68 percent of the MBA students in a negotiation class predicted that their bargaining outcomes would fall in the upper 25 percent of the class. These students also expected that they would learn more than their classmates, achieve more unique results, and contribute more to the class experience. This optimism can easily lead to turning down the best job offer that you will receive, turning down an offer on your house (when no better offer is coming), and a variety of other regrettable behaviors.

Illusion of Control

People falsely believe that they can control uncontrollable events (Crocker, 1982), and they overestimate the extent to which their actions can guarantee a certain outcome (Miller and Ross, 1975). Evidence suggests that experienced dice players believe that "soft" throws are more likely to result in lower numbers being rolled (Taylor, 1989). These gamblers also believe that silence by observers is relevant to their success.

FIGURE 4.2 Perceived versus Objective Logic Ability

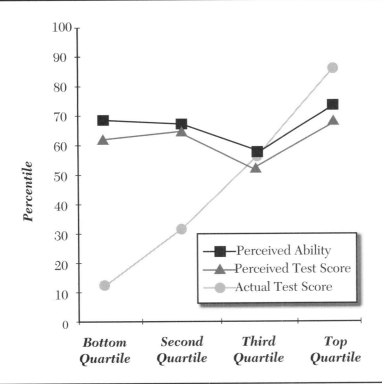

SOURCE: Kruger and Dunning (1999).

Langer (1975) found that people have a strong preference for choosing their own lottery card or numbers, even when this has no effect on improving the likelihood of winning. Similarly, despite the fact that outcomes are random, allowing subjects to spin a wheel of fortune themselves increased their perceived chance of winning (Wohl and Enzle, 2002). Many superstitious behaviors are the result of an illusion of control. Obviously, these illusions can have strongly adverse effects on gamblers and managerial risk-takers.

Self-Serving Attributions

People interpret the causes of events in a biased manner. Specifically, we tend to take a disproportionately large share of the credit for collective successes and to accept too little responsibility for collective failures (Kramer, 1994). Kramer (1994) notes that John F. Kennedy was describing this effect when he said, "Victory has a thousand fathers, but defeat is an orphan" (Sorenson, 1965, p. 322). Similarly, when successful negotiators are asked to explain their results, they tend to give internal attributions—reasons related to their own decisions. When asked about a failure, however, they tend to cite external factors; they attribute the failure to an unfortunate situation in which they found themselves. Self-serving biases lead people to focus on the aspects of a problem that allow them to avoid blame, thus enabling them to protect a positive self-image. Kramer (1994) argues that self-serving attributions lead individuals to overestimate their contribution to their organization. Self-serving attributions also lead people to overestimate their likelihood of success and to underestimate the time it will take to complete a project—a pervasive miscalculation in organizations. When organizational members are contaminated by self-serving attributions, they are more likely to be dissatisfied with their actual outcomes and to disappoint other members, including their bosses.

Positive Illusions in Groups and Society

Positive illusions are not limited to the individual. Kramer (1994) argues that people extend self-enhancement to the groups to which they belong. People tend to believe that members of their group are more honest, more cooperative, more trustworthy, more diligent, and more industrious than members of other groups (Brewer, 1986; Kramer, 1994). Thus, desirable behaviors on the part of in-group members are likely to be attributed to internal, dispositional causes, while similar behaviors by out-group members are likely to be attributed to transitory or situational causes (Brewer and Kramer, 1985).

Not only do we tend to generalize positive illusions to members of our group, but we also tend to invert this pattern in assessing opponents. Frequently, decision makers negatively distort information about their adversaries. Salovey and Rodin (1984) found that individuals tend to denigrate others who are more successful than they are. Kramer (1994) reports that less-successful MBA students disparaged the performance of more-successful students in a negotiation class. These less-successful students were more likely to attribute the success of other students to uncooperative and unethical bargaining tactics, to ascribe more negative motivations to successful negotiators, and to rate them as excessively competitive and self-interested. Similarly, both Diekmann (1997) and Tenbrunsel (1995) have found that while students rate themselves above the mean of their class on a variety of positive attributes, they rate their specific negotiation opponent below the mean on these attributes. Kramer (1994), basing his argument partially on Janis's (1962) analysis of political events, ties this pattern of behaviors to tragic mistakes made in the political arena. For example, Kramer suggests that the Nixon administration's mismanagement of the Watergate embarrassment was partially the result of Nixon and others close to him denigrating the competence and motivation of his critics.

Kramer, Newton, and Pommerenke (1993) argue that this pattern of opponent denigration can be dangerous in the context of negotiation. They maintain that negotiators' willingness to reveal information about their own interests may be contingent upon their expectation that the other party will reciprocate such disclosures or, at the very least, not exploit them to their own advantage. As a consequence, individuals' judgments regarding such attributes as the other party's cooperativeness, fairness, and trustworthiness might be expected to play an important role in their negotiations. With the combined effects of self-enhancement and the denigration of opponents, negotiators who see themselves as better than others may undermine their ability to appreciate or fully empathize with the perspective of the other party. This may help explain why negotiators are not very good at understanding the cognitions of the other party. Both parties to a negotiation may feel that they tried harder to reach agreement and offered more substantial concessions than the other party, and that it was only the opponent's recalcitrance that forestalled agreement.

Positive illusions may also lead to dysfunctional societal behaviors. In the realm of social responsibility, positive illusions may cause people to believe that their behaviors and attitudes are more environmentally sensitive than those of most people. People may think they are doing their fair share of sacrificing and working toward the resolution of environmental problems, but their self-assessments are likely to be inflated (Wade-Benzoni, Thompson, and Bazerman, 2005). Consistent with Allison et al. (1989), Wade-Benzoni et al. found self-assessment of environmental sensitivity to depend on how much ambiguity surrounds the self-assessment. Specifically, individuals maintain unrealistically positive beliefs about their degree of environmental sensitivity when their self-evaluation is difficult to disconfirm, but possess more realistic assessments of themselves when they are constrained by the objectivity of the evaluation. For example, assessments of general beliefs such as one's awareness of, concern for, understanding of, and interest in environmental issues and problems are difficult to confirm or disconfirm. In contrast, assessments of how well one performs on specific activities such as recycling, donating money to environmental organizations, and using energy-saving light bulbs can be checked against objective measures. If individuals define their environmental sensitivity in terms of general (not easily confirmable) behaviors instead of specific (objectively measurable) behaviors, their self-evaluations are likely to be inflated.

In Wade-Benzoni et al.'s (2005) study of environmental behaviors, a strong correlation exists between how subjects rate their actions regarding the environment and their judgments of the importance of that action to society. Presumably, positive illusions enable subjects to believe that they are doing well relative to others on important activities, though they may admit to doing less well on activities they consider to be less important. These biases may cause individuals to think that their positive contributions to environmental issues are more important than the contributions of others. For example, an individual who puts a lot of effort into recycling, but refuses to take public transportation, may justify this decision by convincing himself or herself that recycling is the most important way of addressing the environmental crisis. Because individuals have the liberty to judge what they already do (which may be what is most convenient for them) as more important than behaviors that may call for inconvenient lifestyle changes, they are able to maintain positive views of themselves with minimal lifestyle adjustment. Overall, this pattern of self-enhancement may provide people with an easy way out of engaging in more responsible societal behaviors.

Are Positive Illusions Good For You?

A common view among social psychologists is that positive illusions are adaptive (Taylor, 1989). These illusions are said to contribute to psychological well-being by protecting an individual's positive sense of self (Taylor and Brown, 1988, 1994). In addition, Taylor and Brown argue that positive illusions increase personal commitment, help individuals persist at difficult tasks, and facilitate coping with aversive and uncontrollable events. Certainly, it is reasonable to argue that positive illusions help create entrepreneurs who are willing to discount risks. Positive illusions allow us to maintain cognitive consistency, belief in a just world, and perceived control (Greenwald, 1980).

Seligman (1991) advocates the selection of salespeople based on the magnitude of their positive illusion—what he calls "learned optimism." He argues that unrealistically high levels of optimism bolster sales-force persistence.

I believe that each of these findings is true and that in some specific situations (e.g., severe health conditions), positive illusions may prove beneficial. In addition, positive illusions may help people cope with tragic events, particularly when they have few alternatives and are not facing any major decisions. However, I also believe that this adaptive story is incomplete, and dangerous in most decision-making environments. Every day, people invest their life savings in new businesses that have little chance of success. Similarly, falsely assuming that they are irreplaceable, people make ultimatums to their employers and often end up losing their jobs.

Positive illusions are hazardous when they cause people to temporarily fool themselves. Because positive illusions may provide a short-term benefit with larger long-term costs, they can become a form of emotional procrastination. Robins and Beer (2001), in a study of college students, found that positive illusions are associated with higher levels of self-reported well-being and self-esteem in the short term. But, over time, individuals are frustrated as they encounter data that tells them that they are not as good as they think. These long-term realizations are often associated with long-term drops in well-being and self-esteem.

My cynicism about the adaptive role of positive illusions is shared by a number of scholars who caution that positive illusions are likely to have a negative impact on learning and on the quality of decision making, personnel decisions, and responses to organizational crises ("the hole in the ozone layer isn't that big"), and can contribute to conflict and discontent (Brodt, 1990; Kramer, 1994; Tyler and Hastie, 1991). Positive illusions lead organizational members to claim an inappropriately large proportion of the credit for positive outcomes, to overestimate their value to the organization, and to set objectives that have little chance of success (Kramer, 1994). Self-enhancing interpretations of negative outcomes also prevent organizational members from learning from their poor decisions.

SELF-SERVING REASONING

- The West blames the Third World for burning the rain forests and for over-population. At the same time, the Third World blames the West for pollution caused by industrialization and excessive consumption.

- A *U.S. News and World Report* survey asked, "If someone sues you and you win the case, should he pay your legal costs?" Eighty-five percent of respondents answered "yes." However, only 44 percent answered "yes" to this question: "If you sue someone and lose the case, should you pay his costs?" (January 30, 1995, p. 52)

- The use of tall smokestacks to reduce local air pollution contributes to the regional problem of acid rain. The higher the air pollution, the farther it travels from its source (Gore, 1992). When Northeastern Canada is affected by acid rain, citizens blame the industrialization of the Northeast and Midwest United States. The United States denies responsibility, claiming acid rain may be caused by the local burning of coal.

Perceptions and expectations are often biased in a self-serving manner (Babcock and Loewenstein, 1997; Diekmann, Samuels, Ross, and Bazerman, 1997). When presented with identical information, individuals perceive a situation in dramatically different ways, depending on their role in the situation. Specifically, individuals first determine their preference for a certain outcome on the basis of self-interest and then justify this preference on the basis of fairness by changing the importance of attributes affecting what is fair (Messick and Sentis, 1983). While people frequently have the goal of reaching a fair solution, their assessments of what is fair are often biased by self-interest. For example, it is common for all parties in a conflict to suggest viable, but self-serving, solutions, which they justify based on abstract fairness criteria. Self-serving reasoning allows people to believe that it is honestly fair for them to have more of a given resource than an independent advisor would judge. The problem lies not in a desire to be unfair but in our failure to interpret information in an unbiased manner (Diekmann et al., 1997; Messick and Sentis, 1983).

Hastorf and Cantril (1954) asked student football fans from Princeton and Dartmouth to view a short film of a football game between the two schools. Although both sides watched the same film, each side thought the opposing team played less fairly and engaged in more aggressive and unsportsmanlike conduct. The researchers observed that the two groups of students "saw a different game." Similarly, in a study of arms control negotiations, Sutton and Kramer (1990) found that both sides of the Cold War attributed failure to reach agreement to the rigidity of the other side. President Reagan told reporters, "We came to Iceland to advance the cause of peace…and although we put on the table the most far-reaching arms control proposal in history, the General Secretary rejected it." On the very same day, General Secretary Gorbachev stated: "I proposed an urgent meeting here because we had something to propose…the Americans came to this meeting empty handed." Kramer (1994) cites these leaders' memoirs as proof that these quotes are more than political representations, but reflect the underlying egocentrism of the diplomatic process.

Diekmann et al. (1998) created a simulation in which MBA students allocated resources across two divisions of a company. "Advantaged" allocation recipients viewed these allocations to be fairer than similar allocations that favored their rivals. Advantaged allocation recipients even considered favorable allocations to themselves to be fair when the degree of favorability exceeded the inequality that they would have created had they been the allocator. Thus, they pointed to the fact that someone else had made the allocation to justify the favorable inequality. Finally, the degree of bias in assessing fairness was greater when the merits of the alternative recipients were ambiguous. This study suggests that justifiability plays a key role in egocentric determinations of fairness.

Diekmann (1997) shows that the degree to which people are self-serving is greater when the favorable outcome that individuals will receive can be attributed to the individual's group rather than to just the individual. Thus, people are more comfortable with their self-serving claims if they can base their biased judgments on their department's need or their family's needs, rather than on their own personal needs. As my colleague David Messick has noted, when a football coach quits one job for a better paying job, we do not hear the coach say, "I wanted more money." Rather, we are much more likely to hear him say, "I wanted to ensure the financial security of my family." In reality, these are very similar statements.

Dawson, Gilovich, and Regan (2002) nicely document our tendency to select standards of evidence in self-serving ways. They note that it sounds completely reasonable to accept an argument when the available data is consistent with the argument. On the other hand, it also seems reasonable to require the data to be overwhelmingly supportive. In fact, Dawson et al. (2002) note that different parts of the U.S. legal system use different standards of evidence. Thus, O. J. Simpson was found not guilty of murder in a criminal trial based on the higher standard of evidence, while being found guilty of the same offense in a civil suit based on the weaker standard. Different standards of evidence are not just a legal issue. Dawson et al. (2002) argue that when we want to believe an argument, we tend to ask "Can I believe this?" When we do not want to believe an argument, we ask, "*Must* I believe this?"

Returning to Enron's collapse, and the other financial scandals that followed, the evidence in this section supports the possibility that most auditors were not guilty of intentional manipulations or cover-ups. Rather, the auditors are much more likely to have been guilty of the motivational bias of interpreting and searching for data favorable to maintaining the client relationship. This section provides an overview of the evidence that virtually all humans tend to view data from a self-serving perspective. Accordingly, my colleagues and I argue, when an auditing firm depends on a client for financial or consulting business, it is not psychologically possible for the auditor to maintain true independence of judgment (Bazerman, Morgan, and Loewenstein, 1997; Bazerman, Loewenstein, and Moore, 2002). Unfortunately, we were unsuccessful in persuading the SEC of this view in 2000; the SEC maintained the status-quo system that kept the nation from having an independent auditing system, and disaster followed. The implications of this result is that restoring auditor independence requires changing the relationship between auditors and their clients such that auditors do not have a goal of keeping the client happy. We will return to this theme in Chapter 8.

AFFECTIVE INFLUENCES ON DECISION MAKING

In Chapter 3, I described the endowment effect (Kahneman, Knetsch, and Thaler, 1990), which describes the fact that the value people place on a commodity is far greater if they own the commodity than if they do not. Lerner, Small, and Loewenstein (2004) have found that emotional state can have a significant effect on the nature of the endowment effect. These researchers explored what happens to selling prices of a commodity (set by those who own the commodity) and choice prices (set by those who are choosing between the commodity and money) if study participants are sad or in a state of disgust, rather than in a more neutral state. They find that disgust triggers the desire to expel, suppressing prices for people who do and do not own the commodity. In contrast, sadness triggers the goal to change one's circumstances, increasing the willingness to pay to buy and decreasing the price demanded to sell.

With this study, Lerner et al. (2004) show how emotions can affect financial decisions. More interestingly, by manipulating emotion in a separate task that occurs prior to the buying and selling of the commodity, they show that we overgeneralize emotional reactions from one context and allow these reactions to influence our decisions in another context. Even more important, this research demonstrates the need for a very clear and precise understanding of how emotion affects decision making. Many scholars have assumed that emotions could be categorized simply into positive and negative emotions. But Lerner et al. (2004) show that two different negative emotions, in this case sadness and disgust, can create two very different patterns of effects.

We are only at the beginning stages of understanding the complex role of emotions on decision making. While this literature does not yet have the clear structure of the cognitive biases reviewed in Chapter 2 and 3, some interesting effects have emerged, some related to the research reviewed earlier in the book. I will examine the role of depression and sadness on optimism and overconfidence, the role of positive and negative moods on stereotyping, and the role that the anticipation of regret can play on decision making.

Over twenty-five years ago, Alloy and Abramson (1979) found that depression was related to greater judgmental accuracy. In an article aptly subtitled "Sadder but Wiser," they found that depressed study participants do not exhibit the positive illusions (reviewed earlier in this chapter) and overconfidence typically of most people (reviewed in Chapter 2). Many scholars interpreted these and related results as evidence that depression and sadness triggered more deliberative thought processes. Yet Bodenhausen, Gabriel, and Lineberger (2000) have shown that sad people are more affected by anchors than are those in a more neutral state, and as a result, make worse decisions. Clearly, the early, broad conclusion linking depression to greater decision-making accuracy was incorrect. While sadness and depression are not identical states, and though the biases studied were different, the distinction between sadness and depression suggests the need for a more detailed understanding of how emotions affect different aspects of decision making.

Bodenhausen et al. (2000) and Lerner et al. (2004) also highlight recent studies that explore how affective states impact optimism and risk taking. They note that people in good moods are more optimistic and that people in bad moods are more pessimistic (Loewenstein, Weber, Hsee, and Welch, 2001). In addition, fear and anxiety create risk-averse behavior (Lerner and Keltner, 2000). Affect may also be useful in predicting when motivational biases occur.

One of the opening quiz items in Chapter 2 focused on a student who writes poetry and is rather shy and small in stature. You were asked whether the student was more likely to major in (A) Chinese studies or (B) psychology. Using stereotypic reasoning, most people answer "Chinese studies," ignoring the enormous difference in the number of people who major in each of these fields. Park and Banaji (2000) found that a happy mood increases reliance on stereotypes, while a sad mood decreases reliance on stereotypes. This result is consistent with other research that generally suggests that happy individuals may be less motivated to expend cognitive effort and more likely to rely on heuristic processing (System 1 thinking), while the reverse is true for sad individuals (Park and Banaji, 2000).

Another area where emotions drive behavior is the anticipation of regret. Consider the following story:

> Imagine that you are at an out-of-town business meeting that runs late. As soon as you can break away, you head to the airport to catch the last flight home. If you miss the flight, which is scheduled to leave at 8:30 P.M., you will have to stay overnight and miss an important meeting the next day. You run into traffic and do not get to the airport until 8:52 P.M. You run to the gate, arriving there at 8:57 P.M. When you arrive, either:

a. You find out that the plane left on schedule at 8:30 P.M., or

b. You see the plane depart, having left the gate at 8:55 P.M.

Which is more upsetting, (a) or (b)? Most people would quickly agree that (b) is more upsetting. Yet, both possibilities create the same net outcome for you—you've missed your flight, and will have to spend the night. Choice (b) simply highlights the counterfactual but infuriating thought that with any minor change in schedule, you could have made the flight (Kahneman and Miller, 1986; Kahneman and Tversky, 1982).

The impact of counterfactual thinking and feelings of regret have been central to the work of Medvec, Madey, and Gilovich (1995), who discovered the fascinating phenomenon that silver-medal winners at the Olympics are less happy with their achievement than bronze-medal winners. Obviously, any athlete would choose to win silver over bronze. However, when these researchers coded the initial reactions and the facial expressions of athletes as they received their medals, they found that the bronze medal winners appeared to be happier. Medvec et al. concluded that while the bronze-medal winners are thrilled simply to be medalists, silver-medal winners regret what might have been—Olympic gold.

Kahneman and Tversky (1982) compared the regret associated with action versus inaction. One investor considers selling her stock, does not sell, and finds out she would have made more money had she sold. Another investor sells his stock and finds out he would have done better had he not sold. Both investors have lost out on the same amount of earnings; objectively, they should experience the same amount of regret. In fact, the second investor invariably feels worse than the first investor! Why? The second investor is more likely to compare his action to the status quo—doing nothing. People feel greater regret for acts of commission (what they did) than for acts of omission (what they did not do) (Spranca, Minsk, and Baron, 1991).

Research on regret, perhaps more than other emotions, highlights how the management of emotions affects decision making (Larrick, 1993). In the absence of feedback on what would have happened had they followed a different course of action, people are able to maintain positive illusions about the quality of their decisions and outcomes. When they expect to receive feedback regarding what they did and did not do, individuals recognize the possibility that they will receive unfavorable comparative information. Larrick (1993) provides evidence that decision makers will distort their decisions to avoid such negative feedback, and he identifies two ways in which they can do so. First, they can choose options that shield them from feedback on foregone alternatives. Second, when feedback on the decision not chosen is inevitable, they can make choices that are likely to compare favorably to foregone options.

Larrick and Boles (1995) examined choices made between a certain alternative and a risky alternative. Each participant played a recruit in a simulated negotiation with a prospective employer called Alpha. In both conditions, recruits knew that they would receive an offer from another firm, Beta; the amount of the bonus from Beta had an expected value of $10,000 but was uncertain. In the first condition, participants would later find out the outcome of the risky choice, regardless of the outcome chosen. In the second condition, participants found out the outcome of the risky choice only if they selected that choice. Recruits who knew that reaching an agreement with Alpha would likely preclude finding out the details of Beta's offer were more willing to make concessions to get an agreement with Alpha than were recruits who knew they would find out Beta's offer regardless of their choice. Larrick and Boles argue that recruits who would not find out the details of Beta's offer if they reached an agreement with Alpha could settle for less and still assume that they made a wise decision— they would not receive contradictory evidence. However, when recruits would find out Beta's offer regardless of whether they reached agreement with Alpha, they had to worry about how their agreement with Alpha would compare to the foregone outcome with Beta. This led them to be less concessionary and to hold out for a better deal from Alpha.

Overall, the studies reviewed in this section highlight the effects that emotions can have on decision making. Awareness of this interesting pattern of effects should create a new set of warnings for decision makers. Yet, this area is just beginning to blossom, and I am confident that we will soon have clearer structures to organize this knowledge.

SUMMARY

Too often, people view emotions as uncontrollable. The fact is, even if we can't stop ourselves from feeling, we may be able to limit the negative effects of our emotions on the quality of our decisions. Johnson and Tversky (1983) and Lerner, Goldberg, and Tetlock (1998) note that people are typically unaware of the influence of their emotions on their decisions. Thus, though we may feel that we are angry, we may falsely believe that we can make a decision independent of that anger. Perhaps a better appreciation of the literature can help create the knowledge that, "Just like everyone else, I am affected by my emotional state." We have all heard the idea of "counting to ten" before acting, but most of us assume that it is other people who need this advice.

Another strategy to manage emotions is to find a way to make the decision makers accountable for their choices. Lerner and Tetlock (1999) have found that study participants who must in some way justify their decisions learn to hold their emotions in check and move toward more systematic, System 2 thinking. Accountability can mean reporting your rationale to a boss, to yourself, or just writing down an explanation for your decision. Logically and empirically, the simple cognition of accountability has the ability to reduce the likelihood of acting on emotions in ways that you will later regret.

Finally, it may be possible to institutionalize controls on emotion. It is widely known that government policies can be overly influenced by the vividness of various issues (see Chapter 2). As a result, we as a society tend to allocate scarce resources to vivid concerns rather than to the issues where scarce resources would do the most good. Why? Vivid stories create emotional reactions; these emotions, in turn, lead us to misallocate scarce resources. Sunstein (2002) argues, "Just as the Senate was designed to have a 'cooling effect' on the passion of the House of Representatives, so cost–benefit analysis might ensure that policy is driven not by hysteria or alarm, but by a full appreciation of the effects of relevant risks and their control." Essentially, Sunstein suggests that institutionalizing the use of logical decision-making processes would protect our society from being overly influenced by temporary emotions.

This chapter has offered a very different perspective to biased decisions than was offered in the first three cognition-oriented chapters. Specifically, it focused on biases that emanate from motivational and affective influences within the individual. I have reviewed the motivational pressures of momentary desires, the need to view ourselves in a positive manner, the tendency to view events the way we would like to see them turn out, and how affect can change decisions in systematic ways. Certainly, other motivational and affective influences exist. This chapter simply serves to highlight the additive role of motivation and affect, beyond the role of cognition, in understanding unusual patterns in our decision-making processes. While it may be difficult for us to control our emotional and affective responses, a fuller understanding of how they affect our choices is certain to improve our decisions.

CHAPTER FIVE

The Nonrational Escalation of Commitment

If at first you don't succeed, try, try, again. Then quit. No use being a damn fool about it.

—W. C. Fields

*I*n the previous chapters, we examined single decisions and the ways in which judgmental and motivational biases and the framing of information can influence our responses to them. However, many critical managerial decisions concern a series of choices rather than an isolated decision. We are prone to a particular type of bias when approaching decisions serially—namely, a tendency to escalate commitment to our initial decision. I open this chapter with an explanation of the individual tendency to escalate behavior. In the second section, I demonstrate how a competitive environment increases the tendency to escalate. In the third section, I provide a taxonomy of explanations for the psychological tendency to escalate and offer recommendations for eliminating nonrational escalation behavior.

Consider the following examples:

- You personally decided to hire a new manager to work for you. Although you had expected excellent achievement, early reports suggest that she is not performing as you had hoped. Should you fire her? Perhaps her current level of performance is becoming a financial drain. On the other hand, you have invested a fair amount in her training, and she may just be in the process of learning the ropes. You decide to invest in her a bit longer and provide additional resources to help her succeed. Two months later, her performance is still sub par. Although you have more reason to "cut your losses," you also have a greater investment in this employee. When should you give up on your "investment"?

- You accept a position with a prestigious consulting firm, believing that the job offers an excellent career opportunity in a firm that you can grow with. Two years later, you have not progressed as rapidly as you had expected. Anxious to demonstrate your worth to the company, you decide to invest large amounts of unpaid overtime to get ahead. Still, you fail to get the recognition you think you deserve. By now, you have been with the organization for several years and would lose numerous benefits, including a vested interest in the company's pension plan, if you decide to leave. You are in your late thirties and feel you have invested your best years with this company. Do you quit?

- You work for a private equity firm and make a decision to invest $2 million in a start-up venture. You personally argued for this investment against some skeptics in your firm. One year later, the CEO from the start-up shows up in your office and says: "I have bad news, and I have good news. The bad news is that the company is running out of cash. Without additional funds, we will definitely go under, and you will lose the $2 million. The good news is that I am quite confident that if you invest another $1 million, we can work out the bugs in our invention and still be a great success." Do you invest the additional $1 million?

Although each of these decisions represents a very different situation, they share a number of common elements. In each case, you have a decision to make as a result of a previous decision. You hired the employee. You took the job. You made the investment. In each case, you have invested a great deal of time, effort, and resources in your selected course of action, and now things are not working out in an optimal way.

We frequently face similar decisions of varying importance. Should you sink more money into that old wreck you call a car? How long should you stay on hold with an airline before hanging up? When an investment starts to fail, should you stick with it? If you think about your own career and life, you will see that situations of this type are common. Inertia frequently leads us to continue on our previously selected course of action, or we may feel we have "too much invested to quit." How do you know when to quit? At what point does continuing on the same course of action become irrational? And why, when such behavior becomes irrational, is it so common? These are the central questions of this chapter.

Although we are taught from an early age to "try, try again," the fact is that misdirected persistence can lead you to waste a great deal of time, energy, and money. However, directed persistence can lead to commensurate payoffs. The key to making intelligent decisions in dynamic contexts such as those presented above is being able to discriminate between situations in which persistence will pay off and situations in which it will not.

A variety of authors from different fields have presented ideas relevant to the three hypothetical situations described above, using a number of different terms (such as escalation, entrapment, and persistence) to describe commitment to a previously selected course of action. Without presenting the diversity of definitions used in the literature, this chapter defines nonrational escalation as the degree to which an individual escalates commitment to a previously selected course of action to a point beyond that which a rational model of decision making would prescribe.

Accountants and economists provide insight into how to handle these scenarios. Experts from these areas tell us that in such situations we need to recognize that the time and expenses already invested are "sunk costs." That is, these costs are historical, irrecoverable, and should not be considered in any future course of action. Our reference point for action should be our current state, and we should consider all alternative courses of action by evaluating only the future costs and benefits associated with each alternative. For example, if you are considering whether to quit a doctoral program, it is irrelevant whether it took you six months or four years to get to the point you are at now; the key decision involves the future costs and benefits of exiting versus the future costs and benefits of continuing.

While accountants teach their students to recognize sunk costs in an accounting context, the decisions of managers trained in accounting suggest that the textbook advice to ignore sunk costs seldom translates to solving real-world problems. Why is it so hard for managers to absorb the sunk-cost concept in a lasting manner? One deficiency in the typical training of the sunk-cost concept is the lack of descriptive identification of why we intuitively tend to include sunk costs in our calculations. To eliminate escalatory behavior, we need to identify the existing nonrational behavior within ourselves, "unfreeze" that behavior, and prepare for change.

Decision makers who commit themselves to a particular course of action have a tendency to make subsequent decisions that continue that commitment beyond the level suggested by rationality. As a consequence, they often allocate resources in a way that justifies previous commitments, whether or not those initial commitments now appear valid. The following section examines the components of this behavior in more detail.

THE UNILATERAL ESCALATION PARADIGM

Put yourself in the equity firm officer's predicament again. My description of the escalation situation has probably biased you to assume that it would be "bad" for you to escalate your commitment to the first investment by granting another one. The fact is, it might be economically rational to continue your investment in the start-up. After all, it is not always wise to quit at the first sign of failure. Many would argue that doing so is a sign of a serious psychological deficiency.

How do you separate the rational from the nonrational tendency to escalate? One body of knowledge suggests that you should try to determine the rational course of action, ignoring the fact that you personally made the initial monetary commitment. A number of studies have attempted to separate the effect of being the person who made the initial commitment. These studies have investigated the difference between how two groups of decision makers make a second decision that follows an initial failure. One group has already made the initial decision, while the other group inherits the initial decision.

In Staw's initial study of this type (1976), one group of participants (labeled the high-responsibility participants) was asked to allocate research and development funds to one of two operating divisions of an organization. The participants were then told that, after three years, the investment had either proven successful or unsuccessful and that they were now faced with a second allocation decision concerning the same division. A second group (labeled the low-responsibility participants) was told that another financial officer of the firm had made a decision that had been either successful or unsuccessful (the same content information about success or failure was provided to this group as to the previous one) and that they were to make a second allocation of funds concerning that division. When the outcome of the previous decision was negative (an unsuccessful investment), the high-responsibility participants allocated significantly more funds to the original division in the second allocation than the low-responsibility participants did. In contrast, for successful initial decisions, the amount of money allocated in the second decision was roughly the same across participants. Given that the greater escalation of commitment occurred only for the participants who had made a previously unsuccessful decision, Staw concluded that the mechanism underlying escalation is self-justification. That is, once an individual makes an initial decision to embark on a course of action, negative feedback is dissonant with the initial decision. One way to eliminate this dissonance is to escalate commitment to the initial action in the belief that it will eventually lead to success.

We also know a fair amount about the conditions that tend to lead people to escalate commitment to a chosen course of action. Staw and Ross (1978) found that the tendency to escalate commitment was pronounced when the failure could be explained away with a causal account unrelated to the individual's initial decision (e.g., a shift in the economy instead of poor market appeal). Bazerman, Giuliano, and Appelman (1984) found that groups are less likely than individuals to escalate commitment; however, groups that escalate tend to do so to a greater degree than individuals. Apparently, the presence of multiple members increases the likelihood that the group will recognize the irrationality of escalating commitment to previous unsuccessful actions. If this realization does not occur, however, the group dynamic reinforces support for the initial decision and increases the level of rationalization to escalate commitment. Schoorman (1988) found that supervisors who participate in a hiring or promotion decision, and who agree with the eventual decision to hire or promote, positively bias that employee's subsequent performance appraisals. In addition, supervisors who participate in such a decision and disagree with the eventual decision to hire or promote bias subsequent performance appraisals for that employee in a negative direction.

Staw and Hoang (1995) found that National Basketball Association teams escalate their commitment to their draft choices. The sunk costs that teams incur are the use of draft choices and money to select and sign players. Staw and Hoang found that draft order had strong effects on playing time, likelihood of being traded, and survival in the league, even after controlling for the performance of players. Friedman's (1996) account of the decisions of mountain climbers to go for the peak provides chilling insight into the role of escalation in vivid life-and-death situations. Interestingly, Friedman presented his paper at a conference in memory of Jeffrey Z. Rubin, a noted escalation scholar and mountain climber who died in a 1995 climbing accident. Rubin's climbing partner had turned around prior to the fall, believing the weather conditions to be too dangerous.

Taken together, the foregoing evidence suggests that managers should beware of the difficulty of separating initial decisions from related future decisions. Steps can even be taken within an organization to combat nonrational escalation of commitment. Some hedge funds rotate portfolios on a regular basis so that the same trader who bought a commodity does not also make the decision to sell. Of course, mechanisms such as this are not amenable to situations where it is necessary for one person to make a string of related decisions. In general, we should try to be cognizant of the fact that our decisions will tend to be biased by our past actions, and that we have a natural individual tendency to escalate commitment, particularly after receiving negative feedback.

THE COMPETITIVE ESCALATION PARADIGM

In the unilateral escalation paradigm just described, justifications for nonrational escalation lie within the individual; we escalate because of our own previous commitments. In the competitive escalation paradigm, additional competitive forces feed the escalatory process. This section examines the process of escalation in competitive situations.

Imagine that two companies, A and B, are the most important in a given industry, while Company C is their potential target, an important third player, a key supplier, or a key buyer. C is worth $1 billion as a stand-alone company and would be worth $1.2 billion if managed by A or B, as a result of the synergy in the possible combination of A and C or of B and C. Assume that if A were to acquire C, B would be at a catastrophic disadvantage and would lose $0.5 billion. It would be similarly destructive to A if B were to acquire C; A would also lose $0.5 billion. Finally, assume that if either A or B makes an offer on C, the other company will learn of the offer. Question: As the head of Company A, what do you do?

A typical response by executives to whom I have posed this problem is to offer C $1.1 billion, which if accepted, would create a $100 million benefit to A and C. However, this offer, once made, creates a problem for B: if B does not act, B loses $0.5 billion. So, rather than suffering a $0.5 billion loss, B offers $1.2 billion to break even. Now, A has a problem: If A does not act, A loses $0.5 billion. So, A offers $1.3 billion to limit their losses to $100 million, rather than suffering a $0.5 billion loss. The problem is now B's, and we can easily see the auction escalating to an amount around $1.7 billion, where both A and B end up losing $0.5 billion in this competition. Any party quitting below that amount would still suffer a $0.5 billion loss.

This story is consistent with the lack of profit obtained by buyers in the merger mania of the 1980s—in the aggregate, the synergy that was obtained in acquisitions went to the sellers. This story is also consistent with a classroom auction that I have run many times: Imagine yourself in a room with thirty other individuals. The person at the front of the room takes a $20 bill out of his/her pocket and announces the following:

> I am about to auction off this $20 bill. You are free to participate or just watch the bidding of others. People will be invited to call out bids in multiples of $1 until no further bidding occurs, at which point the highest bidder will pay the amount bid and win the $20. The only feature that distinguishes this auction from traditional auctions is a rule that the second-highest bidder must also pay the amount that he or she bid, although he or she will obviously not win the $20. For example, if Bill bid $3 and Jane bid $4, and bidding stopped, I would pay Jane $16 ($20 – $4) and Bill, the second-highest bidder, would pay me $3.

Would you be willing to bid $2 to start the auction? (Make this decision before reading further.)

I have run this auction with undergraduate students, graduate students, and executives. The pattern is always the same. The bidding starts out fast and furious until it reaches the $12 to $16 range. At this point, everyone except the two highest bidders drops out of the auction. The two bidders then begin to feel the trap. One bidder has bid $16 and the other $17. The $16 bidder must either bid $18 or suffer a $16 loss. The uncertain option of bidding further (a choice that might produce a gain if the other guy quits) seems more attractive than the current sure loss, so the $16 bidder bids $18. This continues until the bids are $19 and $20. Surprisingly, the decision to bid $21 is very similar to all previous decisions: You can accept a $19 loss or continue and reduce your loss if the other guy quits. Of course, the rest of the group roars with laughter when the bidding goes over $20—which it almost always does. Obviously, the bidders are acting irrationally. But which bids are irrational?

Skeptical readers should try out the auction for themselves. The bidding typically ends between $20 and $70. However, my highest auction ended at $204, and I have had fifteen auctions hit the $100 mark. In total, I have earned over $30,000 running these auctions in classes over the last twenty years. (Note: While I win this money fair and square, I do not keep it. The money has either been used to provide food and beverage for the class or immediately given to charity.)

Shubik (1971) introduced the dollar auction. I adjusted the auction from $1 to $20 for inflation and to sharpen the impact. Teger (1980) has used the paradigm extensively to investigate the question of why individuals escalate their commitment to a previously selected course of action. Teger argues that participants naively enter the auction not expecting the bidding to exceed $1 (or $20); "after all, who would bid more than a dollar for a dollar?" The potential gain, coupled with the possibility of "winning" the auction, is enough reason to enter the auction. Once an individual is in the auction, it takes only a few extra dollars to stay in the auction rather than accept a sure loss. This "reasoning," along with a strong need to justify the bidder's entering the auction in the first place, is enough to keep most bidders bidding for an extended period of time. Recently, with more senior executive groups, I have shifted to $100 auctions, in $5 increments. The basic pattern remains unchanged.

Thoughtful examination of the dollar auction suggests that individuals who choose to bid are entering into a trap. While it is true that one more bid may inspire the other party to quit, if both bidders hold this belief, the result can be catastrophic. Yet, without knowing the expected bidding patterns of the opponent, we cannot conclude that continued bidding is clearly wrong. What is the right course of action? Successful decision makers must learn to identify traps, and the key to the problem lies in identifying the auction as a trap and never making even a very small bid. One strategy for identifying competitive traps is to try to consider the decision from the perspective of the other decision maker(s). In the dollar auction, this strategy would quickly tell you that the auction looks just as attractive to other bidders as it does to you. With this knowledge, you can accurately predict what will occur and stay out of the auction.

You can also develop strategies that discourage escalatory behavior by your competitors. In the $20 bill auction, one class member could organize the class to collude against me. That class member could arrange for one member to bid $1, everyone else to refrain from bidding, and the class could later divide the $19 profit—communication can be a very effective tool. The same is true of the earlier scenario involving companies A, B, and C. In 1995, the basic pattern of this story played out with American

Airlines, United Airlines, and USAir. USAir, the nation's fifth largest airline, announced that it was for sale at the right price. Analysts quickly speculated that the two industry leaders, United and American Airlines, were likely to be interested. However, their analyses were limited to the expectation that the value of USAir was higher to United or American as an acquisition than as a stand-alone company. These analyses ignored information suggesting that United and American would be extremely motivated to avoid losing a bidding war, since the sale of USAir to American would be a major setback for United, and the sale of USAir to United would be a similarly damaging blow to American. As the head of American or United, what would you do?

American developed a strategy aimed at avoiding the escalatory war described above. Robert Crandall, the chairperson of American, wrote an open letter to his company's 118,000 employees that stated, "We continue to believe, as we always have, that the best way for American to increase its size and reach is by internal growth—not by consolidation. . . . So we will not be the first to make a bid for USAir. On the other hand, if United seeks to acquire USAir, we will be prepared to respond with a bid, or by other means as necessary, to protect American's competitive position" (*Chicago Tribune*, November 10, 1995, p. B1). Although the letter was addressed to American Airlines employees, it was obvious that the most important target of this message was United. The message was clear: Keep things as they are, or we will both end up in a money-losing battle. Crandall's letter was very effective in avoiding an escalatory war (no offers were made on USAir in 1995). Five years later, when United made a preemptive bid on USAir for 232 percent of the company's stand-alone value, both United and American stock prices fell sharply.

Also failing to learn from Crandall's successful strategy, a year later, Norfolk Southern railroad acquired Conrail at a price far in excess of Conrail's market value. Esty (1998) traces this overpayment to a bidding war between CSX Corporation and Norfolk Southern. Because both companies were aware that the loser of the bidding war would incur a loss of market value once the bidding got started, each had an incentive to continue bidding beyond the value of Conrail. As a result, Esty (1998) shows that Norfolk Southern lost value by overpaying, while CSX lost value by losing the bidding war. In takeover contests where the losing bidder faces a loss in market share or competitive position, the natural outcome can be overpayment for target firms. Bidders become indifferent between winning the auction by overpaying and losing the auction and suffering a loss in competitive position.

In both the $20 auction and in corporate bidding wars, bidders have typically failed to consider the decisions of the other party, and continue to bid to justify their initial strategy. Finally, the auction moves to very high levels of financial loss when the two parties forget their original objective of earning money and switch to the objective of beating the other party. As an auctioneer, this is when I do very well!

The competitive-escalation paradigm has much in common with Staw's unilateral paradigm. In both cases, the decision maker makes an initial decision that he or she feels a need to justify through future decisions, and reaches a point where he or she has "too much invested to quit." However, there is one major difference between the two paradigms. In the dollar auction, competition with the other party—that is, the desire to "win"—serves as added motivation to escalate commitment.

WHY DOES ESCALATION OCCUR?

Each of the previous sections has provided some clues about the conditions under which nonrational escalation of commitment occurs. The first step toward eliminating escalation from our behavioral repertoire is to identify the psychological factors that feed it. The existing literature clearly suggests that there are multiple reasons why escalation occurs. Building on findings presented in earlier chapters, this section provides a taxonomy of these reasons. The first three classes of explanations—perceptual biases, judgmental biases, and impression management—are general to all of the examples of escalation presented. The fourth class of explanations, competitive irrationality, differentiates the unilateral escalation paradigm from the competitive escalation paradigm. After presenting each class of explanations for this phenomenon, I consider the implications for the elimination of escalation.

Perceptual Biases

Consider the case at the beginning of this chapter, in which you made the decision to hire the employee who subsequently performed below your expectations. Evidence presented earlier in this chapter suggests that your perception of the employee's performance may be biased by your initial decision. That is, you may notice information that supports your hiring decision, while ignoring information that stands against your initial decision. Similarly, in the start-up venture case, after making the initial investment decision, you may have a greater tendency to notice positive information about the start-up than negative information about it. This phenomenon can be predicted by the suggestion in Chapter 2 that we pay more attention to confirming than disconfirming information. Similarly, Staw (1980) suggests that administrators often protect their initial decisions by actively seeking out information that supports these decisions—for example, information that suggests an employee is performing well. Caldwell and O'Reilly (1982) empirically show that participants who freely choose a particular course of action will then filter information selectively to maintain commitment to that course of action.

The perceptual biases that result from our commitment to a particular course of action suggest a number of corrective procedures. As recommended in Chapter 2, when we are making a decision, we need to search vigilantly for disconfirming information to balance out the confirming information that we intuitively seek. This need is particularly pronounced in serial decisions, where we have a natural tendency toward escalation. In addition, establishing monitoring systems that help us check our perception before making subsequent judgments or decisions could prove useful. For instance, if an objective outsider could evaluate our openness to disconfirming information, our perceptual barrier to nonescalatory behavior could be reduced or eliminated.

Judgmental Biases

Once we have filtered the information that we will use to make a subsequent decision, we still have to make the decision. The central argument of this section is that any loss from an initial investment (such as bidding more than $20 in the competitive-escalation paradigm, or more than the initial research-and-development funding in Staw's unilateral escalation paradigm) will systematically distort judgment toward continuing the previously selected course of action. The logic of this prediction lies in the framing concepts developed in Chapter 3.

As you will recall, individuals tend to be risk averse to positively framed problems and risk seeking to negatively framed problems. As the private equity executive described at the beginning of the chapter, you made an initial investment of $2 million to the start-up venture. After a short period of time, you are faced with the decision of accepting a loss of that $2 million or risking an added $1 million in the hope that this added investment will turn things around. The risk-averse response is to accept the sure loss of $2 million, while the risk-seeking action is to try to recover the initial funds by allocating an additional $1 million. From Chapter 3, we know that most of us tend to be risk seeking in the domain of losses. Based on this systematic preference, we would expect most individuals to lean toward investing the additional $1 million if the expected value of the decision was anywhere close to being equal. Now reconsider the problem assuming that someone else in your firm made the initial investment. You are now likely to evaluate the potential benefit of the second loan from a different reference point. From this reference point, the decision is either to quit now or to invest $1 million in a start-up that has run into significant problems. Without having made the initial decision, more people would choose against investing more funds—the reference point has changed. Following this line of reasoning, high- and low-responsibility participants in Staw's paradigm may have been responding to the negative frame of the allocation problem.

Individuals should learn to assess the new decision from a neutral reference point that eliminates the extreme risk-seeking behavior observed among high-responsibility participants (that is, decision makers who have already committed funds or resources to a course of action). This reference-point shift can be accomplished by convincing the decision maker that the initial investment has proven to be a loss and that the second decision represents a new problem to be examined objectively. If this shift is not feasible, a new decision maker should step in to make the subsequent decision.

Impression Management

Returning to the hiring decision from the beginning of this chapter, even if your perception and judgment led you to the conclusion that that the underachieving employee should be fired, you might not choose to fire her. Why not? Firing the employee would be tantamount to a public announcement that your earlier decision was a mistake. You might decide to keep the employee on simply to "save face." Caldwell and O'Reilly's (1982) work shows that individuals not only selectively perceive information, but also selectively provide information to others. Specifically, individuals who make an initial commitment to a particular course of action are more likely to provide confirming, rather than disconfirming, information to others. Thus, managing the impressions of others serves as a third reason for escalating commitment.

In addition to not wanting to admit failure to others, we also try to appear consistent to others. Increasing our commitment to our previous actions is one sign of consistency. Staw and Ross (1980) suggest that our society perceives that administrators who are consistent in their actions are better leaders than those who switch from one line of behavior to another. As support for their position, they offer the following excerpts from the press's evaluation of Jimmy Carter:

> Carter has exacerbated many of the difficulties he has faced. His most damaging weakness in his first two years has been a frequent indecisiveness. ("The State of Jimmy Carter," 1979)

> A President must, plainly, show himself to be a man made confident by the courage of his clear convictions. . . . The American people find it easy to forgive a leader's great mistakes, but not long meanderings. (Hughes, 1978)

Indecision was also cited as the second most common reason for dissatisfaction with Carter in a Gallup poll taken after the president's first year in office (Staw, 1981). In his book *Profiles in Courage*, John F. Kennedy wrote that the most courageous decisions politicians must make are those favoring an action that they believe to be in the best interests of their constituency, yet that they know will be disfavored by that very same constituency. Staw and Ross's findings suggest that this conflict is particularly severe when an action consists of turning one's back on a previously supported course of action.

An interesting paradox results: Making the best decision for your organization means that you should focus on future costs and benefits, ignoring any previous commitments. Yet empirical evidence shows that you are more likely to be rewarded for escalating commitment than for changing course (Ross and Staw, 1986). From an organizational standpoint, this suggests that we need to replace systems that encourage impression management with those that reward good decisions. To do this, managers must convey to all members of the organization that impression management at the expense of high-quality decisions will not be tolerated. Second, organizations should strive to make the employees' values closer to those of the organization by modifying reward systems. The organization wants managers to make smart organizational decisions; managers want to make decisions that will further their careers. When rewards are based on results, employees will hide a bad result by escalating commitment. When management determines rewards by looking at the decision process, not at the outcome, employees will be motivated to make the best possible decisions at different stages, whether or not their initial decisions have been judged to be correct (Staw and Ross, 1987).

Competitive Irrationality

The previous three explanations for escalation can be generalized to both the unilateral and competitive paradigms. Research on competitive irrationality, however, adds an additional insight that distinguishes between the two paradigms. Specifically, competitive irrationality refers to a situation in which two parties engage in an activity that is clearly irrational in terms of the expected outcomes to both sides, despite the fact that it is difficult to identify specific irrational actions by either party. Many people would argue that getting involved in the dollar auction is an irrational decision, and while this is a very reasonable perspective, the argument is not completely valid. If it makes sense for you not to play, then it does not make sense for anyone else to play. If no one else plays, then you can bid a small amount and get a bargain. This reasoning sounds logical, but once you make the initial bid, another individual inevitably bids, and the bind that I have already described emerges. I argued earlier that continuing to bid then depends on your estimation of the likelihood that the other party will quit. Obviously, the same reasoning applies to the other party. If it is possible for someone to get a very cheap $20 (for $1, for example), then it must be rational for one individual to be able to bid. Yet we know the pitfall that results when multiple individuals adopt this attitude. Thus, in many ways, competitive irrationality presents an unresolved paradox, other than as an explanation of escalation. The main recommendation that can be derived from the competitive irrationality explanation of escalation is that many situations may look like opportunities but prove to be traps unless the actions of others are fully considered.

INTEGRATION

This section has suggested four additive causes that contribute to our tendency to escalate commitment to a previously selected course of action. By referring to the four causes as additive, I am calling attention to the fact that they are rarely mutually exclusive. Each one can cause escalation independently, but they more often act together to increase a decision maker's nonrational tendency to continue a previous mistake. To reduce escalation, we must attack each cause at the individual and organizational levels. In doing so, we must remember that we are trying to counter the nonrational commitment to a course of action. Continuing commitment may make sense in many contexts.

Overall, the findings on the tendency to escalate suggest that managers need to take an experimental approach to management. That is, as a manager, you should make a decision and implement it, but be open to dropping your commitment and shifting to another course of action if the first plan does not work out. This means constantly reassessing the rationality of future commitments and learning to identify failures early.

Finally, a caveat: While this chapter has dealt with situations in which commitment is taken too far, it is also important to consider the other side of the spectrum. In certain scenarios, people should maintain or even escalate their commitment to a chosen course of action, primarily to keep their options open. From business to personal relationships, individuals may feel as if they should give up when conditions become mediocre or even just okay. It is important to realize, however, that by ending a commitment, you may lose out on all future benefits from the relationship. Often, maintaining a relationship provides you with more options as you move forward. This advice may seem to run contrary to the discussion of escalation of commitment. One argument seems to urge caution while the other supports taking chances. In fact, they can be reconciled. The key is to make decisions without undue weight on the past and with expectations about the future that are as accurate as possible.

Fairness in Decision Making

You are graduating from a good MBA program. Following your discussions with a number of firms, one of your preferred companies makes you an offer of $90,000 a year, stressing that the amount is not negotiable. You like the people. You like the job. You like the location. However, you find out that the same company is offering $95,000 to some graduating MBAs from similar-quality schools. Will you accept the offer?

Hurricane Andrew hits southern Florida, leaving many people homeless. For many commodities such as building materials, demand is up and supply is down. This is a condition that leads economists to predict an increase in prices. In fact, in the aftermath of the hurricane, a small building-supply company more than doubles its prices on many items that are in high demand, such as lumber. Are the price increases fair? Are they rational?

In the first story, many students are very bothered by the difference between their salary and the salary of others, even if they learn that the difference does not predict how the company will treat them in the future. In the second story, most people believe that it is not fair for the company to raise its prices. In addition, there are reasons to believe that raising prices may not be rational either.

Concerns about fairness are central to a complete understanding of decision making. Research on fairness has focused on either the distribution of scarce resources (Messick, 1991) or the fairness of the distribution procedures (Lind and Tyler, 1988). This chapter gives you the opportunity to examine the consistency of your fairness judgments, just as earlier chapters have encouraged you to explore other components of judgment. Most fairness research has avoided making evaluative statements about the rationality of fairness judgments. This silence has inhibited our understanding of how our cognitive processes create anger, jealousy, and inefficiency. If we are to reduce or eliminate our dysfunctional perceptions of fairness, we need to confront the limits to rationality in these perceptions.

Fairness considerations may account for some of the limitations of the explanatory power of economic models. Kahneman, Knetsch, and Thaler (1986) argue that fairness considerations inhibit employers from cutting wages during periods of high unemployment, despite changes in supply and demand, and explain the lack of price adjustment in the consumer domain. In this chapter, I examine three systematic ways in which fairness considerations lead our decisions to deviate from a simple rational action model. First, I describe situations in which individual judgment deviates from the expectations of supply and demand considerations. Second, I examine how people respond to ultimatums and why we may make choices inconsistent with our own economic self-interest. Third, I consider how social comparison processes lead to decisions that may clash with our underlying preferences.

WHEN DO WE ACCEPT THE ROLE OF SUPPLY AND DEMAND?

In a provocative set of experiments, Kahneman et al. (1986) demonstrated that fairness considerations can dominate economically rational choices in decision making. Consider the action of the hardware store owner in the following scenario:

> A hardware store has been selling snow shovels for $15. The morning after a large snowstorm, the store raises the price to $20.

Would you rate this action as fair or unfair? From an economic perspective, the price should go up. When demand increases relative to supply, an increase in price is expected. However, despite the economic rationality of raising the prices of snow shovels, 82 percent of respondents viewed raising the price of snow shovels to be unfair. And, of the individuals who said it was fair, many would not think it fair for a hardware store to raise the price of generators after a hurricane, even though the logic is the same. Thus, fairness considerations lead to systematic departures from the predictions of economic models.

An interesting reversal of the snow shovel problem emphasizes the importance of thinking about the fairness concerns of others. Assume that you own the hardware store and have twenty-five remaining shovels. Should you raise the price by $5? Even if you believe that the market is a fair measure of the value of the commodity, the answer may be no. By ignoring concerns for fairness, you might raise the price and collect an additional $125 on the shovels. However, the loss of future business from angry customers may cost you more than $125. It does not matter that you think your customers should understand the nature of the supply and demand relationship. If they think the price increase is unfair, they may react to this perception of unfairness in the future. Thus, someone who acts in an economically rational manner (e.g., increases the price of the shovels) may underperform those who consider norms of fairness, since other parties (e.g., customers) may punish a party for the perceived unfairness of an economically rational action.

Cognitive biases also influence people's perceptions of fairness. For example, fairness judgments seem to be susceptible to the effects of framing (see Chapter 3). Consider Kahneman et al.'s (1986) following two problems:

> **Problem A.** A company is making a small profit. It is located in a community experiencing a recession with substantial unemployment but no inflation. Many workers are anxious to work at the company. The company decides to decrease wages and salaries 7 percent this year.

Sixty-two percent of respondents thought the company's behavior was unfair.

Problem B. A company is making a small profit. It is located in a community experiencing a recession with substantial unemployment and inflation of 12 percent. Many workers are anxious to work at the company. The company decides to increase wages and salaries 5 percent this year.

In this case, only 22 percent of the participants thought the company's behavior was unfair. Despite the similar changes in real income, judgments of fairness were strikingly different. A wage cut was perceived as an unfair loss, while a nominal gain that does not cover inflation was more acceptable. We seem to carry around with us certain rules of fair behavior, such as the rule that wages should go up and not down. Thus, when economic conditions change for the worse, it is very difficult for employees to regard a pay cut as fair. Our tendency to rely on nominal quantities, known in the economics literature as a "money illusion," makes Problem B seem fair, even though it is essentially equivalent to the wage change in Problem B. It is logical to think about money in terms of its real buying power (real dollars), rather than the arbitrary unit of a dollar (nominal dollars), which changes in value as a result of inflation. In contrast, our assessments of fairness are largely built around whether the nominal dollar amount of our salary is increasing and decreasing. Instead of rationally adjusting for inflation before making the judgment, we follow our intuitive social rules.

Consumers show similar inconsistencies when thinking about discounts and price increases. Consider the following scenarios from Kahneman et al. (1986):

Scenario 1: A shortage has developed for a popular model of automobile, and customers must now wait two months for delivery. A dealer has been selling these cars at list price. Now the dealer prices this model at $200 above list price.

Scenario 2: A shortage has developed for a popular model of automobile, and customers must now wait two months for delivery. A dealer has been selling these cars at a discount of $200 below list price. Now the dealer prices this model at list price.

The majority of individuals view the action in the first scenario to be unfair (71 percent), yet consider the action in the second scenario to be fair (58 percent). Consumers seem to grant special status to the manufacturer's list price, even if they do not expect to pay that amount. The list price acts as a critical anchor for assessments of fairness. It is unacceptable to exceed that amount. Yet, there is no normative basis for the manufacturer's list price having this special value.

The pattern that emerges is that individuals are very concerned with departures from the status quo and that economically justifiable behaviors will often be perceived as unfair. We seem to place special value on list prices, current prices, and so forth, and to develop fairness rules around these numbers. Regardless of whether the reader follows the judgmental patterns just described, it is critical to recognize the existence of such patterns in a world where fairness judgments affect the behavior of others.

Thaler (2004) documents multiple examples where consumers do not defer to the market. Rather, they use their affective response to decide what is fair. He cites Delta's attempt to charge $2 per ticket extra for tickets not purchased on the Internet, First

Chicago's idea of a $3 charge for doing business with a human teller, Coke's development of vending machines that change price based on demand level, and American Airlines' enormous bonuses to executives at the same time the company asked union employees for substantial wage concessions. In each case, there was no evidence that these actions violated market pricing, but most people sense intuitively that these were bad business ideas at best.

THE INFLUENCE OF ULTIMATUMS

Consider the following opportunity:

> You are traveling on an airplane, sitting in an aisle seat next to an eccentric-looking woman in the middle seat (Vivian). Next to her, in the window seat, is a rather formal-looking businessperson (Mark). About thirty minutes into the flight, Vivian interrupts you and Mark, and explains to you that she is quite wealthy, becomes bored easily on flights, and likes to pass the time by playing games. She then pulls fifty $100 bills out of her wallet and makes the following proposition. "I will give the two of you this $5,000 provided that you can agree on how to split the money. In splitting up the money, however, I will impose two rules. First, Mark must decide how the $5,000 is to be split between the two of you. Then, you (the reader) will decide whether to accept the split. If you do accept, then you and Mark will receive the portion of the $5,000 based on Mark's allocation. If you do not accept the split, then you and Mark will each receive nothing." Both you and Mark agree to play the game. Mark thinks for a moment and then says, "I propose that the $5,000 be split as follows: I get $4,900 and you get $100." Now it is up to you: Will you agree to this split?

If you are like most people, you will probably reject this split. Why? Obviously, rejecting such a deal is inconsistent with the notions of economic rationality, because each party would be better off (+$4,900 for Mark and +$100 for you) if you were to accept it. However, you might choose to reject this offer for a variety of reasons that lie outside self-interested wealth maximization. Reasons for rejecting the $100 include not wanting to accept an unfair allocation and not wanting Mark to benefit from your acceptance. Alternatively, some may argue that you are doing society as a whole a favor by punishing Mark for giving an unfair offer. Any of these possibilities show that fairness somehow comes into play. If you were unaffected by fairness considerations, you would accept the $100. After all, $100 is better than nothing.

This story points out the importance of understanding the role of fairness and equality in decision making. Assume that the roles were reversed: You could determine the allocation and Mark would have the option of accepting or rejecting it. What would you decide? If you did not factor in fairness considerations, it would be easy to conclude that the other party would accept the $100 or even less. However, this proposal would very likely leave you with $0 because Mark would probably reject your offer. In contrast, a consideration of fairness and emotion would lead you to anticipate the likely response of the other party and consequently improve the expected value that you would receive out of this transaction by offering the other party significantly more than $100.

A number of researchers have systematically studied how people respond to ultimatums that are similar to this fictional airplane story (Guth, Schmittberger, and Schwarze, 1982; Roth, 1991). In these studies, Player 1 divides a known, fixed sum of money any way he chooses by filling out a form stating, "I demand X." Player 2 either accepts the offer and receives her portion of the money as allocated by Player 1, or rejects the offer, leaving both parties with nothing. Traditional models of rational actors predict that Player 1 will offer Player 2 only slightly more than zero, and that Player 2 will accept any offer greater than zero. The results, however, show that individuals incorporated fairness considerations into their offers and choices. The average demand by Player 1 was for less than 70 percent of the funds, both for first-time players and for players repeating the game one week later. In addition, individuals in the role of Player 2 rejected profitable but unequal offers.

People often rely on attaining what they consider to be a fair or justifiable result. As a result, they are often willing to pay to punish their opponent if he or she asks for too much. Ochs and Roth (1989) studied a situation in which Player 2 could reject the allocation offer of Player 1, then counterpropose an allocation. However, the amount of funds available was reduced if Player 2 rejected the first offer. The researchers found that in such ultimatum games, 81 percent of rejected offers were followed by disadvantageous counteroffers in which parties who rejected the initial offer demanded less than they had just been offered. Ochs and Roth argue that players' utilities for fairness may explain the results. However, they also argue that a simple notion of equality does not explain the data, since in most cases Player 1 asks for more than 50 percent of the resources in the first stage. Rather, parties realize that the other side may very well refuse offers perceived as unfair despite the economic rationality of accepting them.

Ochs and Roth had participants play either an ultimatum game like the one just described, or a "dictator" game in which Player 1 could simply decide how the resources would be split without Player 2's acceptance. They found that while many Player 1s chose a 50:50 split in the ultimatum game, none proposed a 100:0 split. By contrast, under the dictator format, 36 percent of all Player 1s took 100 percent. When acceptance was required, proposals became more equal. However, in the dictator game, when acceptance by the other party was not required, 64 percent still chose to give the other party some portion of the resources. These results demonstrate that both a desire to be fair and the realization that being unfair can generate future costs led to choices that deviated from rational models in systematic and predictable directions.

Murnighan and Pillutla (1995) argue that the psychology behind ultimatum game behaviors is more complicated than a concern for fairness and a concern for future costs associated with being unfair. Specifically, they suggest that Player 1s view these games quite differently than Player 2s. Player 1s tend to analyze the game strategically, while Player 2s tend to define the situation morally and reject profitable offers when they find the behavior of Player 1 to be immoral. This inconsistency in the definition of the situation can lead to unhappiness for both parties, both in terms of the bargaining result and the destruction of the future relationship. We will return to the problems created by inconsistent and self-serving interpretations of competitive situations in Chapter 10.

Support for the affective component of ultimatum games has been found through the use of neuroimaging techniques. New advances in MRI technology allow scientists to see how blood flows to different parts of the brain in real time. Decision scientists who are interested in the mechanisms behind the observed choices of their subjects have used MRIs in order to determine which part of the brain is activated under different conditions. Sanfey et al. (2003) scanned players' brains as they received ultimatum game offers either from another person or from a computer. They found that activation of the brain was greater for unfair offers than for fair offers, and greatest when these unfair offers came from another person than when they came from a computer. A region connected with negative emotional states was stimulated when players considered unfair offers, as was another region that the authors hypothesized was connected to the cognitive demands of the task, namely the desire to make as much money as possible. The greater emotional response for unfair offers provides concrete evidence that emotional processes are involved in this type of decision making.

The discussion of availability in Chapter 2 showed that a vivid example can overwhelm a rational assessment of a decision. Kramer, Shah, and Woerner (1995) found that the vividness of the examples used to explain ultimatum games influences the aggressiveness of study participants. For example, Kramer et al. showed that individuals exposed to President Kennedy's successful ultimatum in the Cuban Missile Crisis (1962) were far more aggressive than individuals exposed to air controllers' unsuccessful ultimatum in their 1981 strike. Blount and Bazerman (1996) and Boles and Messick (1990) also noted inconsistency in how managers respond to the ultimatum game. When individuals are asked for the lowest amount they will accept in an ultimatum game, they specify a higher amount than the minimum they will actually accept when asked to make a choice between accepting or rejecting an ultimatum.

While priming can cause differences in ultimatum game behavior, there is a surprising amount of cross-cultural consistency in the way people play the game. Heinrich et al. (2001) conducted studies that included the ultimatum game in fifteen small-scale societies all over the world. This research found no support for the classic economic view of self-interest; fairness was found to be an important factor in these economic games for each of the societies tested. However, the researchers did find that while economic and demographic variables did not predict how the ultimatum game was played, the patterns of everyday interaction explained variations. From this field data, it appears that fairness is much more than a modern invention. Instead, it is a universal concept affecting decisions that depends on norms influenced by cultural behavior.

Player 2's expectations in ultimatum games are partially affected by a norm of equality. In the ultimatum game, expectations of fairness lead to the rejection of economically desirable offers, but it also possible that the same norms of equality can cause us to accept "fair" situations too prematurely. Messick (1991) identifies many contexts in which individuals expect an even split, even when a rational analysis would not support such a split. The ease with which individuals accept an equal allocation of pleasure and pain probably accounts, in large measure, for the common use of the compromise solutions in decision making. Consider the following situation:

> You visit a car dealer and go on a test drive. You return to the salesperson's cubicle in the showroom. The car has a list price of $18,000. After a short discussion, you offer $15,500. The salesperson counters with $17,600, you counter with $16,000, he counters with $17,200, you counter with $16,400, and he reduces his price to $16,800. You act as if you will not make another move and threaten to visit another dealership. The salesperson then says

earnestly, "You look like a nice person, and I can see that you really like the car. My main concern is that you get the car that you want. I assume that you are a reasonable person, and I want to be reasonable. How about if we split the difference—$16,600?"

Many of us would quickly accept the salesman's offer. After all, a 50:50 split sounds fair. Yet, careful consideration reveals that this 50:50 split, like most 50:50 splits, is quite arbitrary. The final two numbers on the table could have been $16,000 and $16,400, and the 50:50 split would have sounded just as fair, but the resulting price would have been $16,200, or $400 less. The fairness of a 50:50 split depends on the comparative fairness of the two numbers used as anchors for the split. A rational decision maker must be aware of the influence of a seemingly fair 50:50 split, and realize that other 50:50 alternatives are easy to generate. Just because an offer can be considered fair does not mean that it is optimal. Other equally fair outcomes may exist that would be better for you.

Again, we see that fairness concerns do affect decisions, and that ignoring these concerns in the decisions of others can be detrimental to your own outcomes. Readers are entitled to their own assessments of fairness. However, we must all realize that others may have very different norms about how to respond to an ultimatum; the goal of maximizing their own outcomes may not fully describe their fairness models.

CONCERN FOR THE OUTCOMES OF OTHERS

People care about what happens to other people. Individuals may suffer intentional losses to harm an adversary or forgo gains to help a loved one. In addition, people are concerned about how their own rewards compare to the rewards of others. Recognizing these concerns, organizations create elaborate job grade systems to specify the compensation available to employees at each level within the organization. Salaries, bonuses, and benefits are carefully calculated within these specified parameters so employees will believe they are being fairly compensated relative to others in comparable positions. In addition, organizations strive to conceal salary data to avoid social comparisons and perceptions of unfairness. This elaborate behavior is justified by findings of a positive correlation between pay equity of a corporation and the quality of its products (Cowherd and Levine, 1992). Similarly, Depken (2000) shows a negative relationship between the size of pay differentials within a Major League Baseball team and how well that team performs, judging by the objective standard of winning percentage. The smaller the gap between the highest-paid and the lowest-paid members, the better a group as a whole works together. Clearly, across a broad variety of situations, individuals not only exhibit concern for how their own rewards compare to those of relevant others, but show resulting changes in their behavior as well.

As recent college graduates entering the workforce often experience, significant differences in payment exist across industries. Those who go into investment banking might earn $60,000 or more in their first year while their similarly qualified peers in publishing make less than half that amount. How can that unfair difference persist in the market? Two particularly interesting facts about this cross-industry wage differential can be explained by how concerns for fairness are formed. First, there is an observed correlation between high-profit industries and high wages. Second, if one job within an industry is highly paid, other jobs in that industry tend also to be highly paid. Perceptions of the fair comparison wage are related to the profitability of a given firm and what other individuals in closely related jobs can earn (Akerlof and Yellen, 1990). This means that people make comparisons within the firm and to other firms in the industry, not across industries. This may account for the acceptance of differences in payment between industries such as banking and publishing.

Chapter 3 shows that people often compare outcomes against an anchor, or reference point. The reference point usually represents the status quo, such as your present wealth (Kahneman and Tversky, 1979). Loewenstein, Thompson, and Bazerman (1989) argue that the outcomes of others commonly act as a key reference point in interpersonal decision settings, and that interpersonal comparisons can overwhelm concern for personal outcomes in rating potential resolutions of a dispute. For example, in an experiment that asked participants to assess multiple outcomes to a dispute, one at a time, typical individuals rated $500 for self and $500 for another person as a more satisfactory outcome than $600 for self and $800 for the other. Yet, I would like to believe that I would choose $600 for myself and $800 for another person over $500 for myself and $500 for another person.

Bazerman, Loewenstein, and White (1992) combined the logic on how concerns for others influence our decisions with the work on joint-versus-separate preference reversals from Chapter 3 to examine when people are concerned with the outcomes of others. In the first empirical demonstration of joint-versus-separate preference reversals, Bazerman et al. (1992) showed that while individuals care far more about social comparisons when rating a specific outcome, absolute individual outcomes are more important in actual choice behavior. Seventy percent rated the outcome of $400 for self and $400 for the other party as more acceptable than $500 for self and $700 for the other party when asked to evaluate these outcomes separately. However, only 22 percent chose $400 for self and $400 for the other party over $500 for self and $700 for the other party when asked to choose between the two. This basic pattern is consistent across many other comparisons and across a wide variety of contexts. When a series of joint outcomes are evaluated individually, the outcomes of others become the reference point. When choosing between two outcomes for oneself, the outcomes of others are not needed as a reference point, since the two outcomes can be easily compared. In this type of situation, the outcomes of others become less relevant. Instead, the salient attribute in a choice task is outcome to self.

Blount and Bazerman (1996) extended this result to a real situation involving real payoffs. They agreed to recruit participants for a colleague's experiment. One group of potential participants was offered $7 to participate in a forty-minute experiment, knowing that all participants would be receiving $7. A second group was offered $8 to participate in a forty-minute experiment, knowing that some participants were arbitrarily (based on the last digit of their social security number) being offered $10. A third group was given an opportunity (1) to participate in a forty-minute experiment in which everyone was being paid $7, (2) to participate in a forty-minute experiment in which some participants, including themselves, would receive $8 and others would receive $10, or (3) not to participate. Although significantly more participants in the first group chose to participate (72 percent) than in the second group (55 percent), the majority of participants in the third group (56 percent) chose to participate in the experiment that gave them $8 while some others were given $10 (16 percent chose the experiment in which everyone received $7; 28 percent chose not to participate in either). Thus, in evaluating whether to participate in one specific experiment, the outcomes of other potential participants were critical. However, when multiple opportunities were available, participants were able to compare what they would receive across the multiple experiments, and the outcomes of others became less important.

In a related set of studies conducted in the fall of 1991, Bazerman, Schroth, Pradhan, Diekmann, and Tenbrunsel (1994) asked second-year MBA students at the Kellogg Graduate School of Management whether they would, under a deadline, accept or reject a hypothetical job offer from a consulting firm. Some participants were presented with one offer at a time, while others were given two job offers at a time. In both cases, they were told to imagine that it was January 15 of their graduating year, that the job offer(s) expired today, and that they needed to either accept one of the offers or reject the offer(s) and remain on the market. Two of the jobs were described as follows:

> **Job A:** The offer is from Company 4 for $75,000 a year. It is widely known that this firm pays all starting MBAs from top schools $75,000. (Additional descriptive information about the firm is then provided.)

> **Job B:** The offer is from Company 9 for $85,000 a year. It is widely known that this firm is paying some other graduating Kellogg students $95,000 a year. (Additional descriptive information about the firm is then provided.)

The study was interested in how MBA students discriminated between the two jobs; it was not concerned with single-choice participants who accepted neither or both job offers in a pair, or with multiple-choice participants who rejected both offers. Of the thirty-two participants who accepted one of the two jobs listed above in the single-choice condition, twenty-two accepted Job A and ten accepted Job B. In contrast, of the thirty participants who accepted one of the two jobs in the multiple-choice condition, five accepted Job A and twenty-five accepted Job B. Consistent with the earlier Blount and Bazerman (1996) study, this study generalizes the findings to a realistic context with participants who could easily identify with the decision context.

We also explored the question of whether social comparisons are simply one of many possible sources of social information that people use inconsistently. When individuals are assessing any single outcome to self and lack a metric to assess the worth of that outcome, they will search for some social information to make sense of the outcome. However, when they are evaluating more than one option, comparing outcomes to self across multiple options provides evaluative information about each option. Specifically, we examined whether procedural justice information would create effects similar to those caused by social comparison information. The procedural justice literature suggests that individuals value the procedures used to create justice, as well as the justice of the outcomes obtained. However, in past studies, procedural justice research presented participants with one situation at a time, never allowing them a choice between options (Lind and Tyler, 1988). Thus, one interesting question is whether procedural justice is considered valuable only in contexts where decision makers are deprived of the information necessary to assess the worth of their outcomes by more important standards.

To address this question, we substituted procedural justice information for social comparison information and asked MBA students to assess either six single job offers or three pairs in the same format as described in the previous experiment. As shown in the following pair of offers, the jobs were set up to create a conflict between obtaining procedural justice and maximizing salary:

Job A (lower salary, high procedural justice): The first offer is from Company 1 for $60,000 a year. New associates are given the opportunity to participate in decisions typically made by upper management. New associates are allowed to voice their preferences regarding client and project assignments. The firm encourages all consultants, both junior and senior, to voice their opinions for changes and improvements in the company's policies.

Job B (higher salary, low procedural justice): The second offer is from Company 2 for $75,000 a year. New associates are assigned by senior partners to specific clients, projects, and engagement teams in which a senior partner is in charge and from which they are not allowed to request changes. Decisions involving company policies, including MBA training, job objectives, career advancement, and salary increases, are made by senior management. The new MBAs are not encouraged to voice their opinions or objectives.

It was expected that when individuals assessed jobs individually, procedural justice information would be more important than when individuals assessed pairs of jobs. In the single condition, of the forty MBA students who accepted one of the two preceding jobs, twenty-nine accepted Job A and eleven accepted Job B. In contrast, in the multiple condition, of the thirty-seven MBA students who accepted one of the two jobs, fourteen accepted Job A and twenty-three accepted Job B.

These findings are consistent with the affect heuristic introduced in Chapter 1, with the work on joint-versus-separate preference reversals introduced in Chapter 3, and with the want/should distinction developed in Chapter 4. When we assess one option at a time, social comparisons create a quick affective response, which significantly influences the acceptability of that option. But when multiple options exist, a more cognitive assessment occurs, and we place a smaller weight on more affective information—comparison salary information or issues of procedural justice.

SUMMARY

Judgments of fairness permeate organizational life. Comparisons of pay raises, the distribution of scarce budgets, promotions, grades, and prices are just a few of the many situations in which we make fairness judgments that affect our emotions and behavior. Judgments of fairness are based on more than objective reality. This chapter provides an introduction to the cognitive patterns that lead to perceptions of unfairness.

It would be impossible to eliminate concerns for fairness and social comparisons from our decision-making repertoire. Ample evidence supports the argument that people will use fairness and social comparison information to interpret their world. Thus, understanding how you and others judge fairness may help you make better managerial and life decisions. Concerns for fairness will not end with this chapter, but will become a central ingredient when we explore "bounded ethicality" in Chapter 8.

CHAPTER SEVEN

Common Investment Mistakes

*I*magine that you have placed most of your retirement investments in an index fund, a relatively "boring" investment that seeks to match the performance of a large group of stocks (for example, the entire Standard & Poor's 500 index of large U.S. companies). Your best friend, learning of your investment practices, argues that a bright person like you should be able to outperform that boring index fund. When you counter that you don't enjoy spending time searching for the best investment, he advises you simply to switch your retirement funds to the actively managed mutual fund that he uses. An actively managed fund is run by professional stock-pickers who trade stocks on a regular basis, seeking to own the right ones at the right time. His mutual fund, it turns out, beat your index fund by two percentage points last year.

A year goes by, and your friend brags to you that his fund had another great year, beating the market by 4 percent (over the overall percentage that the market returned that year). He tells you it's time to switch—that you're losing too much money. Still, you decide to stick with your index fund. Another year goes by, and your friend is back to brag about outperforming the market for the third year in a row—this time by 2 percent. Is it time for you to listen to him?

Now consider some more data. In recent years, the Vanguard Index 500 fund, which tracks the S&P 500, has outperformed about 75 percent of the actively managed mutual funds in existence each year. Of course, you do not plan on investing in one of the 75 percent of funds that performs worse than the market; you plan to choose among the top 25 percent like your friend. The only problem is that substantial evidence demonstrates that past stock performance is not predictive of future performance (Bazerman, 1999). While some research suggests minor relationships between past and future performance, these relationships have been small and inconsistent. But, on the other hand, your friend's fund has been consistent!

Now consider that there are a lot of funds—approximately 8,000—and that all of them are being managed by people who would like you to believe they can outperform the market, though only an average of 25 percent will succeed in any given year. In other words, each year approximately 2,000 of these 8,000 funds will outperform the market. Of these, 25 percent, or 500, will outperform the market again the next year. And among these winners, 25 percent, or 125 funds, will again outperform the market for a third year in a row. The key lesson is that there will always be funds that outperform the market for multiple years in a row, but this trend will happen roughly at random, and past performance will still have little predictive power.

By contrast, index funds are certain to perform at the level of the overall market to which they are indexed, minus a very small operating fee. One reason index funds outperform the majority of mutual funds is simply that their fees are so low—often below 0.2 percent. Actively managed mutual funds have far higher expenses—often as high as 2 percent annually, or up to ten times higher than some index funds. What's more, the actively managed funds often trade stocks faster, leading to higher brokerage costs that are subtracted from their returns. By definition, the aggregate of active funds (in which managers choose stocks) is likely to match the market, before fees are subtracted (Sharpe, 1991). In the end, high expenses significantly reduce the returns of these actively managed funds.

But it was your friend who told you to switch from an index fund to actively managed mutual funds three years ago, and you trust your friend. This is not unusual. Lots of people rely on others for investment advice. Of course, those friends whose choices underperform the market eventually become too sheepish to make recommendations; we only continue to hear from those who have been lucky. Friends are not the only source of tips on the past performance of mutual funds. Ads in magazines, in newspapers, and on television promote mutual funds that have done very well over the last year and try to make investors feel guilty for not having chosen that fund earlier. In fact, in any given time period, any large family of mutual funds (Fidelity has over 150 funds) will always have some funds that have performed well above the market and some that have performed well below the market. The mutual-fund company, of course, will advertise only those funds that performed above the market. If all large mutual-fund companies selected their portfolios by throwing darts at dartboards, companies could still advertise the funds with the luckiest dart throwers. In all likelihood, this system would produce the same numbers of winners and losers as under the current system—but it would be difficult for the dart throwers to justify charging high operating fees for their "expert" opinions.

This may be true, but you, like your friend, are investing for the long term, and you plan to select one of the most successful actively managed mutual funds. This is possible—but not likely! An amazingly small number of funds outperform the S&P 500 index over longer stretches. For the period 1982–1992, for example, forty-eight of the 205 leading mutual funds underperformed the S&P 500 by at least three percentage points per year, while only three of the 205 funds outperformed the market by at least three percentage points per year (Bogle, 1994). Thus, as the time span lengthens, the performance of actively managed mutual funds looks even worse.

While you might hope to invest in one of the three mutual funds that perform three percentage points or more above the index, don't forget that every other investor who is picking actively managed funds also intends to pick a winner. Of course, you might choose a fund that boasts of having outperformed the market over the last ten or even twenty years. Be careful, Bogle (1994) warns:

Marketers of mutual funds have a fairly easy time achieving—and then bragging about—returns that mark their fund as '#1.' Here is the strategy: Select a fund that ranks first in any class of funds with similar objectives and asset size . . . over any specified period of time (the past quarter or year or even twenty-five years). Advertise it as #1. When the ranking subsequently drops (and it will), select another fund... and advertise it as #1... These promotions provide simplistic information that is easily manipulated and has absolutely no predictive value... Similar rankings published in the financial press lack the fund sponsor's bias... However, these rankings are also utterly without predictive value....

Bogle's evidence is very good. For the twenty-year span of 1972–1992, he found that the average of the twenty best-performing mutual funds for the first ten years was ranked 142 out of 309 in the next ten years. While this performance is marginally better than that of the average fund, it is a far worse deal than buying into an index fund and avoiding expenses. Specifically, while the average total return of these "top" twenty funds during the second decade (+14.3 percent) beat the allfund average (+13.1 percent), it was far short of the +16.2 percent return of the unmanaged S&P 500 Index (Bogle, 1994).

More recently, the *New York Times* provided performance results for the portfolio selections of five investment pros—Eric Kobren, Sheldon Jacobs, Jack Brill, Russel Kinnel, and Harold Evensky—for a seven-year period ending June 30, 2000 ("A Seven-Year Lesson in Investing," Carole Gould, 9 July 2000, p. B18). All five portfolios were invested primarily in stock funds for the seven years, and the decision makers were financial experts regularly featured in the press. The seven-year returns achieved by the five portfolios were 210 percent, 204 percent, 200 percent, 147 percent, and 124 percent, respectively. These numbers sound good—but how did the Vanguard 500 Index do over the same period of time? This unmanaged, low-cost, boring index fund provided a return of *278 percent* for the same seven-year period. Yet another victory for less management and lower fees.

Why *do* people buy actively managed mutual funds, despite this strong, easily available evidence that they are getting a bad deal? Jason Zweig (2000) warns in *Money Magazine,* "The folks who run mutual funds have always been good at cooking up clever ways to gouge you on fees, confuse you about performance, make you pay unnecessary taxes and goad you into buying funds you don't need." Mutual-fund companies also engage in creative strategies to help them look like they are performing better than an objective assessment would suggest. In addition to advertising their winners, mutual fund companies can take their losers out of business—and they do! In 1996, 242 of the 4,555 stock funds tracked by Lipper Analytical Services were merged or went out of business (Damato, 1997). Note, these funds did not go out of business at random; they were the laggards, and the fund companies were ashamed of their performance. When a fund dissolves, its old track record is erased from history, removed from the databases kept by research organizations like Morningstar and Lipper. Thus, because dropped funds are not part of the analysis, the average performance of a mutual-fund company is often much lower than the company typically reports it to be.

You may argue that some analysts offer good advice and are capable of identifying the few long-term best funds—after all, they are quoted in financial magazines and newsletters and interviewed on television. Perhaps it is possible to form a fund managed by allstar portfolio analysts selected on the basis of their long-term performance.

Bogle (1994) describes a fund that was actually created in this manner. A good idea? Maybe, but in this case it just didn't work. The unmanaged S&P 500 beat the experts by more than one percentage point per year (13.9 percent versus 12.8 percent) between 1986 and 1992.

No individual who buys an active mutual fund expects that it will perform far worse than average. Yet, lots of people buy actively managed funds and continue to hold onto them long after receiving evidence of their failure. The cost of these mistakes adds up to billions of dollars. Why do people make these mistakes? While I believe the answers can be found in the first six chapters of this book, researchers have developed a related field of inquiry: behavioral finance.

Essentially, behavioral finance is an application of what we know about common judgment errors to the world of investment. In the 1980s and early 1990s, behavioral decision research was applied most extensively to the area of negotiation (which we will cover in Chapter 9). In recent years, the most active area for new insights has been in the area of investments. This research gives us a better understanding of an important set of life decisions, and also offers clear evidence that the decision errors described in this book are broad in scope. Behavioral finance focuses on how biases affect both individuals and markets. This chapter focuses on the former application; Shleifer (2000) and Shefrin (2000) are good sources on the latter.

In this chapter, we will specifically: (1) apply some of the core findings from earlier chapters to investment decisions, (2) explore the scary practice of daytrading that became popular in the late '90s, (3) consider the role of investment groups (have you heard of those nice grandmothers from Beardstown?), and (4) close with some clear, common-sense investment advice. As you read, I encourage you to compare these insights to your own beliefs about investing and to your current investment portfolio.

THE PSYCHOLOGY OF POOR INVESTMENT DECISIONS

Investors love new books promising that the market will go up by 300 percent or 1,000 percent in the next year. Glassman and Hassett's (1999) *Dow: 36,000*, for example, received enormous media attention. Such titles achieve their success by tapping into the psychological mistakes of investors. This is a great development for the authors who get rich from these books, but this success is unlikely to be passed along to the books' readers. As shown in earlier chapters, even very bright people make poor decisions that cost time, profitability, and in some cases, their financial future.

As you read this chapter, my argument against active investing may sound too strong. However, the evidence is amazing, and it contradicts the massive amount of money and advice changing hands in financial markets. Investors pay high fees to actively managed mutual funds, to brokers to pick stocks, and to electronic trading companies to make frequent trades. These fees are how funds, brokers, and companies make their money. Are all of these investors making mistakes? The great majority of them are! Incorporating the themes of previous chapters with new research on investors, this section will document how investment decisions are affected by: (1) over-confidence; (2) optimism; (3) denying random events and the regression to the mean; (4) anchoring, the status quo, and procrastination; and (5) prospect theory.

Overconfidence

Chapter 2 demonstrated that people are generally overconfident in their decision making. In the area of investing, this overconfidence translates into a tendency to believe that you can pick mutual funds or stocks that will perform better than the market. This overconfidence leads people to engage in more active investing. Why should you be concerned about overconfidence? Because it is likely to lead you to believe that the stocks or actively managed mutual funds that you pick will perform better than they actually will, while also leading you to discount the likelihood of failure. In the investment arena, an additional pattern is vicarious overconfidence. That is, we overestimate the likelihood that our friends or our investment adviser will outperform the market.

Overconfidence is especially pertinent to stock-market investing strategies. The expense associated with owning individual stocks is largely created by the costs of buying and selling them. These expenses, which include transaction costs and differences between buy and sell prices, are dramatically higher for investors who make frequent trades. Collectively, these expenses can add up to a surprisingly large amount of money over time. While I have argued that investing in an index fund is a better strategy than frequent stock trades, it is not your only good option. For an investor with a moderate amount of wealth, a low-cost alternative to an index fund would be to buy a diversified portfolio of stocks and hold them for many years. Thanks to the emergence of a variety of investment vehicles designed to help you build a portfolio cheaply and conveniently, this strategy is becoming easier and more commonplace (Zweig, 2000).

Unfortunately, many stock-market investors fail to recognize the advantages of following this pattern. Barber and Odean (2000a) studied 66,465 households that held an investment account with a large discount broker during the period 1991–1996. In contrast to the buy-and-hold strategy, the average account turned over 75 percent of its portfolio annually. That is, on average, investors with this brokerage house sold 75 percent of their investments in any given year. Similarly, Carhart (1997) reports that the average turnover of mutual funds is 77 percent annually, while the New York Stock Exchange (2000) determined that in 1999, its total turnover rate was 78 percent. These numbers mark a dramatic increase since 1970, when the turnover rate for the New York Stock Exchange was 19 percent, and in 1980, when it was 36 percent. This growing frenzy can be attributed in part to bright people thinking they can predict the moves of the market. Are they right?

The average investor in the Barber and Odean (2000a) database earned a return of 16.4 percent during a booming market, just 1.5 percent lower than the overall market return of 17.9 percent for this same period. Most interesting are the 20 percent of accounts (more than 12,000 accounts) that had the highest turnover rates—those who actively traded stocks. Presumably, these investors believe they can assess the direction stocks will take, and are willing to incur the costs of buying and selling stocks to own the "right" portfolio at the right time. On average, the 20 percent with the highest turnover earned a return of just 11.4 percent. Thus, in comparison to the overall market return, by spending time and money trying to track, buy, and sell stocks, investors *lost* 6.5 percentage points. If active trading is so hazardous to your wealth, why do so many people engage in it? One simple explanation is that they are overconfident in their ability to outperform the market.

Overconfidence does not affect the genders equally. Examining 35,000 investment accounts at a large discount brokerage, Barber and Odean (2001) sorted the accounts by gender and found that women achieved better results than men. In comparison to the market as a whole, women underperformed the return that they would have obtained by holding the same portfolio for a year by 1.72 annual percentage points, while in a similar comparison, men lost 2.65 percentage points. Does this mean that women pick better stocks than men? No! Actual returns of stocks picked by men and women were not significantly different. Rather, turnover patterns differed; the men had a harder time sitting still. Women had average turnover rates of 53 percent annually, while male turnover rates were 77 percent annually. It was the added costs of these more frequent trades that led men to underperform women; with each trade, the brokers got richer while the investors themselves fell further behind. Barber and Odean conclude that overconfidence among men leads to increased turnover, which in turn leads to lower performance after brokerage costs are carved out of the returns. Before women readers become overly confident about these findings, it is important to note that Barber and Odean are describing men performing worse than women whose results are *already far behind* those of the market. In other words, women did less badly than men—not an achievement worth celebrating.

Optimism

If you have money invested in the stock market, what was the total percentage return of your portfolio last year? Did you beat the market—in other words, did your performance compare favorably to the S&P 500? Now, go check your answers based on the actual data: Look up your account statements or call your brokerage or fund adviser, and don't forget to ask for last year's return on the S&P 500. How did your memory of your performance compare to your actual performance? My guess is that your comparison will be consistent with evidence showing that people tend to be optimistic about a variety of behaviors, such as expected career advancement, driving ability, etc. (see Chapter 4). Once people make an investment, they tend to be overly optimistic about its future profitability, and later maintain optimistic recollections of the investment's past performance. Optimism is closely related to overconfidence, yet distinct from it. When investors make overly confident decisions, they will hold unwarranted optimism regarding future success; retrospectively, they will maintain this optimism, even when the disappointing results of their investments are easily available.

Moore, Kurtzberg, Fox, and Bazerman (1999) created an investment simulation based on the actual performance of the nine largest mutual funds, plus one index fund, over a ten-year period, 1985–1994. MBA students received a computer disk with an investment assignment. Starting with $100,000, for each six-month simulated period, participants were allowed to invest their balance in any of the ten funds, or in a money market account, with the goal of maximizing their ending balance at the end of the simulated ten years. (The entire task took the typical student forty-five minutes to complete.) After making a six-month investment decision, participants received extensive feedback on their return, the return of all funds, and the return on the overall market; they were then prompted to place their next six-month investment. Investing the entire account in the index fund for the entire ten-year period would have led the $100,000 initial portfolio to grow to $380,041. However, the average investor ended up with only $349,620 in his or her account—a return consistent with the evidence from real-world databases presented earlier. The typical investor made too many trades, incurring far too many fees.

False optimism was clearly a factor in the participants' investment strategies. Despite the fact that the market performed very well overall during this ten-year period (1985–1994), participants consistently predicted that their portfolios would grow faster for the next six-month interval than they actually did. Specifically, participants predicted that their portfolios would rise 8.13 percent per six-month period; in fact, they grew by only 5.50 percent. Even more interesting, participants had optimistic illusions about their past performance: At the end of the game, most participants reported that they had matched the market's performance. In fact, participants obtained an average return 8 percent *below* the market. More specifically, Moore et al. (1999) asked participants whether they had performed (1) more than 15 percent below the market, (2) 10–15 percent below the market, (3) 5–10 percent below the market, (4) within 5 percent of the market, (5) 5–10 above the market, (6) 10–15 percent above the market, or (7) more than 15 percent above the market. On average, participants overstated their performance by one entire level.

In a parallel study, Goetzmann and Peles (1997) obtained very similar results. Participants remembered obtaining more favorable returns than they actually obtained. Goetzmann and Peles conclude that optimism helps investors justify their past behaviors, allowing them to maintain illusions about the superiority of their investment strategy. I argue that optimism also encourages investors to continue active trading, rather than pursuing wiser, time-saving investments in index funds.

By the way, before reading this chapter, had you ever compared your investment decisions to the market? Most investors have not. Why not? I argue that most investors want to protect their overly optimistic view of their investments—and are willing to pay a high price to maintain their illusions. Similarly, if you use an investment adviser, have you ever instructed this "expert" to provide systematic follow-up on his or her recommendations? It might be instructive for you to ask the adviser to compare the returns on his or her advice to the market's performance during the same period of time. The psychological need to perceive good news may be insulating you—and your hired experts—from the truth about investing, and costing you a great deal of money in the long run.

Plenty of external sources encourage investors' natural optimism. Financial magazines remind us of the wise advice they provided in the past, but generally neglect to mention the advice that was flat-out wrong. These publications also tend to supply anecdotal evidence of past success, rather than risking their reputation by tracking it in a systematic manner. Overall, I have to admit that this is a wise business strategy:

If they revealed the true returns on their past advice, they would probably sell fewer magazines.

Denying that Random Events Are Random

As we saw in Chapter 2, people tend to deny that random events are random, and find patterns where none exist—such as having a "hot hand" in basketball. When investors are led to believe that a specific fund is "hot," they will become more willing to pay the fees associated with active investing. For example, when a fund outperforms the market two years in a row, investors rarely attribute its success to random variation. It is more likely that they will overgeneralize from these few data points and assume that the manager of the fund has great skill and is therefore worthy of their investment. In fact, there is a great deal of randomness in the investment arena, and even more denial of this randomness by investors. In their eagerness to outperform the market, most investors are unwilling to accept that performing at the level of the market, while minimizing expenses, may be a level of performance that they should be happy to accept. The most important conclusion? Be wary of any advice that predicts the market's future based on past performance.

Consistent with research by Bogle (1994), Carhart (1997), and Thaler and DeBondt (1992), in the ten-year database used in the Moore et al. (1999) study (1985–1994), the performance of mutual funds tended to regress to the mean. Nevertheless, study participants expected their portfolios' future performance to be highly correlated with past performance. In fact, their expectations were negatively correlated with actual returns. Overall, participants expected "hot" funds to stay hot, usually because they think talent lies behind the investment decisions. This is the same false assumption that leads real-world investors to hold onto expensive funds.

There is some minor evidence that past performance of stocks predicts their future performance. Jegadeesh and Titman (1993) document a momentum effect in which stocks that have done well continue to do well the next year. The only problem is that this pattern then reverses itself in following years (DeBondt and Thaler, 1985). Odean (1999) argues that biased investors who expect past patterns to continue in the future may influence a stock's performance. However, after the last of these momentum traders enter the market and push the value of the stock beyond the underlying value of the company, the price will begin to fall, causing the inevitable reversal.

DeBondt and Thaler (1985) compared the future performance of two groups of stocks: one group of extreme losers from the past three years and one group of extreme winners from the past three years. They found that, over the following five years, the "loser" portfolio dramatically outperformed the "winner" portfolio. DeBondt and Thaler (1985) attribute reversals to the tendency of investors to assume that the past is a good predictor of the future, and thus to their penchant for overbuying winners and overselling losers. The market eventually adjusts, and owners of the underpriced "loser" portfolio will find themselves with a better set of investments than owners of the overpriced "winner" portfolio.

Inspired by Jegadeesh and Titman's (1993) results, you might be tempted to adopt the strategy of buying recent stock-market winners. On the other hand, DeBondt and Thaler's (1985) findings might motivate you to buy recent losers. Unfortunately, it is extremely difficult to predict when the last momentum buyers have entered the market. Once again, the past is not an accurate predictor of the future. Personally, I am more comfortable admitting that I have no way of knowing which stocks will do better in the future and sticking with index funds.

Anchoring, the Status Quo, and Procrastination

Much of this chapter suggests that many investors think too much about their investments, frantically trading stocks and shifting mutual funds based on the most recent advice of too many experts. However, evidence also exists that most people think too *little* about the type of assets they should hold. Thinking through one's asset allocation and developing a long-term plan makes a great deal of sense. This is where investment advice (e.g., free software programs provided by many mutual fund companies) may be helpful. For example, Shefrin (2000), Belsky and Gilovich (1999), and most other sources of good financial advice suggest that most people place too little of their *long-term* investments in stocks. This observation is based on the amazing long-term superior performance of stocks over bonds and other standard investments. Yet, people use fairly naïve strategies for asset allocation, sticking with what they or others have decided in the past; in other words, their investment decisions tend to be fairly mindless.

In a study of scholars who enroll in retirement plans offered by TIAA-CREF, Benartzi and Thaler (1999) found that most professors, facing a choice between investing their retirement funds in either TIAA (bonds) or CREF (stock), commonly allocated their money 50:50 to the two accounts. In addition, the median number of changes that professors made to this allocation over their career was zero. That is, professors (maybe not the smartest of people, but also not the dumbest) made a fairly naïve allocation, and then never adjusted their decision—even as their life circumstances changed over time.

The professors' 50:50 allocation meshes with another of Benartzi and Thaler's (1999) findings: When firms offer a choice of investment options for retirement accounts, the percentage of stock funds offered is an excellent predictor of the percentage of dollars that employees will choose to invest in stocks. That is, if a company offers four funds, three stock and one bond, employees put about 75 percent of their money into the stock funds. In contrast, if the company offers one stock fund and three bond funds, then employees hold, on average, 75 percent of their retirement investments in bonds. Thus, people choose their investments the way many diners order food in a Chinese restaurant: one dish from the "Vegetables" column, one from "Chicken," one from "Beef," and so on. That may be a good way to pick a satisfying meal, but it's not the best investment strategy; history shows that if your money will remain invested in a retirement fund for decades, stock funds will offer the best return. The point is that people should think carefully about this allocation, rather than being led naïvely by the choices their employers offer them.

By this point in the chapter, I hope that many of my readers are reconsidering their investment decisions. However, there is a strong force competing against change—the status quo bias. This is the effect that prevented Benartzi and Thaler's (1999) professors from making even one allocation change in a lifetime. Samuelson and Zeckhauser (1988) find that people tend to keep their investments the way that they are. In an experimental study, they presented a thought exercise to a group of individuals with a working knowledge of economics and finance. The participants were asked to imagine that they had inherited a large amount of money from a great uncle, and were asked which of four possible investments they would pick: (1) a stock with moderate risk, (2) a risky stock, (3) U.S. Treasury bills, and (4) municipal bonds. Each investment was described in a bit of detail. Four other randomly selected groups were told that they inherited an investment from their great uncle, and that it consisted of one of the four investments listed above (one group was told that they inherited a stock with moderate risk, a second group was told that the inherited a risky stock, a third group was told that they inherited a U.S. Treasury bill, and a fourth group was told that they inherited a municipal bond). These participants were asked whether they would keep the investment or trade it for one of the three other investments listed above. They chose overwhelmingly to keep the investment that they received, rather than picking the investment best suited to their unbiased preferences. Essentially, the study participants accepted the status quo, rather than switching to the investments that best suited their particular needs.

Finally, the bias against action also leads many people to procrastinate making investments in the first place. Studies of automatic enrollment in 401(k) employee savings plans powerfully illustrate just how passive people can be about very important economic decisions. 401(k)s are attractive savings vehicles not only because taxation is deferred until the money is withdrawn, but because some companies offer to match the contributions of their employees up to a certain amount. Most companies use an "opt-in" savings plan, which means that their employees must enroll in the 401(k) on their own initiative, usually by filling out a form or calling a phone number. Others use automatic enrollment, where the default is enrollment at a set contribution rate. In this scenario, an employee must make an extra effort if he or she does not want to contribute. The difference in employee enrollment rates between these two different types of enrollment schemes is striking. Madrian and Shea (2001) found that initial enrollments in 401(k)s jumped from 49 percent to 86 percent within the same company when they switched from an opt-in system to automatic enrollment. Choi, Laibson, Madrian and Metrick (2003) found that a third alternative, no default, which forces the employee to think about the decision, also increases enrollment, but not as much as automatic enrollment (Choi et al., 2003).

Similarly, it is not uncommon for people to hold a large amount of money in their checking, savings, or money market account with the intention of investing it soon. Months pass, and they find themselves facing the same decision—but suddenly the market has gone up in value by 6 percent, and they've missed out on a great opportunity. By procrastinating, you may be sacrificing your long-term financial well-being. Somewhat paradoxically, investors procrastinate on making allocation decisions, while being overly active in moving funds within a category (e.g., stocks)—thus putting too much effort into the less important financial decisions and not enough effort into the far more vital ones.

Prospect Theory, Selling Winners, and Keeping Losers

Consistent with Shefrin and Statman (1985), Odean (1998) found that investors have a strong preference to hold on to stocks that are selling below purchase price, so that they will avoid becoming "losers," and to sell stocks that are selling above the purchase price, so that they will come out "winners." Similarly, Barber, Odean, and Zheng (2000) show that investors tend to hold on to losing mutual funds and oversell winning mutual funds. If your goal is to make as much money as you can, then the choice of whether to buy or sell a fund should be based solely on how much you expect its value to increase in the future. Thus, the price at which you bought it is an arbitrary and meaningless reference point, except with regard to taxes. From a tax perspective, when you sell a winner, you must pay taxes on your earnings, and when you sell a loser, your taxes are reduced. Therefore, with respect to taxation, it makes sense to sell more losers than winners. In addition, Odean (1999) finds that the winners that investors sell end up outperforming the losers that they keep. In sum, when investors seek to become winners, stock selection and taxes actually increase their chances of being losers.

Why do investors follow this losing pattern? As we learned from prospect theory in Chapter 3, decision makers tend to compare outcomes to a reference point. For most investors, the most common reference point is the price that they paid. Investors holding stocks valued at a price higher than they paid for them are faced with a sure gain (selling now and becoming a "winner"), or holding the stock and risking the current gain for an unknown return. With gains, we tend to be risk averse; investors tend to sell to guarantee the gain. Investors holding stocks valued lower than their initial purchase price, on the other hand, are faced with a sure loss (selling now), or holding the stock for an unknown return. With losses, we tend to be risk seeking; investors tend to take the risk of holding onto the loser in the hope of becoming a winner. This pattern is also consistent with a regret minimization strategy—an effort to avoid "booking" a loss. As long as you let the loss "ride," you can pretend it doesn't exist; but once you sell the stock, you have to enter it, in your mental accounts, on the loss side of the ledger. However, for three reasons, this pattern leads investors to lose money relative to the market's overall performance: high costs associated with making trades, selling the wrong stocks, and paying too much in taxes. Recognition of these errors should encourage investors to adopt wiser and simpler strategies.

ACTIVE TRADING

Starting in the late 1990s, online trading became the dramatic growth area of the investment world. Electronic trading was, and still is, simply cheaper than going through a stockbroker, and as more people began to trade online, the costs went down. From 1996 to 1998, the average online trading commission fell by 75 percent. In addition, the Internet has enabled regular people to have access to a vast amount of financial data, research, and tools, including up-to-date information, low-cost trades, and almost instantaneous transactions.

First, the good news about online trading. If you are planning to invest in stocks, bringing your costs down will be a key to your success. So, for those investors who follow a long-term buy-and-hold strategy, investing online rather than through a full-service broker makes a great deal of sense. However, buy-and-hold is not the strategy of the typical online trader. Especially during the late 1990s bull market, online traders tended to be actively engaged in trading stocks. In the worst case, they quit their jobs to be professional traders. Many of them were headed for disaster!

The typical investor who engaged in online trading around this time was someone whose trades had recently beat the market (most likely because they were lucky). In a 1992–1995 sample of online trading, Barber and Odean (2002) found that the average new online trader outperformed the market by two percentage points the year before switching to online trading. Note that these investors' confidence was further bolstered by the fact that these were very good years for the stock market. Unfortunately, after switching, these traders' average performance regressed to the mean and was further lowered by the costs of frequent trades. As a result, these online traders lagged the market by three percentage points.

Lagging a very successful market by three percentage points is no disaster, particularly if you engage in online trading in your spare time. However, because online traders tend to be the most overconfident of investors, many of them quit their regular professions to trade full-time, becoming members of the now notorious pseudo-profession called daytrading. Under the strict definition of "daytrading," individuals initiate and close out high-volume positions by the end of the same trading day, but the term refers to extremely short-term trades in general. Daytraders try to capitalize on price fluctuations of highly volatile, usually technology-related, stocks.

The extreme frequency of their trades doomed these full-time traders to underperform the market by even more than three percentage points. Jordan and Diltz (2003) studied records of 324 daytraders during 1998 and 1999, the time of an immense stock market bubble, and found that only 36 percent made money during this heady period. In addition, nearly all of a daytrader's profits are short-term capital gains, which are taxed as ordinary income (with a tax rate of up to 35 percent, depending on the investor's income bracket); a more patient investor would be taxed on long-term gains at a much lower 15 percent. In addition, nearly all of a daytrader's profits are short-term capital gains, which at that time were taxed at the highest marginal rate (up to 39.6 percent); a more patient investor would be taxed on long-term gains at a much lower 20 percent. Even before the market plummeted, one particularly distraught Atlanta daytrader went on a shooting spree after a streak of "bad luck." Tragically, when the market went down, many more sad stories emerged about those who had quit their jobs and subsequently lost life savings by daytrading.

What caused reasonably smart people to decide to become daytraders? In Chapter 2, I presented evidence that people respond to vivid data. Barber and Odean (2000b) document the barrage of ads that made daytrading success vivid to all Americans. In one commercial, Discover Brokerage introduced us to an intrinsically motivated tow-truck driver with a postcard on his dashboard. "Vacation?" his white-collar passenger asks. "That's my home," the driver responds. "Looks more like an island," comments the passenger. The driver explains, "Technically, it's a country." Where did the driver get his wealth? Online trading, of course—it was that easy. This type of commercial, as well as real-life stories of the lucky, inspired more and more people to trade online, leading in many cases to tragic consequences.

When I used to run into daytraders (they were often also taxi drivers), I liked to ask them why they thought they knew more than the party on the other side of the trade. Most of the daytraders I met had never considered this question. When they asked me to clarify, I tried to explain: When a daytrader is buying a stock, it is because someone else has sold it. Similarly, when a daytrader sells a stock, someone else is buying it.

Odds are that the other party is an institutional investor of some sort. Thus, most day-traders are typically paying fees to make an exchange with someone who has better information, more experience, and quicker hardware to make the trade than they do. Overall, I argue, this sounds like a bad bet. But, as I will explain in Chapter 10, people are not very good at considering the other side of a transaction.

These days it is rare to hear dinner-party guests boast of quick online profits. Dreams of buying a laptop and earning a living by trading on a remote tropical island have been mostly forgotten. I hope the lessons of the aftermath of the bubble will stick around, however, because the low costs of online trading remain. The tendency to trade too actively may still be enticing to the uninformed. Believe it or not, with the market picking back up, there are a handful of individuals who are stepping back up to the daytrading plate, willing to take another swing at making a huge profit. Perhaps they are goaded on by their past successes or urban legends of someone else making it big. I wish them luck; both history and data show they are going to need it.

THE BEARDSTOWN GANG AND OTHER GROUPS THAT LIMIT INVESTMENT RETURNS

Perhaps, you think, you can get better returns on your investment by pooling your knowledge with others. That's the core concept of investment groups. In fact, a group of nice grandmothers from Beardstown, Indiana, wowed investors with reports of very high returns. Their bestseller, *The Beardstown Ladies' Common-Sense Investment Guide*, claimed that the club's members had outperformed the market and made a 23.4 percent return on their investments over a ten-year period by following the simple, straightforward strategy of investing in well-known companies (such as McDonald's and Wal-Mart). The women appeared as investing experts on many of the most popular talk shows and were profiled by film crews from Great Britain, Germany, and Japan. They produced five books, a video, and a Web site, and held numerous book signings, seminars, and speaking engagements.

In the midst of the media frenzy, Shane Tritsch, a reporter for *Chicago* magazine, noticed a curious disclaimer on the copyright page of the 1996 edition of the Beardstown Ladies' book. Clarifying a detail not mentioned in previous editions, the disclaimer stated that the members' dues were included in the club's annual return figure. In other words, the Beardstown Ladies calculated their annual returns quite differently from the way mutual funds (and virtually all professionally run investments) calculate theirs. The Ladies set returns equal to the sum of stock appreciation plus dividends plus monthly dues; by contrast, the returns of mutual funds are based only on stock appreciation plus dividends. According to Price Waterhouse, from 1984 to 1993, the decade covered by the Beardstown Ladies' *Investment Guide*, the club's average annual return, as it should have been calculated, was actually *only 9.1 percent*—far below the 23.4 percent return they reported, and also significantly lower than the 15 percent average return of the overall stock market from 1984 to 1993.

While the Beardstown Ladies' investments underperformed the market, the American public's desire to believe in their incredible story turned out to be a cash cow for the retirees, whose book royalties more than made up for returns. Readers shelled out money for the book, and many of them made far poorer investments as a result.

Why did the media and the public fall for this story? One possibility is that investors fail to accept the true difficulty of outperforming the market. False optimism allowed the public to believe the story, rather than double-check the amazing record.

Nevertheless, the false claims from Beardstown fueled the growth of investment clubs nationwide; from 1994 to 1998, the number of such groups rose in the United States from 13,000 to 35,000 (Barber and Odean, 2000b). In a study of 166 investment clubs from 1991 to 1997, Barber and Odean found that the groups earned a 14.1 percent annual return, while the S&P index returned 18 percent and individual investors earned 16 percent. All told, 60 percent of the clubs underperformed the index. The investment clubs turned over their investments far too often (65 percent annually), causing them to pay too much in brokerage costs.

There are a variety of reasons to join an investment club. Perhaps your friends are tired of hearing you talk about investments. Perhaps you like the people in the club, or maybe they serve good food. But if you belong to the investment club to increase your return, it may be time to rethink your investment strategy.

ACTION STEPS

More than any other chapter in this book, the ideas presented in this chapter have action implications for virtually all readers. I hope I have provided a thorough overview of mistakes that many people make and explained the psychology behind those mistakes. Now that we have observed these mistakes in the investing context, I close with some specific thoughts to consider as you strive to reduce the biases that affect your investments. I begin with the issue of saving for retirement and then close with broader investment advice.

In Chapter 1 of this book, I argued that a key aspect of making more rational decisions is to clearly identify your final goal. Many investors have never put much thought into this issue. Some may have the goal of "accumulating as much money as possible." But, if you are able to take this goal to the extreme—by earning a good income, living frugally, and investing your savings wisely—you could end up dying with mountains of money in your accounts. A different goal is to acquire the funds you need to buy whatever bundle of goods you want to surround yourself with for the rest of your life. This goal is the central theme of the investment bestseller *Die Broke* by Pollan and Levine (1997). I have no objection to a mixed strategy of buying the goods you desire and providing funds for other people and charitable organizations. However, many of us fail to think even this far about our monetary objectives.

The goal of investing to acquire the funds you need for a comfortable retirement seems straightforward. However, a 1997 survey found that only 6 percent of U.S. citizens felt they had surpassed their retirement savings goal, while 55 percent felt that they were behind (Laibson, Repetto, and Tobacman, 1998). Laibson et al. (1998) report that the median U.S. household retires with liquid wealth of $10,000 and net worth of $100,000 (including house equity and autos). This finding is consistent with a broad array of evidence that Americans are saving too little for retirement.

Assuming that we are capable of saving more, why do we fail to do so? Perhaps the most critical answer comes from the want/should distinction developed in Chapter 4. People know that they *should* save more for retirement, but they *want* to consume more now (to buy a new TV, eat dinners out, etc.). The evidence in Chapter 4 suggests that our desires typically overcome what we think we should do, particularly when the benefits of listening to our "should self" are decades in the future. This will be particularly true for those who avoid financial planning; the less we plan, the more we allow our desires to gain the upper hand. To assist our want self in defeating our should self, people become overly optimistic that solutions for retirement will suddenly appear. This optimism works out fine for a small minority of citizens—maybe Uncle Edgar will keel over and leave you a fortune in his will, or your numbers will come up in Powerball—but the majority may be in for a rude awakening upon retirement.

With regard to investments, the U.S. government provides support for people who want to make conscientious decisions about their futures by offering tax incentives for retirement investments—IRAs, Keoghs, etc. By investing in these plans, you are not only acting wisely from a long-term perspective, but getting a bonus from the government as well. Quite simply, virtually all readers should be investing as much money as they can to reduce their taxable income.

What's more, your own employer probably gives you incentives to save. As mentioned previously, many 401(k) retirement plans allow you to contribute a portion of your salary and then have your employer "match," or augment, a portion of that money. Some employers match 25 percent, 50 percent or more—instantly and automatically turning each dollar you contribute into $1.25, $1.50, or even higher rewards. The power of the status quo bias has already been discussed in reference to enrollment in 401(k) plans. When enrollment in a lucrative plan is not the default, many people never take the initiative to participate.

Unfortunately, participation is only the first hurdle. After deciding whether to join, you must then decide what percentage of your income to save. If you are not contributing the maximum percentage of your salary that your plan allows, then you are missing out on one of the best and safest ways to build your long-term wealth. Yet, among the too few who do participate in 401(k)s, most are contributing too little. A large percentage of people think that they do not save enough, but they lack the willpower to do anything about it. A parallel problem is procrastination. People think they will increase their savings rate, but never get around to it.

Benartzi and Thaler have found a way to help overcome the lack of self-control and initiative preventing optimal contribution rates (Thaler and Benartzi, 2001). Using the psychological principles described in this book, they motivate people to increase their contributions to their 401(k)s through a program called "Save More Tomorrow." Under this program, workers commit ahead of time to increase their contribution rates a set amount every time they receive a raise. The success of the program is dependent on its understanding of the concepts of hyperbolic discounting, procrastination, and loss aversion. Their design makes the program easy to adopt, because it's easier to make difficult choices when you are discussing future rather than present events. It remains effective, because it's very rare that people will take the initiative to opt out of the program once they have started. Finally, it is not that difficult for the saver to stomach; because the savings rate increases just as the size of their paycheck does, they will never experience a decrease in their disposable income. The Save More Tomorrow plan more than tripled the savings rates of those who joined in just over two years. It is an important example of how knowledge of our psychological biases can help improve our decision making and, specifically, financial planning. The principles of Save More Tomorrow can easily be applied to your own personal savings. Think ahead about how to schedule savings increases to coincide with windfalls, and construct ways to prevent avoiding these deadlines when the time comes.

Once you have allocated money to savings, decisions regarding where you place your retirement money should be based on a clear asset allocation plan. Benartzi and Thaler (1999) make a convincing case that most people have far too low a percentage of their retirement funds in stock. The fact that retirement funding is for the distant future means that it should be easier to accept the higher risk of stock in return for the higher returns that stocks achieve over a long period of time. A few bad years are unlikely to lead stocks to underperform bonds between now and the time when most readers will retire. As you approach retirement, it may make more sense to move more money into bonds to reduce risk.

As retirement approaches, for those investors with the goal of buying their desired bundle of life goods, annuities also make a great deal of sense. In return for a lump sum of money, the investor gets a guaranteed amount of funds periodically for the rest of their life. If you die ahead of schedule, you lose—but then again, you won't need the money anyway. However, if you outlive expectations, you will get a great return, and you are more likely to need these additional funds. Green (2000) argues that annuities are underused in comparison to the financial benefits that they create. In addition, annuities are now provided by a number of charitable organizations, allowing you to obtain guaranteed income for life and tax benefits, and to provide funds to your preferred charity. These annuities create more total benefit than what you could obtain privately, while making a similarly valued contribution to society. However, while annuities will be logical for many investors, you need to choose them carefully. Some annuities, pushed by the sleaziest outfits in the financial business, come with a slick sales pitch and are wildly overpriced. I recommend sticking with a highly reputable, well-known mutual-fund family that charges low fees, such as T. Rowe Price, Schwab, or Vanguard.

Beyond retirement, the key argument of this chapter is that very bright people are currently paying billions of dollars per year for collectively useless advice. Why? Because they are committing the errors described throughout this book in the area of investing. Now that you understand the psychology behind these mistakes, you must learn to confront them and identify a better plan for the future. This plan should include taking the time to formulate an asset allocation plan. You should strive to achieve this allocation in a low-cost manner; avoid paying fees to people and companies who do not truly add value. While many investors now know to avoid "loads" (commissions that are paid when you buy a mutual fund), far too many are still buying funds with very high annual expense ratios (Barber, Odean, and Zheng, 2000). Once you have your plan in place, continue to invest on a regular basis. If you combine these three tasks—appropriate asset allocation, low-cost investing, and adding regular investments—you are well on your way to an excellent investment strategy. Then relax, go back to work on tasks that you enjoy, or play more tennis—there is little reason to be thinking about your investments more than a few hours per year.

Some final words of caution: Changing your allocation of funds according to the advice in this chapter does require some care on the tax front. Before selling securities that have appreciated in value, you must first seek to understand the taxable consequences of doing so; you may want to check with your accountant. The advice in this chapter is relevant to existing investments, but must be applied to them with care. It should be easiest to follow when you are thinking about making new investments.

CHAPTER EIGHT

Bounded Ethicality[1]

*F*ollowing the many corporate scandals that coincided with the start of the new millennium, the media looked for the underlying cause of the unethical behavior that caused them. Popular targets of the media's blame included a few "bad apples" within firms such as Enron and Arthur Andersen, gatekeepers within these companies, and failed governmental regulation. Business leaders were blamed for their role in the presumed ethical decline, and business schools were criticized for failing to provide ethical training to future leaders. The media implied that the key to stemming the tide of financial scandals was to figure out how to keep corporate actors from explicitly engaging in unethical behavior.

In this chapter, I will challenge this ethical perspective on corporate scandals. I am in favor of changing the incentives of organizational actors to encourage more ethical behavior, and would be delighted to see genuine corporate criminals serve time in prison. But recent research provides a compelling case that the vast majority of unethical behaviors occur without the conscious awareness of the actor engaging in these behaviors.

This chapter focuses on the cognitive biases that lead honorable people to engage in unethical behavior without realizing that they are doing so. Chapter 6 examined the ways in which fairness judgments depart from standard economic models. The topic of this chapter is related, but distinct. This chapter considers how cognitive biases allow us to act in ways that contradict our own intended standard of ethics. These deviations from our intended standard of ethics are systematic and predictable, just as the biases from rationality discussed in Chapters 2 and 3 are predictable and systematic. Rather than concentrating on intentionally corrupt behavior, I will discuss recent research that identifies the types, magnitude, and causes of unethical behavior that occur without the awareness of the actor—what my colleagues and I refer to as

---

1. The term "bounded ethicality" comes from coauthored work (Chugh, Bazerman, and Banaji, 2005). Much of the material in this chapter is based on my collaboration with Dolly Chugh and Mahzarin Banaji. In addition, seeds of this works were influenced by my earlier collaboration with David Messick (Messick and Bazerman, 1996).

bounded ethicality (Chugh, Bazerman, and Banaji, 2005). This perspective diverges from standard treatments of ethics, which assume the explicit analysis of appropriate action by the individual, yet complements this traditional view.

Our central argument is that understanding and changing the ethicality of human action requires going beyond the common assumption that ethically challenged behavior results from people choosing self-rewarding behavior over what is right. The assumption of the conscious agent as the sole determinant of human action has been clearly refuted (Fiske, 2004). New evidence points to the limitations of the conscious mind, while emphasizing the power of the unconscious mind to create unethical behavior (Banaji and Bhaskar, 2000; Murnighan, Cantelon, and Elyashiv, 2001; Wegner, 2002).

My colleagues and I use the term "bounded ethicality" in a precise manner; it refers to the systematic and predictable psychological processes that lead people to engage in ethically questionable behaviors that are inconsistent with their own preferred ethics. Bounded ethicality comes into play when an executive makes a decision that not only harms others, but is also inconsistent with the decision maker's conscious beliefs and preferences. Managers and executives develop protective cognitions that lead them to engage in behaviors that they would condemn upon further reflection or awareness. For example, Chapter 3 reviewed the omissions bias, which shows that people feel less responsible for harms caused by inaction than for harms caused by action. When managers become aware of an ethically questionable situation that is not formally part of their responsibility and fail to get involved, they may be quick to justify inaction as ethical, when greater reflection would prove inaction to be more harmful than many errors of action. Chugh (2004) argues that bounded ethicality is exacerbated by the demands of executive life, which cause System 1 thinking (discussed in Chapter 1) to take over. System 1 thinking allows the biases created by bounded ethicality to develop, which in turn lead to decisions that deviate from one's personal standards.

Like the other biases reviewed in this book, the biases emanating from bounded ethicality apply to the best and the brightest among us. In March 2004, Justice Anthony Scalia denied a motion from the Sierra Club to recuse himself from an upcoming Supreme Court case, *Cheney v. U.S. District Court for D.C.* Scalia had hunted ducks in Louisiana with Vice President Dick Cheney in January 2004, just three weeks after the Supreme Court agreed to consider whether Cheney should be forced to provide information about the energy task force he led as the Bush administration formulated its environmental policy. The Sierra Club argued that Scalia and Cheney's friendship led to questions about Scalia's objectivity. "If it is reasonable to think that a Supreme Court justice can be bought so cheap, the nation is in deeper trouble than I had imagined," Scalia wrote in defense of his decision (*New York Times*, 19 March 2004, p. A1). His friendship with the vice president would not intentionally distort his judgment, Scalia argued, and did not violate the Supreme Court's rules on conflicts of interest.

But the rules governing the Supreme Court, like most guidelines, rules, and laws that protect against conflict of interest, were generated to guard only against intentional corruption (Banaji, 2004). Scalia's comments indicate that he rejects or is unaware of the unambiguous evidence on the psychological aspects of conflict of interest. In this chapter, I will provide evidence that even the strictest of conflict-of-interest guidelines are not sufficient to address those conflicts of interest that escape the awareness of the professional being affected. Specifically, psychologists have shown that a friendship between two people makes it impossible for one friend to objectively assess issues involving the other.

This chapter overviews five examples of bounded ethicality: overclaiming credit without realizing that you are doing so, implicit attitudes, in-group favoritism, overdiscounting the future, and the influence of conflicts of interest. In each case, I present research showing that such behaviors occur beyond the actor's conscious awareness.

OVERCLAIMING CREDIT

Coauthors often overclaim credit for their joint work. If two coauthors are asked to estimate their own contribution to the finished product, the two percentage estimations have a strong tendency to total more than 100 percent (Taylor, 1989). Harris (1946) even found evidence of egocentrism between cowinners of the 1923 Nobel Prize for the discovery of insulin. After receiving the prize, Banting, one of the winners, contended that his partner, Macleod, who was the head of the laboratory, was more of a hindrance than a help. In turn, in speeches describing the research that led to the discovery, Macleod managed to forget to mention that he had a partner.

Overclaiming credit is not limited to Nobel Prize winners. When four group members each claim they did 30 percent of the work on a project, it becomes impossible to split the proceeds in a manner that everyone will deem equitable. With multiple parties clamoring for what they believe to be their entitlement, conflict inevitably erupts. Since the original demonstration by Ross and Sicoly (1979) that married couples overestimate their unique contribution to shared household activities, overclaiming has been demonstrated in academia (Ross and Sicoly, 1979), athletics (Brawley, 1984; Forsyth and Schlenker, 1977), and fundraising (Zander, 1971), just to name a few fields (see Caruso, Epley, and Bazerman, 2005b for a review). The roots of overclaiming are the self-serving biases reviewed in detail in Chapter 4. Even honest people believe they contributed more to an enterprise than they actually did. So, the next time a member of your group makes a claim that you view to be outrageous, before arguing, consider that you might also be guilty of the tendency to overclaim credit. In addition, remember, it is far more likely that your colleague is biased than dishonest.

Can anything be done to stop such overclaiming? Caruso, Epley, and Bazerman (2005a) recently asked Harvard MBA students to estimate how much of the work done in their study groups was done by them. When we added up members' claims by group, the average total was 139 percent. In other words, the members of the average group believed that they were responsible for 139 percent of the 100 percent of work completed. However, when we first asked group members to think about the contribution of each member, including themselves, the average total of the claimed work done by the group fell to 121 percent. While "unpacking" individuals' contributions to the group effort did not cause the overclaiming of credit to disappear, it did at least reduce the magnitude of the bias. Extending work on academic authorship to papers with between three and six authors, we found that overclaiming was rampant and that unpacking reduced overclaiming. In addition, the greater the magnitude of overclaiming, the less parties wanted to work together in the future. Essentially, improving the perspective-taking skills of group members can help reduce overclaiming and raise group performance. In addition, overclaiming may have important implications for the longevity of groups.

Overclaiming can also be critically important at the firm level. Researchers have puzzled over the question of why joint ventures so often result in disappointment. One possible drawback of strategic partnerships is that parties are often skeptical that the other side is doing their share. It is a widely known problem that joint venture partners often contribute mediocre talent to the enterprise, rather than their firms' best talent. Why? Part of the reason is that each party has an incentive to save their best talent for projects that they are fully invested in, rather than on projects of which they own only half. When we factor in the tendency of each side to overclaim credit for their own contribution, it becomes apparent that they will feel entitled to reduce their contribution. Consequently, each side views the other side's behavior to be unfair and its own behavior to be justified; the escalation of sinister attributions about the other party spirals downward.

IMPLICIT ATTITUDES

John Smith, a venture capitalist, was faced with a choice between allocating his firm's current funds to one of two businesses. One entrepreneur had an exciting concept that focused on online education, while the other had a very successful chain of local restaurants, with plans to go national. The online-education entrepreneur was a white male and the restaurateur was a black female, but John considered these facts irrelevant. Many of the standard analyses that John and his partners crunched out favored the restaurateur over the online educator. In the end, without being able to easily articulate his reasons, he decided to go with his gut: he said "yes" to the online educator and "no" to the restaurateur.

Soon after, John and Jim, his partner, were filling out an internal form that summarized the firm's recent funding decisions. In the ethnicity column, John noticed that every project he had selected was headed by a white male like himself. Few proposals had come from women and minorities, but John recalled that these entries were finalists in almost every case. "I guess they were just not as strong as their competitors," he said to his partner.

The data on ethnicity and gender in the funding decisions made John feel guilty. He was proud of his long history of publicly supporting affirmative action. John's guilt intensified a month later, when he saw a segment of "Dateline NBC" that referred him to the Implicit Association Test (IAT) Web site at Harvard University (http://implicit.harvard.edu). This site, which I encourage the reader to explore before reading further, provided an experiential tool to identify racial and gender biases that are not cognitively available to the test-taker. John decided to take the test to prove to himself that he had no bias against African-Americans.

The first computerized test that John selected required him to make rapid classifications of photographs of African-Americans and European-Americans. Using two computer keys, John identified faces as either "black" or "white." At times, he was asked also to identify whether words that appeared on the screen represented concepts that were positive ("good") or negative ("bad"). Words such as "peace," "love," and "joy" were easy to classify as "good," while words such as "bomb," "devil," and "awful" were easy to classify as "bad." As the test continued, the two types of trials—African-American/European-American faces and good/bad words—merged. Now John was asked to tap one computer key to judge when a face that appeared was "black" and the same key when a word that was "bad" appeared. He was to tap a different key to judge when a "white" face appeared and the same key when a "good" word flashed on the screen. This task seemed easy as well.

Halfway through the test, a small change was made to the pairing: Now "black" was paired with "good," and "white" was paired with "bad." Once he started, John found this task to be much harder than the previous one. He made more errors and, to make sure he answered correctly, he had to slow down a great deal. By the time he was done with the task, John had the distinct sense that the two tasks, while seeming to be small variations of each other, were in fact quite different. The first task was simple; the second was annoyingly tricky.

The test results appeared on the screen, and John was not pleased. Because he was able to respond more quickly in the black/bad version than in the black/good version, he showed a moderately strong association between "black" and "bad" and between "white" and "good." In other words, John's implicit attitude, or preference, favored whites over blacks, though he didn't endorse such a preference in his conscious mind. Did these implicit associations in John' mind also affect his investment decisions?

A significant amount of recent research suggests that John's associations may have affected his decisions, and that he is not alone in this respect. Most of us, including those who view themselves as progressive on issues of race and gender and hold no explicit hostility toward other races or the other gender, may be out of touch with our more implicit feelings and preferences. The study of stereotyping and prejudice has revealed the power of the unconscious mind. The Implicit Association Test (IAT; Greenwald, McGhee, and Schwartz, 1998), which the aforementioned Web site exemplifies, allows researchers to measure thoughts, and specifically to contrast explicit thinking, or mental processes operating within our awareness, with implicit thinking, or mental processes operating outside our awareness. Explicit attitudes are defined as thoughtfully formed attitudes that the decision maker is aware of endorsing, while implicit attitudes are automatic attitudes that the decision maker is unaware of and does not necessarily endorse (Banaji, Bazerman, and Chugh, 2003). Both explicit and implicit attitudes affect behavior. For most people, the surprise lies in the important effects that result from implicit attitudes.

Because implicit attitudes are rooted in ordinary mental processes of categorization, perception, memory, and judgment, Banaji (2001) has called the use of these attitudes "ordinary prejudice." She argues further that the word "ordinary" captures the likelihood that, if ordinary mental processes are involved in expressions of stereotypes and prejudice, then ordinary managers, executives, and other professionals will demonstrate them. Prejudice is so ordinary that Nosek, Banaji, and Greenwald (2002) report that roughly three quarters of the whites who visit their Web site (http://implicit.harvard.edu) exhibit pro-white implicit attitudes. And, implicit attitudes predict behavior. Rudman and Borgida (1995) have found that implicit stereotypes predicted discrimination against female job applicants. Rudman and Glick (2001) found that study participants who held strong implicit attitudes connecting women with communal traits (e.g., helpful) and men with agentic, or individualistic, traits (e.g., ambitious) were more likely to view a female exhibiting ambition as having poor social skills than were participants with weaker implicit attitudes on this dimension. McConnell and Leibold (2001) found that implicit attitudes were highly predictive of nonverbal behaviors toward different groups of people. Finally, Asendorpf, Banse, and Muecke (2002) discovered that implicit attitudes are more predictive of spontaneous behaviors and that explicit attitudes are more predictive of thoughtful behaviors. This effect implies that implicit attitudes are more likely to occur when decision makers are operating under System 1 than under System 2 thinking.

Many researchers have noted a societal shift over the last few decades from "old-fashioned racism" to "modern racism" (Brief, Dietz, Cohen, Pugh, and Vaslow, 2000; Chugh, 2004). Old-fashion racism is explicit and accompanied by hostility. Modern racism is more subtle, afflicting decision makers when ambiguity allows them to deny responsibility for racist behavior, perhaps by claiming they were only following orders (Brief et al., 2000). One likely possibility is that explicit measures of assessing racism (i.e., asking people about their preferences for one group over another) were sufficient for diagnosing old-fashion racism, but more implicit strategies (such as the IAT) will be needed to undercover and address modern racism.

In July 2004, Morgan Stanley paid $54 million to settle a sex discrimination suit filed on behalf of some of its female executives by the Equal Employment Opportunity Commission. The commission argued that much of the problem at Morgan Stanley, and at other investment banks, is that the mostly white men who are in charge do not seem to recognize the existence of inequities in their operations (*New York Times*, 14 July 2004, p. C1). Hydie Summer, who previously received $2.2 million from Merrill Lynch as a result of arbitration associated with sex discrimination, commented, "[The brokerage managers] really don't believe they are discriminating. If you come in and you look like they want you to look—probably a white male profile—they'll project success for you. They have a specific view of what a successful broker or manager will look like, and it is not usually a woman or a black or Hispanic." Rather than simply waiting for evidence of explicit prejudice to emerge, individuals and organizations need to learn to confront their own implicit attitudes.

IN-GROUP FAVORITISM

Think about some of the favors you've been asked to perform in recent years, whether for a friend, a relative, a friend of a friend, or a friend of a relative. Have you helped someone get concert tickets, an apartment rental, admission to a school, or a job? Most of us are glad to help out with such favors. More often than not, we have done them for people like ourselves—people who went to the same college, people we work with, or people who happen to be of the same race. A basic psychological finding is that we tend to identify with people who are a lot like us. In addition, we are more comfortable doing favors for those with whom we identify than for those noticeably different from us. Thus, we tilt toward helping people who share our nationality, religion, race, gender, or alma mater. This all sounds rather innocent. What's wrong with asking your neighbor, the admission's officer at the nearby college, to check up on a coworker's son's college application? Isn't it just "networking" to recommend a former sorority sister for a job, or to talk to your cousin the banker when a friend from church gets turned down for a home loan? A favor is a favor no matter who you're helping, right?

Few people set out to exclude underrepresented minorities through such acts of kindness. But when those in the majority tend to favor people who are similar to them when allocating scarce resources (such as jobs, college admissions, and mortgages), they effectively discriminate against those who are different from them. Consistent with the work on implicit attitudes discussed above, Dasgupta (2004) has reviewed almost one hundred research studies that show that people have a greater tendency to associate positive characteristics with their "in-groups" (groups they belong to) than with "out-groups" (groups they do not belong to), and to more easily associate negative characteristics with out-groups than with their in-groups. These patterns can result from both automatic, implicit processes and thoughtful, explicit processes.

One fascinating manifestation of these patterns is the tendency of people to do favors for members of their in-group without recognizing the harm that these favors may create for out-group members. Even as we congratulate ourselves for doing something nice for a member of our "community," we overlook the unethical favoritism we perpetuate in the process. In-group favoritism, or giving "extra credit" for shared demographic traits, is equivalent to punishing people for being different from you. Yet helping people who are like us is viewed by society as a nice thing to do, while discriminating against those who are different is viewed as unethical.

Over the last decade, studies have repeatedly shown that banks are much more likely to deny a mortgage to an African-American than to a Caucasian, even after controlling for a variety of factors, including income, house location, and so on. The common view is that banks are overtly hostile to the African-American community. For some banks and some loan officers, this may very well be the case. But Messick and Bazerman (1996) argue that a much more common—and insidious—cause of discriminatory mortgage lending is likely to be in-group favoritism. Thus, white loan officers may be making too many loans to unqualified whites. Given a limited pool of resources, fewer funds remain available for nonwhite applicants.

DISCOUNTING THE FUTURE

People generally believe that we ought to leave the natural environment in as good a state as we inherited it. People also generally believe that we should not treat the earth "as if it were a business in liquidation" (Herman Daly, cited in Gore, 1992, p. 191). These explicit values concern future generations. In contrast, our bounded ethicality allows us to make ongoing decisions that are inconsistent with our explicit views. Rather than making decisions aimed at sustainability, we choose to consume environmental resources at an ever-increasing rate. Our explicitly stated concern for the future collides with our implicit desire to consume and, too often, our implicit desires win out. We discount the future, and future generations, in ways inconsistent with our explicit environmental attitudes.

Research documents extremely high discount rates regarding the future (Loewenstein and Thaler, 1989; Bazerman, Wade-Benzoni, and Benzoni, 1996). Most homeowners do not sufficiently insulate their attics and walls. They also fail to buy more expensive, energy-efficient appliances, even when they would recoup the extra costs in less than a year. Organizations are also guilty of discounting the future. A great university in the United States began an extensive effort to improve its infrastructure but, due to a shortsighted concern for the bottom line, administrators failed to use building materials that would be the most cost-efficient over the long term. The university placed a very high implicit discount rate on its construction decisions, reducing present costs by increasing future expenses on energy consumption. At the same time, the investment arm of the university certainly would have been delighted to receive the returns that were available by buying more efficient products. In most cases involving energy and the environment, myopic decisions result in a waste of resources and environmental degradation.

Loewenstein (1988) argues that very high rates of discounting the future occur partially due to the widespread human bias toward increasing consumption. Our ever-increasing desire to consume more than we did in the past causes us future harm; for example, by spending more now, we sacrifice the funds we need for a comfortable retirement. When the natural environment is involved, our discounting crosses generations. Despite our explicit concerns for preservation, our ethicality becomes bounded, and we too often engage in environmentally destructive behaviors.

THE PSYCHOLOGY OF CONFLICT OF INTEREST

Financial advisers often earn fees based on the transactions they recommend you follow. Surgeons often earn higher fees when they operate, and doctors are often paid for recommending patients for clinical trials. Commission-paid lawyers are more likely to recommend settling a case than are lawyers paid by the hour. Real estate agents earn their living from our housing purchases. Merger and acquisition experts typically are paid only when a transaction occurs, and sometimes Supreme Court justices rule on cases involving their friends.

Most members of these professions would agree that conflict of interest exists in many of these examples, but assume that they themselves are immune. Likewise, it would be natural for me to believe that the similarity of a job candidate's research to my own would never affect my opinion in a faculty hiring decision. After all, I consider myself to be an honest and objective person. Not only do we believe that we ourselves are immune from conflicts of interest, but we believe that the professionals giving us advice can overcome them as well.

This common belief in our objectivity and the objectivity of our advisers belies the clear evidence that conflicts of interest are less likely to lead to conscious corruption than they are to distort our judgments in ways that we are not even aware are occurring. When a real estate agent advises you to raise your offer beyond what a rational assessment would suggest, the point is not that she is corrupt, but simply that she is human, and therefore implicitly motivated to maximize her own returns from the deal. So, she learns over time that buyers are happier paying a bit more than running the risk of losing the house, regardless of what is objectively true. When we are motivated to interpret or alter data in a direction that will benefit us, we are not capable of providing others with an objective assessment (Moore, Cain, Loewenstein, and Bazerman, 2005). This is true of doctors, lawyers, auditors, and all other professional advisers.

Moore, Loewenstein, Tanlu, and Bazerman (2004) gave students a complex set of information concerning the potential sale of a company and asked them to estimate the company's value. There were four different roles in the simulation: buyer, seller, buyer's auditor, and seller's auditor. All participants read the exact same information about the company. Consistent with research on self-serving biases, sellers thought the company was worth more than buyers did. In addition, the judgments of auditors were strongly biased toward the interests of their clients. It is not terribly surprising that sellers' auditors concluded that the firm was worth more than did buyers' auditors. More interestingly, auditors' private judgments about the company's value were also biased in their clients' favor. Auditors were asked to estimate the company's true value, their judgments were compared to those of impartial experts, and they were rewarded for the accuracy. Even with this incentive for accuracy, the estimates of the sellers' auditors averaged 30 percent higher than those of the buyers' auditors.

We also examined the decision making of actual auditors. We presented 139 auditors employed by one of the largest U.S. accounting firms with five ambiguous auditing vignettes and asked them to judge the accounting decisions made in each one. Half of the participants played the role of an auditor hired by the company whose financial statements were described in the vignettes; the other half played the role of an auditor hired by a different company, one that was conducting business with the company whose financial statements were described. In addition, half the participants in each of these two groups generated their own auditing numbers before examining the firm's financial statements, then stated whether they believed the statements complied with generally accepted accounting principles (GAAP). The other half of each of the two groups performed these two tasks in the reverse order, examining the statements first and then generating their own numbers.

Across the five vignettes, auditors were on average 30 percent more likely to find that the accounting behind a company's financial reports complied with GAAP when they were playing the role of auditor for that firm than when they were disinterested third parties. In addition, the auditors who generated their own numbers *after* assessing the company's financial statements tended to come up with numbers that were closer to the client's numbers than did the participants who generated their own numbers before looking at the financial statements. Thus, we concluded that experienced auditors are not immune from bias and that they are more likely to accede to a client's biased accounting numbers than to generate such numbers themselves. This study did not involve a real audit, but one could argue that the lack of real incentives created by a real client should minimize rather than exaggerate the bias. The evidence suggests that even the possibility of a hypothetical relationship between an auditor and a client distorts the auditor's judgments. One can only imagine the degree of distortion that must exist in a long-standing relationship involving millions of dollars in ongoing revenues.

Many believe that the solution to conflict of interest problems is disclosure. However, we sign disclosure forms all of the time, with little impact on our judgment. In most states, real estate agents for the buyer and the seller are required to have their customer sign a disclosure statement clarifying that the real estate agent earns a percentage of any sales transaction. Most people sign such agreements, and never again think about the conflict of interest that exists between themselves and their agent. They really believe that their real estate agent is giving them objective data and advice.

Cain, Loewenstein, and Moore (2005) suggest that disclosure could actually increase auditor bias. Auditors who expect that disclosure will lead investors to discount or otherwise make adjustments for auditors' public statements may feel less duty bound to be impartial. In their study, Cain et al. paired participants and assigned one member of each pair to the role of estimator and the other to the role of adviser. The estimator viewed several jars of coins from a distance, estimated the value of the money in each, received advice on her estimate from an adviser who was allowed to study the jars close up, and was paid according to how close her estimates were to the jars' true values. The adviser was paid not according to the estimator's accuracy, but according to how high the estimator's guesses were; in other words, advisers had an incentive to mislead the estimators into guessing high. In addition, Cain et al. (2005) told half of the estimators about the advisers' pay arrangement; but said nothing about it to the rest of the estimators. The researchers found that advisers whose motives were disclosed provided much more biased guesses (i.e., high estimates of coin jar values) than did advisers whose motives were not disclosed. In addition, disclosure did not cause estimators to substantially discount their advisers' advice. Thus, disclosure led advisers to make much more money and estimators to make much less. This raises the real possibility that auditors who are forced to disclose conflicts of interest might exhibit greater self-serving bias than those who do not make such disclosures.

How did the corporate scandals reviewed in Chapter 1 occur? Why did Arthur Andersen accept Enron's blatantly flawed accounting? Auditors have long claimed that they can make independent and unbiased judgments about the books of firms that they want to maintain as clients, sell consulting services to, or later seek jobs from. It is quite possible that most auditors are honest enough to avoid the incentives that could lead to intentionally corrupt audits. But as long as auditors are dependent on their clients for future contracts, it is not possible for them to be completely unbiased. Contrary to the focus of the press and the Bush Administration on finding and punishing the few bad apples damaging the U.S. financial system, the research evidence makes it clear that deeply ingrained institutional conflicts of interests that reward auditors for pleasing their clients were largely responsible for the crisis.

Soon after the auditor scandals broke, the lack of analyst independence in investment banks became a focus of media attention and another vivid example of conflict of interest in the business world. Former acting SEC Chairperson Laura Unger cited a 2000 survey documenting that, at the same time that the NASDAQ was dropping 60 percent, 99.1 percent of brokerage-house analysts' recommendations were still "Strong Buy," "Buy," or "Hold." Brokerage firms often tied analyst compensation to the amount of brokerage business done by firms being analyzed, obviously providing analysts an incentive to maintain positive relationships with these companies.

What can be done about conflicts of interest? First, we can try to eliminate them by avoiding advice from biased sources. Second, recognize that honesty does not solve the problem of conflicts of interest—even honest people are biased. Finally, do not make the mistake of viewing yourself or your adviser as immune from the pernicious effects of conflicts of interest.

CONCLUSION

Throughout the corporate scandals that have scarred corporate America in recent years, the U.S. government has consistently tried to blame a few "bad apples" for the crisis. Yet when we examine each scandal, it becomes clear that it would not have been possible for just a few people to create the problems if others around them behaved ethically. From the classic experiments of Milgram (1963) on obedience to authority, to Latane and Darley's (1969) repeated demonstrations of bystanders' inaction to cries of help, to the contemporary research on implicit social cognition reviewed in this chapter, social psychologists have shown again and again that humans make systemic errors, inconsistent with their own desired ethics, that can profoundly harm others.

Much of this book considers the systematic and predictable errors that we make against the criterion of rationality. In this chapter, I have focused on the ethical errors we make against the criterion of our intended ethicality. I have documented perceptual and cognitive errors that lead our ethicality to be bounded in ways that contradict our typical assumption of unbounded ethicality. Most people hold a stable view of themselves as moral, competent, deserving, and thus immune from ethical challenges (Banaji, Bazerman, and Chugh, 2003). This very high self-esteem keeps us from monitoring our own behavior and makes bounded ethicality all the more likely.

Observing that people often fail to notice the ethical components of decisions, Tenbrunsel and Messick (2004) suggest that bounded ethicality is based on the innate tendency for individuals to engage in self-deception. They argue that we engage in "ethical cleansing" to transform, often unconsciously, ethical decisions into ones that lack ethical implications. This self-deception has important implications for ethical training. Educating people about ethics will be useful only if individuals can be taught to overcome the ethical cleansing process that allows them to ignore their biases and to learn to identify the true ethical implications of their actions. "Typical instruction includes an overview of ethical theory, discussion of ethical principles, and applications of such principles using the case-based method," write Tenbrunsel and Messick (2004). "Such instruction assumes that by highlighting and emphasizing the moral components of decisions, executives will be more likely to choose the moral path."

But at least some knowledgeable observers argue that ethics training has shown a limited ability to improve behavior (Badaracco and Webb, 1995). Like Tenbrunsel and Messick (2004), I believe that most ethical training focuses too narrowly on explicitly unethical behavior. The concepts of bounded ethicality and ethical cleansing confront unethical behavior that escapes the actor's conscious awareness.

Most managers are not ethically challenged at an explicit level, and they may question why they should waste their time listening to explicit messages. Meanwhile, those who are most ethically challenged at an explicit level may be the least open to the important messages of ethics training. The concepts presented in this chapter highlight ethical concerns that are likely to have escaped the attention of honest and dishonest managers alike.

Almost a decade ago, David Messick and I (1996) argued against the perspective that questions of executive ethics can be boiled down to explicit tradeoffs between ethics and profits. Rather, we asserted that a focus on psychological tendencies will lead to improved ethical decision making. I now believe that it is the unconscious aspects of these psychological tendencies that offers the best hope for improving individual and organizational ethics.

CHAPTER NINE

Making Rational Decisions in Negotiations

When two or more parties need to reach a joint decision but have different preferences, they negotiate. They may not be sitting around a bargaining table; they may not be making explicit offers and counteroffers; they may even be making statements suggesting that they are on the same side. But as long as their preferences concerning the joint decision are not identical, they have to negotiate to reach a mutually agreeable outcome.

Many of our managerial decisions are made in conjunction with other actors who have preferences different from our own. In this respect, negotiation is central to organizational life. Yet, just as our individual decisions are subject to irrationalities, so, too, are negotiated decisions. Negotiation outcomes are affected not only by your decisions, but by the decisions of other parties. Making more rational decisions increases the likelihood of reaching an agreement when it is wise to do so, and increases the quality of negotiated outcomes.

People often believe that the outcomes they reach in a negotiation were inevitable. In fact, in most negotiations, a wide variety of outcomes are possible. When teaching negotiations to MBA students and executives, I typically use simulations in which half of the participants play one role and the other half play another role. All dyads negotiate the same problem and have access to the same data. When the participants reach an agreement or an impasse, they record their results on the chalkboard. The amazing result is that even within fairly homogenous groups, the range of outcomes obtained is enormous. The lesson? The decisions of each negotiator matter!

While the first eight chapters of this book have focused on biases and irrationalities affecting individual decision making, this chapter and the next one examine judgment in multiparty contexts. This chapter outlines a framework for thinking rationally in two-party negotiation contexts. Chapter 10 uses this framework to examine how our individual biases and heuristics are manifested in the negotiation context. It also provides information on cognitive biases created by the competitive environment. Essentially, this chapter provides a structure for System 2 thinking in negotiated environments, while the next chapter highlights some of the biases that occur due to System 1 thinking.

The goals of this chapter are to give you a framework for thinking about two-party negotiations and to introduce prescriptive suggestions for improving decision making within this context. This chapter seeks to improve the quality of your outcomes as the "focal" negotiator. In addition, the chapter will recommend ways to improve the total outcomes for all parties and, hence, increase societal gains. These goals are achieved by learning how to reduce the likelihood of impasse when it is in the interest of all parties to reach a settlement, and by expanding the total range of benefits that both parties can receive.

Economists were the first to provide prescriptive advice to negotiators. The most well-developed component of this economic school of thought is game theory. In game theory, mathematical models are developed to analyze the outcomes that will emerge in multiparty decision-making contexts if all parties act rationally. To analyze a game, specific conditions are outlined that define how decisions are to be made—for example, the order in which players get to choose their moves—and utility measures of outcomes for each player are attached to every possible combination of player moves. The actual analysis focuses on predicting whether or not an agreement will be reached, and if one is reached, what the specific nature of that agreement will be. The advantage of game theory is that, given absolute rationality, it provides the most precise prescriptive advice available to the negotiator. The disadvantages of game theory are twofold. First, it relies on the ability to completely describe all options and associated outcomes for every possible combination of moves in a given situation—a tedious task at its best, infinitely complex at its worst. Second, it requires that all players consistently act in a rational manner. Yet, as we have seen in earlier chapters, individuals often behave irrationally in systematically predictable ways that are not easily captured within rational analyses.

A DECISION-ANALYTIC APPROACH TO NEGOTIATIONS

As an alternative to game-theoretical analyses of negotiations that take place in a world of "impeccably rational, supersmart people," Raiffa (1982; 2001) has developed a decision-analytic approach to negotiations. Such an approach focuses on how "erring folks like you and me actually behave" rather than "how we should behave if we were smarter, thought harder, were more consistent, were all knowing" (1982, p. 21). Raiffa's decision-analytic approach seeks to give the best available advice to negotiators involved in real conflict with real people. His goal is to provide guidance for you as the focal negotiator, given the most likely profile of the other party's expected behavior. Thus, Raiffa's approach is prescriptive from the point of view of the party receiving advice but descriptive from the point of view of the competing party.

Raiffa offers an excellent framework for approaching negotiations. The analytical structure of this approach is based on assessments of three key sets of information:

- Each party's alternative to a negotiated agreement
- Each party's set of interests
- The relative importance of each party's interests

Together, these three sets of information determine the structure of the negotiation game (Lax and Sebenius, 1986). Negotiation analysis considers how a rational negotiator should think about the structure of the negotiation and the other negotiator (Raiffa, 2001), and the common errors that negotiators and their opponents make (Bazerman and Neale, 1992; Thompson, 2001; Bazerman, Curhan, and Moore, 2000; Bazerman, Curhan, Moore, and Valley, 2000).

Alternatives to a Negotiated Agreement

Before we begin any important negotiation, we should consider what we will do if we fail to reach an agreement. That is, we must determine our *Best Alternative To a Negotiated Agreement,* or BATNA (Fisher and Ury, 1981). Why is this important? Because the value of a negotiator's BATNA provides a lower bound for determining the minimum outcome we require of a negotiated agreement. We should prefer any negotiated agreement that provides more value to us than our BATNA over impasse; likewise, we should decline any negotiated agreement that provides less than our BATNA. This assessment logically determines the negotiator's *reservation point* (also called an indifference point)—the point at which the negotiator is indifferent between a negotiated agreement and impasse.

Imagine that you believe the other side has made their final offer, and all you have to do is accept or reject it. How do you decide? The BATNA concept makes this a fairly clear decision. If the offer is better than your BATNA, accept. If not, reject it. Yet many people say "no" to final offers that are better than their BATNA, and say "yes" to offers that are worse than their BATNA. Why? When you have failed to carefully consider your BATNA, it is easy for emotions to hold sway.

Alternatives to agreement take a variety of forms. For example, rather than buy a specific new car, you may decide to continue to use mass transit. Alternatively, your BATNA may be to buy the same car from another dealership at a price that you have been offered in writing. Notice that in the second situation, it is far easier to determine your reservation price. However, whether you have an easy-to-assess reservation price, or whether you seem to be comparing apples and oranges, you should always determine your BATNA and your best estimate of the value of your opponent's BATNA. While this analysis may be difficult, it will provide a better basis for negotiation than your intuitive, unprepared assessments. Often the critical issue will be whether or not to walk out on the negotiation.

The Interests of the Parties

To analyze a negotiation, it is necessary to identify all of the parties' interests—and yet, the fact is that negotiators are not always fully aware of the other side's interests. How can this be? There is a difference between the parties' stated positions and their underlying interests. Positions are the claimed requirements that parties demand from the other side. Interests are ancillary or underlying issues behind these positions that could matter to the negotiators if they were made aware of them. As the following sections highlight, sometimes a focus on deeper interests can identify a more useful set of concerns to the parties and form the basis of a more reasonable bargaining platform.

Recently, the chief purchasing officer for one of my consulting clients (a *Fortune* 100 organization) participated in negotiating contract terms for the firm's purchase of a new health-care product ingredient from a European company. Both sides agreed to a price of $18 per pound for a million pounds of product per year. However, conflict arose over exclusivity; the European firm would not agree to sell the ingredient exclusively to my client. My client could not afford to invest in producing a new product based on this ingredient if competitors had access to the same ingredient. When the chief purchasing officer arrived in Europe, the argument over exclusivity continued. Finally, he asked the producer why they would not provide exclusivity to a major corporation that was offering to buy as much of the ingredient as he could produce. The producer explained that exclusivity would require him to violate an agreement with his cousin, who currently purchased 250 pounds per year to make a locally sold product. Once this piece of information emerged, the purchasing officer was able to quickly wrap up an agreement that provided exclusivity, with the exception of a couple hundred pounds annually for the producer's cousin—and the celebration began. The key to this agreement was the chief purchasing officer's decision to ask about the producer's interest (selling a small amount of the ingredient to his cousin), rather than staying focused on the producer's stated goal (not providing exclusivity). Interestingly, the chief purchasing officer is viewed within his corporation as a negotiation genius, and part of his reputation is based on his ability to resolve this dispute. Yet, as he puts it, "All I did was ask them why they didn't want to provide exclusivity."

The Relative Importance of Each Party's Interests

Even when we are aware of our interests, we may not have thought through the relative importance of each issue. To be fully prepared to negotiate, we must become aware of how important each issue is to us. The best agreements are reached by trading off relatively unimportant issues for more important ones. For example, when negotiating a new job offer, you may realize that health benefits are more important to you than an extra three days of personal time, or you may be more interested in postponing your start date in exchange for fewer vacation days during your first year. Whatever your preferences, you must prepare yourself ahead of time to recognize which tradeoffs are more and less attractive to you.

Summary

Together, these three groups of information (each party's alternative to a negotiated agreement, each party's set of interests, and the relative importance of each party's interests) provide the building blocks for thinking analytically about a negotiation. A negotiator should assess all components of this information before entering any important bargaining situation. With this information in hand, the negotiator will be prepared for the two primary tasks of negotiation: creating and claiming value (Lax and Sebenius, 1986). As we develop each of these two themes, it is important to remember that creating and claiming value are processes that occur simultaneously in a negotiation. Many of us are good at one but not the other. My goal is to make you comfortable with both aspects of the negotiation challenge.

CLAIMING VALUE IN NEGOTIATION

Consider the following example:

An MBA from a very prestigious school who has a number of unique talents is being recruited for a highly specialized position. The organization and the employee have agreed on all issues except salary. The organization has offered $90,000, and the employee has counteroffered $100,000. Both sides believe they have made fair offers, but they both would very much like to reach an agreement. The student, while not verbalizing this information, would be willing to take any offer over $93,000 rather than lose the offer. The organization, while not verbalizing this information, would be willing to pay up to $97,000 rather than lose the candidate.

A simplified view of the bargaining zone concept describes the recruitment problem:

Bargaining Zone

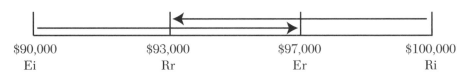

$90,000	$93,000	$97,000	$100,000
Ei	Rr	Er	Ri

Ei = Employer's initial offer

Rr = Recruit's minimum reservation point

Er = Employer's maximum reservation point

Ri = Recruit's initial offer

The bargaining zone framework assumes that each party has some reservation point below (or above) which the negotiator would prefer impasse to settlement. Reservation points are set at the negotiator's BATNA. Notice that the two reservation points overlap. Thus, there is a set of resolutions that both parties would prefer over impasse—in this case, all points between $93,000 and $97,000. This area is known as a positive bargaining zone. When a *positive bargaining zone* exists, a rational model of negotiation would dictate that the negotiators should reach a settlement—it is the rational thing to do. When the reservation points of the two parties do not overlap, a negative bargaining zone exists. In such cases, no resolution should occur because there is no settlement that would be acceptable to both parties.

Many people find the notion of a bargaining zone to be counterintuitive. Having participated in a variety of negotiations throughout their lives, they have reached the conclusion that the reservation points of parties never overlap; they simply meet at the point of agreement. This reasoning is incorrect. In fact, at the point of agreement, when both parties choose a settlement rather than impasse, their actual reservation points are overlapping. This settlement point represents only one of what are often many points within the bargaining zone.

Returning to our recruiting example, we can see that the bargaining zone consists of the range between $93,000 and $97,000. If the employer could convince the recruit that an offer of $93,100 was final, we know the recruit would accept the offer, and the firm would minimize its settlement costs. Similarly, if the recruit could convince the employer that $96,900 was the lowest salary she would accept, we know the employer would accept this figure, and the recruit would maximize her settlement benefit. Thus, one of the key skills of negotiation is to determine the other party's reservation point and to aim for a resolution that is barely acceptable to the other party. This is a delicate process. If one or more of the parties were to misjudge the situation, they might rigidly demand a bargain that is beyond the other party's reservation point, leading to impasse. (Such would be the case if, for example, the recruit holds to a demand of $98,000 and the employer holds to the offer of $92,000—both believing that the other side will "cave in.") When this behavior occurs, the parties act in ways that prohibit the rational choice of a solution within the positive bargaining zone. As Ben Franklin (quoted by Raiffa, 1982) observed:

> Trades would not take place unless it were advantageous to the parties concerned. Of course, it is better to strike as good a bargain as one's bargaining position permits. The worst outcome is when, by overreaching greed, no bargain is struck, and a trade that could have been advantageous to both parties does not come off at all.

CREATING VALUE IN NEGOTIATION

The foregoing analysis dealt with negotiation in a situation in which a single issue (salary) was under dispute. Negotiations are often more complex, involving several or more disputed issues. Consider the Camp David talks in 1978 (documented in Pruitt and Rubin, 1985).

> Egypt and Israel tried to negotiate the control of the Sinai Peninsula, a situation in which it appeared that the two sides had directly opposing goals. Egypt wanted the return of the Sinai in its entirety, while Israel, which had occupied the territory since the 1967 war, refused to return this land. Efforts at compromise failed. Neither side found the proposal of splitting the Sinai acceptable.

An initial examination of this conflict suggests that a negative bargaining zone existed and that a negotiated resolution would not be possible. That is, if we mapped the positions of the parties onto a single scale, the reservation points would not overlap, and impasse would be inevitable.

Who Gets the Sinai?

| 100% to Israel | Ir(?) | Er(?) | 100% to Egypt |

Ir(?) = estimation of Israel's reservation point

Er(?) = estimation of Egypt's reservation point

In contrast to this pessimistic and false prediction, the existence of multiple issues and the development of a creative trade explains the resolution that eventually developed at Camp David.

As the Camp David negotiations continued, it became clear that while the positions of Egypt and Israel were incompatible, the interests of the two countries were compatible. Israel's underlying interest was security from land or air attack. Egypt was primarily interested in sovereignty over land that was part of Egypt for thousands of years. What emerged was the existence of two real issues, instead of one, with differential importance to the two parties: sovereignty and military protection. The solution that emerged traded off these issues. The agreement called for Israel to return the Sinai in exchange for assurances of a demilitarized zone and new Israeli air bases.

To analyze this agreement, examine the more complex diagram presented in Figure 9.1. The utility of an agreement to Israel is represented on the horizontal axis, and the utility of an agreement to Egypt is represented on the vertical axis. Point A represents the solution of giving the land and total control of it to Egypt. Notice that this solution would be completely acceptable to Egypt and completely unacceptable to Israel. Point B represents the solution of Israel keeping the land and maintaining total control over it. This solution would be completely acceptable to Israel and completely unacceptable to Egypt. Point C represents a straight compromise—giving each party control over half of the land. As illustrated in the bargaining zone diagram, this solution fails to meet the reservation points of either Israel or Egypt. It does not give Egypt sovereignty over the Sinai, and it does not give Israel sufficient security guarantees. Point D (the eventual resolution), however, suggests a redefinition of the bargaining zone. In Figure 9.1, a positive bargaining zone exists to the extent that there are solutions that achieve the reservation points of both parties along the dimensions of sovereignty and security. The upper right-hand segment of the figure beyond the dotted lines represents the reservation points of the two parties.

FIGURE 9.1 Integrating Interests in the Israel–Egypt Dispute

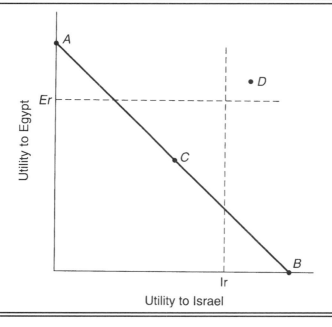

What appears to have occurred in the Camp David accords is that the two parties realized the existence of a positive bargaining zone by considering each other's interests, not just their stated positions. With these interests in hand, it was possible to develop an agreement by trading off the issue that each country cared less about for the issue that each country cared more about.

AN EXTENDED EXAMPLE: THE CASE OF EL-TEK

Virtually all negotiations involve the distribution of outcomes. However, negotiators often overlook the opportunity to create value. In this section, we develop an example that involves both the creation and claiming of value (adapted from Bazerman and Brett's "El-Tek" simulation [1991]).

El-Tek is a large conglomerate in the electrical industry with sales of over $3.1 billion. El-Tek is a decentralized, product-centered organization, in which the various divisions are expected to operate autonomously and are evaluated based on their divisional performance. To preclude competition for sales to external customers, divisions are chartered to sell their products to specific customer groups outside the company.

Recently, the Audio Division (AD) developed a new magnetic material called Z-25. While its corporate charter prevents the division from selling the discovery outside the company, the product is still valuable to AD. It can sell Z-25 within the corporation and also use this magnet to competitively increase the quality of its own audio products. AD has assessed that under this scenario it would earn $5 million from Z-25 over an estimated two years: $1.75 million from selling magnets internally to El-Tek and $3.25 million from product improvements to their audio components that would not be available to their competitors.

While this $5 million is attractive to AD and El-Tek, the Magnetic Division (MD) could generate far more income for El-Tek if it sold Z-25. MD has much better manufacturing capabilities and could sell the magnet to a vast outside market. In fact, MD projects that it could earn $14 million over the same two-year period from this magnetic material. Without Z-25, MD would be using its manufacturing and sales capabilities on an alternative product that is expected to yield a profit of only $4 million.

The parties have agreed to get together to discuss the possibility of AD selling the magnet rights to MD. Both parties already have target prices and reservation points in mind. With this information, the El-Tek situation can be analyzed using the bargaining zone concept diagrammed here:

MD's Payment to AD for Magnet Rights

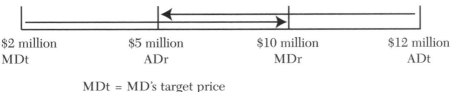

$2 million	$5 million	$10 million	$12 million
MDt	ADr	MDr	ADt

MDt = MD's target price

ADr = AD's reservation point

$$MDr = MD's \text{ reservation point}$$
$$ADt = AD's \text{ target price}$$

Claiming Value

Most people enter into negotiations with some notion of their target outcomes. However, most negotiators fail to think hard enough about their reservation prices and the reservation prices of other negotiators, which are determined by evaluating both parties' BATNAs. In this example, AD can make $5 million without reaching an agreement with MD. MD can make $4 million without Z-25 and thus is indifferent between this option and paying AD $10 million (of the $14 million) for the rights to the magnet. Note that the two reservation points overlap (at all points between $5 million and $10 million), creating a positive bargaining zone. Note further that any agreement within the bargaining zone will lead to a joint surplus of $5 million. (Without the trade taking place, AD can earn $5 million and MD can earn $4 million, for a total of $9 million. By completing a trade, they have a total of $14 million to divide.) Thus, there is a range of agreements that can be very profitable for both sides.

Creating Value by Identifying Additional Issues

So far, our analysis has been limited to just one issue of the negotiation, namely, the distribution of money. By definition, one-issue negotiations claim but do not create value. Through the process of identifying and adding additional issues, the parties will have the potential to create value, thereby increasing the amount of total benefit available.

Remember that one of AD's benefits of not selling the magnet to MD is that it can obtain a competitive advantage from the product improvement. Before entering into negotiations, it might be useful for AD to assess the value of adding restrictions to outside sales of the magnet by MD. For example, AD could create an information table in the form of Table 9.1, which evaluates the expected value to AD of various agreements. The first two outcomes highlight the possible one-issue results. Outcome 1 shows the $5 million profit obtained if AD were to keep the product. Outcome 2 shows that if AD simply transfers the product to MD, AD's profit will be equal to the negotiated transfer price *P*. The remaining outcomes incorporate the sales restriction issue on two levels. These include restricting sales to AD's direct competitors and restricting sales to all El-Tek competitors in general. Each outcome is evaluated in monetary terms that include the expected net profit of the specified restrictions, in addition to the negotiated transfer price *P*. For example, outcome 3 includes the prohibition of sales to AD's competitors for only six months and is expected to yield AD $2 million plus the transfer price. Compare this to outcome 6, wherein sales are restricted to AD's direct competitors for twelve months and all El-Tek competitors for six months. This option is estimated to be worth $2.6 million plus the transfer price. In reviewing each of the outcomes, note that AD is more concerned with prohibiting sales to AD's competitors than to El-Tek competitors. (Compare outcomes 5 and 6, wherein the marginal value of adding a six-month restriction to all El-Tek competitors yields only an additional $100,000.) Note also that the value of this protection has diminishing returns due to obtaining product leadership in a relatively short period of time. (Compare outcomes 3 and 5, wherein the first six months of protection from AD's direct competitors are worth $2 million, but the next six months add only $500,000 in value.)

TABLE 9.1 Audio Division Negotiating Team

Outcome	Lifetime Expected Net Profit to AD
1. AD produces Z-25 and the product is sold only internally.	$5,000,000
2. MD produces and no limitations are put on their distribution efforts.	P
3. MD produces and is prohibited from selling to AD competitors for six months.	$2,000,000 + P
4. MD produces and is prohibited from selling to any El-Tek competitor for six months.	$2,100,000 + P
5. MD produces and is prohibited from selling to AD competitors for twelve months.	$2,500,000 + P
6. MD produces and is prohibited from selling to AD competitors for twelve months, and from selling to other El-Tek competitors for six months.	$2,600,000 + P
7. MD produces and is prohibited from selling to any El-Tek competitor for twelve months.	$2,700,000 + P
8. MD produces and is prohibited from selling to AD competitors for twenty months.	$2,900,000 + P
9. MD produces and is prohibited from selling to AD competitors for twenty months and from selling to other El-Tek competitors for six months.	$3,000,000 + P
10. MD produces and is prohibited from selling to AD competitors for twenty months and from selling to other El-Tek competitors for twelve months.	$3,100,000 + P
11. MD produces and is prohibited from selling to any El-Tek competitors for twenty months.	$3,200,000 + P

Conversely, MD can also assess the costs of having its sales restricted in the same manner. These estimates are shown in Table 9.2; please take a moment to review it. Finally, Table 9.3 combines the assessments of AD and MD from Tables 9.1 and 9.2. This combination allows us to look at how three underlying issues—transfer price, AD's competitor protection, and El-Tek competitor protection—collectively affect the joint surplus available to the parties.

Let's look at this table in detail. First, note that all of the outcomes that prevent MD from selling to any of El-Tek's competitors (outcomes 4, 6, 7, 9, 10, and 11) decrease the joint gain available from this product compared to similar outcomes that prevent MD from selling only to AD's competitors (outcomes 3, 5, and 8). Thus, the two parties are collectively better off not creating restrictions regarding other El-Tek competitors. Furthermore, the highest joint benefit is achieved when the magnet is transferred and MD is restricted from selling to AD's competitors for six months. While this reduces MD's profits (before paying AD) from $14 million to $13.1 million compared to outcome 2, AD's profit increases by $2 million—resulting in an additional $1.1 million of profit to divide. This profit is created by the fact that AD gains more

TABLE 9.2 Magnetic Division Negotiating Team

Outcome	Lifetime Expected Net Profit to AD
1. AD produces Z-25 and the product is sold only internally.	$4,000,000
2. MD produces and no limitations are put on their distribution efforts.	$14,000,000 – P
3. MD produces and is prohibited from selling to AD competitors for six months.	$13,100,000 – P
4. MD produces and is prohibited from selling to any El-Tek competitor for six months.	$10,400,000 – P
5. MD produces and is prohibited from selling to AD competitors for twelve months.	$12,200,000 – P
6. MD produces and is prohibited from selling to AD competitors for twelve months, and from selling to other El-Tek competitors for six months.	$9,500,000 – P
7. MD produces and is prohibited from selling to any El-Tek competitor for twelve months.	$6,800,000 – P
8. MD produces and is prohibited from selling to AD competitors for twenty months.	$11,000,000 – P
9. MD produces and is prohibited from selling to AD competitors for twenty months and from selling to other El-Tek competitors for six months.	$8,300,000 – P
10. MD produces and is prohibited from selling to AD competitors for twenty months and from selling to other El-Tek competitors for twelve months.	$5,600,000 – P
11. MD produces and is prohibited from selling to any El-Tek competitors for twenty months.	$2,000,000 – P

from the six-month restriction than MD loses. However, additional protection beyond six months decreases the joint profit, since additional protection (for example, outcome 5) costs MD more than it benefits AD.

Opportunities to create and claim value in the El-Tek negotiation are shown in Figure 9.2, which plots AD's profit on the vertical axis and MD's profit on the horizontal axis. Lines A and B are the reservation prices that we discussed earlier. Point X is the no-agreement alternative in which AD keeps the magnet. Forty-five-degree lines can be drawn for the various outcomes (2 through 11) that show the possible agreements on the outcomes after *P* is negotiated. For example, the points on the outcome 2 line (C) yield profit of $14 million, while all the points on the outcome 3 line (D) yield profit of $15.1 million. (Of course, more lines can be drawn for all the possible settlements.)

Clearly, it is in the best interest of both negotiators to reach an agreement on the most northeasterly line. As mentioned earlier, one of the key skills of negotiation is to determine the other party's reservation point and aim for a resolution that is marginally acceptable to the other party based on that value. Thus, AD prefers being as close

TABLE 9.3 Joint Profit Resolution (in millions)

Outcome	AD	MD	AD + MD
1. AD produces and sells only internally.	5.0	4.0	9.0
2. MD produces; AD limit equals zero months and other limit equals zero months.	P	14.0 – P	14.0
3. MD produces; AD limit equals six months months and other limit equals zero months.	2.0 + P	13.1 – P	15.1
4. MD produces; AD limit equals six months and other limit equals six months.	2.1 + P	10.4 – P	12.5
5. MD produces; AD limit equals twelve months and other limit equals zero months.	2.5 + P	12.2 – P	14.7
6. MD produces; AD limit equals twelve months and other limit equals six months.	2.6 + P	9.5 – P	12.1
7. MD produces; AD limit equals twelve months and other limit equals twelve months.	2.7 + P	6.8 – P	9.5
8. MD produces; AD limit equals twenty months and other limit equals zero months.	2.9 + P	11.0 – P	13.9
9. MD produces; AD limit equals twenty months and other limit equals six months.	3.0 + P	8.3 – P	11.3
10. MD produces; AD limit equals twenty months and other limit equals twelve months.	3.1 + P	5.6 – P	8.7
11. MD produces; AD limit equals twenty months and other limit equals twenty months.	3.2 + P	2.0 – P	5.2

to MD's reservation price as possible, and MD prefers being as close to AD's reservation price as possible. The task facing the negotiators is to attempt to both create and claim value. Negotiators often make the mistake of focusing on just one dimension, rather than thinking about them simultaneously.

When my students simulate the El-Tek negotiation, a common question from someone who did very well in claiming, but not creating, value (for example, someone playing the role of AD, who received a payment of $9.5 million out of the $14 million on an outcome 2 agreement) is: "Why shouldn't I be happy with this agreement?" In fact, this agreement is typically one of the better outcomes for someone playing the role of AD. The answer is that although this is a fine agreement for AD, if MD settled for this agreement, MD could also have accepted an agreement that called for six months' protection and a payment of $8.3 million. This would have given MD $4.8 million (rather than $4.5 million) and would have given AD $10.3 million (rather than $9.5 million), making both parties much better off!

An agreement is defined as "Pareto efficient" when there is no other agreement that would render both parties better off or one party better off while keeping the second party at the same level. Anytime you have a Pareto-inefficient agreement, there exists an alternative agreement to which the parties can move that would create

FIGURE 9.2 The El-Tek Negotiation

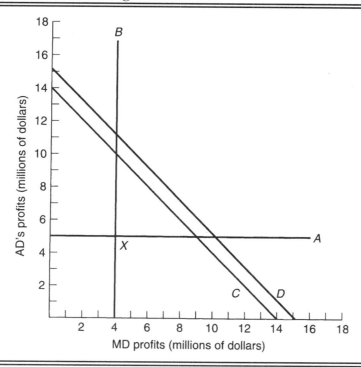

greater joint benefit. In the El-Tek case, the set of outcome 3 agreements between the two parties' reservation prices represents the Pareto-efficient frontier.

When negotiators run into differences with other parties, the common response is to see this as a problem. In fact, differences are opportunities. Effective negotiators understand that the easiest way to create value is to trade issues of differential value. By identifying what you care about and figuring out what the other side cares about, you will be equipped to create value based on these the differences.

While trading issues is the most common way to create value in a negotiation, Sebenius (2000; Lax and Sebenius, 1986) has documented a number of ways in which other differences create opportunity. Perhaps the second most important opportunity is created through the development of bets, or contingent contracts.

Creating Value through Bets

When clients seek advice from me regarding stalled negotiations, it often turns out that a surprisingly large percent of them are arguing needlessly with the other side over their conflicting predictions about uncertain future outcomes. The fact is, our society has developed a very effective technique for dealing with differing predictions: bets.

In the El-Tek simulation, MD had a set of assessments concerning the profitability of various outcomes ($14 million with no restrictions, $13.1 million with a six-month restriction on sales to AD's competitors, and so on). Assume that AD also assessed the profits that MD would receive from the product: $40 million with a six-month sales restriction and $40.9 million with no restrictions. On the surface, this difference in perceptions could create a barrier to agreement. AD might expect a payment of around $20 million—an amount MD would never pay. If trust were lacking, there might be little that MD could do to convince AD of the accuracy of its forecast, and impasse would seem inevitable.

Now consider the following proposal: MD is restricted from selling the magnet to AD's competitors for six months, MD receives the first $9 million of the magnet's profit, and AD receives 80 percent of the profits in excess of $9 million. This agreement allows the parties to bet on their predictions of future events. If MD's forecast turns out to be correct, this agreement would be much better for MD than a 50:50 split of the joint profit. If AD's forecast turns out to be correct, this agreement would be better for AD than a 50:50 split of the joint profit. While at least one of them has made an inaccurate prediction, this "contingent contract" allows for a trade in which both parties believe that they will do very well.

You will recall from the discussion of the endowment effect in Chapter 3 that people commonly overvalue what they own. It is important for sellers to recognize their susceptibility to this effect and adjust their expectations. If such adjustments fail to resolve the dispute, parties may be able to use their difference of opinion to craft a contingent contract that allows each side to bet on its opinion. Consider the case of a television production company negotiating the sale of syndication rights to one of its shows, a major sitcom that had just finished its prime-time run, with a major independent television station in one of the three leading television markets in the United States (Bazerman and Gillespie, 1999, based on a case by Tenbrunsel and Bazerman, 1995). The parties differed in their predictions of the ratings the sitcom would obtain in syndication: the seller argued that the show would receive at least a nine share rating (meaning 9 percent of all American households with televisions would tune into the show), while the buyer countered that they expected the show would obtain no more than a seven share. Both parties agreed that each rating point was worth about $1 million in advertising revenue to the television station. After many heated debates about future ratings, the parties reached an impasse. The show was not aired in this market, and the television station bought a less attractive program. This negotiation failure resulted from an honest difference of opinion about how well the show would perform. Bazerman and Gillespie argue that the parties should have made the price that the station would pay the production company contingent on the show's performance. That is, their disagreement about the expected quality of the show could have been resolved by an agreement where the payment price went up as the ratings went up.

Bazerman and Gillespie (1999) describe a number of ways in which contingent contracts can improve the outcomes of negotiations for both sides, four of which are outlined here.

- **Bets build on differences to create joint value.** Bets can be extremely useful in short-circuiting debates over the likelihood of future uncertain events. Once parties have agreed to disagree, they will be able to design a contingent contract based on their differing predictions.

- **Bets help manage biases.** In previous chapters, I have documented a number of common decision-making biases, including overconfidence, the endowment effect, and egocentric interpretations of fairness. As I will discuss further in Chapter 10, these biases form strong barriers to negotiated agreements. Interestingly, contingent contracts allow agreements to be formed despite these biases. Rather than requiring the parties to be debiased, contingent contracts allow parties to bet on their own (biased) beliefs.

- **Bets diagnose disingenuous parties.** Contingent contracts are a powerful tool for identifying bluffs and false claims by one's negotiation opponent. Returning to the El-Tek story, imagine that AD does not actually expect MD's profits to be as high as $40 million, but presents this number as its estimate in order to persuade MD to agree to higher compensation. In this case, when MD offers AD the majority of the profit above $9 million, and AD turns it down, MD will know that AD was bluffing. Interestingly, when you propose a bet, you do not need to know whether the prediction of other side is sincere. If it is, you have made a nice bet. If it isn't, their rejection of the bet reveals their bluff.

- **Bets establish incentives for contractual performance.** Contingent contracts are also an excellent technique for increasing the incentive of the parties to perform at or above contractually specified levels. Sales commissions are a prevalent example of a contingent contract designed to establish an incentive for high performance. In 1997, professional basketball player Dennis Rodman and the management of the Chicago Bulls were faced with the joint decision-making task of negotiating a contract for Rodman for the 1997–98 National Basketball Association (NBA) season. Given Rodman's increasingly erratic behavior on and off the court, which caused him to miss twenty-seven games during the 1996–97 season, Bulls' management was nervous about signing him on for another year. Rodman, meanwhile, felt confident that his performance in the upcoming season would meet or exceed that of each of his previous eleven seasons. Using a contingent contract to bridge their differences, Rodman and the Bulls hammered out the most incentive-laden deal in NBA history. Only $4.5 million of Rodman's $10.5 million annual contract was guaranteed; the remaining $6 million was dependent on fulfillment of various performance and behavior clauses. This contingent contract worked very well for both parties. Rodman played in eighty of the eighty-two games, won his seventh rebounding title, and collected $10.1 million of his potential $10.5 million salary. With Rodman's help, the Bulls went on to win another NBA championship, generating significant income for team owners.

Using Risk, Temporal, and Other Differences to Create Value

Disagreements about future outcomes are just one type of difference that can be used to improve the outcomes of both parties in a negotiation. In Chapter 3, we saw how individuals' differing tolerance for risk affects their decisions. Risk can play a critical role in negotiations as well. Consider the situation in which both parties in El-Tek agree on MD's forecast of future events. Specifically, they both expect MD to earn $13.1 million with a six-month restriction against sales to AD's competitors; however, they concede that the true outcome could be anywhere from $4.1 million to $22.1 million. In addition, AD is unwilling to accept any agreement that would risk ending up below the $5 million it could earn on its own. MD, on the other hand, is willing to take greater risks in the hope of generating high rewards. Thus, because AD is comparatively more risk averse than MD, AD might reject an offer to split the magnet's profits equally, since in the worst case scenario, profits would be below $5 million.

The parties' differential risk preferences create a new opportunity, specifically, the possibility of a tradeoff that guarantees AD more money and MD more of the upside potential. For example, under one possible agreement, AD might receive the six-months sales restriction, the first $4 million of magnet profits, and 15 percent of profits above $4 million. This deal grants AD its guarantee, while giving MD a higher expected return in exchange for its acceptance of high risk. Risk-sharing strategies such as this allow for trades that might not otherwise occur.

Differences in time preference are another source of tradeoffs in negotiations. These differences might arise from individual, cultural, or situational preferences among the parties. The fluctuation of corporate budget cycles is one common real-world difference in time preferences. When a client complains that their negotiating partner is fixated on meeting a certain budget cycle, I encourage them to view this as an opportunity—in all likelihood, the other side will be willing to make important concessions if you help them solve their budget problems! Future consequences can often be rearranged in a way that gives earlier return to the more impatient party in exchange for concessions favored by the more patient party.

Returning to the El-Tek negotiation, imagine that in the midst of a disastrous year, MD is seeking immediate profitability to keep its recent downturn from being made public. In addition, MD is concerned that most of the fixed costs of manufacturing the magnet will be incurred early to set up the manufacturing process. The two sides might work out an agreement whereby MD receives 75 percent of first-year profits and 20 percent of second-year profits, leaving 25 percent of first-year profits and 80 percent of second-year profits for AD. In this agreement, MD gets the immediate return that it desires, and AD gets a slightly higher return for waiting.

A multitude of differences between parties can enhance negotiation outcomes. Northcraft and Neale (1993) have pointed out that skill differences between parties collaborating on a project—such as a CEO and a COO, two researchers writing a book together, or partners in a strategic alliance—often contribute to the partnership's success. Effectively, complementary skills create the opportunity to make trades in work allocation, to the benefit of both parties. In their discussion of "dealcrafting," Lax and Sebenius (2002) cite a joint venture between auctioneer Butterfields and Internet auctioneer eBay as a successful partnership based on value creation. Butterfields' access to upscale commodities combined with eBay's new distribution mechanism to create value for both companies. Lax and Sebenius (2002) note a variety of other trades that can be enhanced by taking advantage of a wide range of differences, including differences in tax status, accounting treatments, and liquidity. By now, the overarching message of this section should be clear: To the well-informed negotiator, differences are not stumbling blocks, but opportunities.

Gathering Information to Create Value in Negotiation

So far, our discussion of value creation has assumed that both parties have full knowledge of information relevant to the negotiation. In fact, negotiators typically have access only to their own preferences. How can negotiators create value when they lack knowledge of the other side's positions and preferences? I will now review five strategies for collecting that information. While no single strategy is guaranteed to work in a specific situation, they collectively increase the likelihood of reaching a Pareto-efficient agreement.

Build Trust and Share Information

The easiest way for parties to create value in the El-Tek simulation is for the two opponents to share information with each other about their preferences—specifically, the values that they place on different issues. Once this information comes to light, determining the outcome that maximizes joint benefit becomes a simple arithmetic task. Unfortunately, information sharing is easier said than done. We often are reluctant to trust the other side in a negotiation because we believe that giving away information could prevent us from claiming value. Consider this dilemma from El-Tek's overall perspective. For the president of El-Tek, creating value guarantees that the divisions will not jeopardize corporate profitability by focusing on the claiming of value. Therefore, creating value should be the negotiation's primary objective. Even between organizations, firms often develop fully trusting relationships based on kinship, a close subculture, or years of working together. In these cases, the parties learn that the long-term joint benefit of creating value more than offsets the one-time gain that a party might achieve through claiming tactics.

One way to approach information sharing is to discuss a distribution rule in advance of sharing information. If AD fears that it will be at a competitive disadvantage if MD finds out that AD can earn only $5 million on its own, the parties could agree on how to divide any surplus before sharing confidential information. For example, they might agree that AD gets 60 percent and MD gets 40 percent of any surplus. With this understanding established, they can then safely share information to create value. When distrust exists regarding the information-sharing process, the parties could also agree to obtain financial assessments from an independent party.

Ask Questions

Full information sharing will not always be to your advantage. You may have some information that will work against you if the other party obtains it; similarly, the other party also may be unwilling to fully disclose confidential information. What can you do? Ask lots of questions! Most people have a tendency to see negotiating primarily as an opportunity to influence the other party. As a result, most of us do more talking than listening. Even when the other side is talking, we concentrate on what we are going to say next rather than listening for new information. This persuasion process is the basis of most sales training and assists the other party in collecting information from you. In negotiations, however, your goal must be to understand the other party's interests as well as possible.

Asking questions and listening actively are the keys to collecting important new information from the other side. AD might ask, "MD, how much would you lose if you didn't sell to our competitors? How much would a six-month restriction cost you? How much would a twelve-month restriction cost you?" Before you start the negotiation, assess what information you need from the other side; then ask the questions necessary to collect this information. Some of my students have pointed out that, in the real world, the other side won't always answer your questions. That's true. However, the probability that they will answer is higher if you ask than if you do not!

Strategically Disclose Information

Your negotiation does not have a trusting atmosphere, and the other party is not answering your questions in any useful way. What do you do next? Give away some information of your own. Do not tell the other side your BATNA—this will only anchor your final outcome. Rather, reveal information of comparatively minor importance that focuses on the trades you are willing to make. As AD, for instance, you might inform MD that restricting sales to your competitors is more important in the early months of sales than in later months. In disclosing this, you have not given away any information that MD can use unilaterally against you, and you may open up a dialogue.

One benefit of strategically disclosing information is that it can enable you and the other side to expand the pie of outcomes. An additional benefit is that behaviors in negotiation are often reciprocated. When you scream at people, they tend to scream back. When you apologize for a mistake or offense, they may do the same. And when you give them some information about your position, they may return some information of their own. This strategy can create the information sharing necessary to create mutually beneficial agreements.

Make Multiple Offers Simultaneously

Many negotiators try to put an offer on the table early to anchor the discussion. Unfortunately, this offer is often made before the negotiator has worked hard to create additional value. Because the effect of anchoring is so strong it may overshadow subsequent discoveries, you should avoid putting an offer on the table before actively collecting information. In some cases, even after actively pursuing information, you may find that you cannot extend a single offer that creates value for both sides. When this happens, consider the possibility of presenting several offers. Most of us put one offer on the table, and when it is turned down, we know little more than we did before we made the offer. If we had presented several alternatives, we might have learned more.

Imagine that as AD, you present MD with three offers: the transfer of the magnet for $9 million with no restrictions on sales to your competitors, for $7 million with a six-month restriction, or for $6.5 million with a twelve-month restriction. MD refuses all of these proposals. At this point, you ask which of these proposals is closest to being acceptable. MD evaluates the proposals according to Table 9.2 and sees that the proposals provide a net profit of $5 million, $6.1 million, and $5.7 million, respectively. MD answers that, of these unacceptable proposals, the second one is the least unreasonable. As AD, you now have more information to work with in forming a mutually beneficial agreement. Note that all three proposals by AD were equally valuable to AD, and AD did not give away anything that would not be given away by making only one offer. By making multiple offers, AD appears more flexible and collects valuable information. Making multiple offers that are worth the same amount allows you to identify new opportunities for tradeoffs.

Search for Post-Settlement Settlements

Raiffa (1985) suggests that after negotiators have found a mutually acceptable agreement, they should employ a third party to help them search for a Pareto-superior agreement—one that is potentially even better for both parties than the agreement reached. Under this scenario, each negotiator can reserve the right to veto any new settlement proposed by the third party and revert to the original agreement. With this insurance in hand, Raiffa contends that negotiators may be more willing to allow a third party to create a superior agreement. This new agreement is known as a post-settlement settlement (PSS).

Based on Raiffa's insight, negotiators should look for a PSS as a last step in creating value (Bazerman, Russ, and Yakura, 1987). This process does not necessarily require a third party. After an initial agreement is reached, there is often ample opportunity to improve areas of the contract that may not be completely optimal for either party. If you are not confident that you have achieved a Pareto-efficient outcome, it may be in your best interest to propose to the other side a PSS process whereby both parties agree to be bound by the initial agreement if no better agreement is found. If a better agreement is found, however, the two parties will share the surplus. Thus, if AD and MD reached an agreement to transfer the magnet for $7 million with no limits, they could use a PSS process to share information to locate an agreement that would be worth $550,000 more to both sides (outcome 3—$5.55 million and six-month AD protection). A PSS process offers a last attempt, with limited risk to either party, to ensure that a Pareto-efficient agreement has been found. This process can be initiated after an initial agreement by using any of the four previously defined information-building strategies. As Raiffa (1985, p. 9) writes:

> [W]e must recognize that a lot of disputes are settled by hard-nosed, positional bargaining. Settled, yes. But efficiently settled? Often not . . . they quibble about sharing the pie and often fail to realize that perhaps the pie can be jointly enlarged . . . there may be another carefully crafted settlement that both [parties] might prefer to the settlement they actually achieved.

Summary

These five strategies offer a variety of ideas for creating value. No one strategy will work in all situations. Collectively, however, they increase the potential joint benefit that parties will reach through negotiating. It is important to repeat that no strategy eliminates the need to eventually divide value; any advice is incomplete if it fails to deal explicitly with the claiming dimension. Armed with these strategies for creating and claiming value in negotiations, negotiators should be able to improve their performance on both dimensions.

INTEGRATION AND CRITIQUE

This chapter has introduced a number of methods for increasing the potential for successful negotiations. First, I outlined the decision-analytic approach, which focuses on information collection—namely, the importance of establishing reservation points, exploring the underlying interests of the parties, and weighting the relative importance of these interests. The need to think about the creation and claiming of value was discussed, and I introduced the concept of building on differences (such as estimates of future outcomes, risk preferences, and time preferences) as a strategy for uncovering trades. Five information-collection strategies were outlined for uncovering potential to create value in negotiation situations. These include building trust, asking questions, strategically disclosing information, making multiple offers, and searching for post-settlement settlements. Together, these techniques provide a prescriptive framework for thinking rationally about real-world negotiations.

As a teacher of negotiation, I have noticed that students who fail to thoroughly prepare for a simulation are routinely clobbered by their opponent. The assumption that good intuition will allow you to sail through negotiations is simply wrong; preparation is critical. High-quality preparation requires the negotiator to reflect on a number of simple but important questions. The sample list of questions that follows will not cover every negotiation situation, but is a good place to start:

1. What is your BATNA?
2. What is your reservation price?
3. What are the issues in this negotiation?
4. How important is each issue to you?
5. What do you think the other party's BATNA is?
6. What do you think their reservation price is?
7. How important do you think each issue is to them?
8. Are there viable trades that create value?
9. Are you and the other party in disagreement about future events? If so, is a bet viable?
10. How will you go about identifying the information that you do not currently know?

While these questions do not guarantee success, they will improve your odds.

As we saw in the first eight chapters, ours is not a fully rational world, particularly when it comes to our own decision-making processes. A central lesson of this book is that even when you are presented with rational advice, like the decision-analytic approach, your ingrained decision biases may limit your ability to follow this advice. In this sense, the decision-analytic approach is only a first step in helping you to become a better decision maker in multiparty contexts. This approach cries out for additional descriptive models that allow you as the focal negotiator to better anticipate your own likely behaviors and those of the other party. If you or your opponent is not acting fully rationally, what systematic departures from rationality can be predicted? How can you better anticipate the actual behavior of your opponent, and how can you identify and overcome barriers that might prevent you from following decision-analytic advice? The decision-analytic approach tells us that we must consider the actual, but not necessarily rational, decisions of the other side. A useful addition to this approach is to identify the specific deviations from rationality that we can anticipate in our own and in other parties' decision making. This will be the focus of Chapter 10.

CHAPTER TEN

Negotiator Cognition

The decision-analytic approach to negotiation presented in the previous chapter suggests that it is desirable for two parties to strike an agreement whenever a positive bargaining zone exists. Why, then, do actors in negotiations frequently fail to settle? The decision-analytic approach also provides strategies for reaching agreements of great value to both sides. Why, then, do even negotiators who have access to this advice fail to reach Pareto-efficient outcomes?

This chapter explores the most common cognitive mistakes we make in negotiations. Specifically, we will look at seven key issues that affect negotiator cognition: (1) the mythical fixed pie of negotiation, (2) the framing of negotiator judgment, (3) the nonrational escalation of conflict, (4) negotiator overconfidence, (5) self-serving biases in negotiation, (6) anchoring, and (7) the vividness of information. Each section illustrates how the decision-making processes of the typical negotiator diverge from a prescriptive model of behavior and discusses how we as negotiators can correct these deviations.

An understanding of these common mistakes will help improve your negotiating skills in two key ways. First, awareness is an essential step toward avoiding these errors in important negotiations. Second, once you have leaned to identify these errors in your own behaviors, you will be better able to anticipate them in the decisions of other negotiators.

THE MYTHICAL FIXED PIE OF NEGOTIATIONS

Why do negotiators typically fail to reach agreements that create maximum value for both sides? One reason is the fixed-pie assumption, a fundamental, intuitive bias in human judgment that distorts negotiator behavior. When individuals approach negotiations with a fixed-pie mentality, they assume that their interests necessarily and directly conflict with the interests of the other side. Metaphorically, they believe they are both fighting for the biggest piece of the pie.

Agreements in diplomatic situations, solutions to marital disputes, and the creation of strategic alliances are frequently blocked by the assumption that the parties' interests are diametrically opposed. Creative agreements occur when participants discover tradeoffs across issues—but individuals will not search for these trades if they assume the size of the pie is fixed.

The assumption of a fixed pie is rooted in social norms that lead us to interpret most competitive situations as win–lose. This win–lose orientation is manifested in our society in athletic competition, admission to academic programs, corporate promotion systems, and so on. Generalizing from these objective win–lose situations, individuals create similar expectations for situations that are not necessarily win–lose. When faced with a mixed-motive situation requiring both cooperation and competition, the competitive aspect becomes salient, motivating most negotiators to develop a strategy for obtaining the largest possible share of the perceived fixed pie. Such a focus inhibits the search for creative solutions through mutually beneficial tradeoffs.

The destructiveness of the mythical fixed pie is captured in this Cold War–era declaration by Rep. Floyd Spence, R-South Carolina, regarding a proposed arms reduction treaty: "I have had a philosophy for some time in regard to SALT, and it goes like this: the Russians will not accept a SALT treaty that is not in their best interest, and it seems to me that if it is in their best interests, it can't be in our best interest" (originally cited in Ross and Stillinger, 1991). This kind of dangerously confused reasoning—that anything good for the Soviet Union must be bad for the United States—defines the mythical fixed pie assumption.

With the benefit of twenty-first century hindsight, we can easily recognize that treaties like SALT benefited both the United States and the Soviet Union by reducing wasteful defense spending and the specter of nuclear war. And yet, Thompson (2001) has found that even when two sides want the exact same outcome, such as ending the Cold War, negotiators often settle on a different outcome, or reach an impasse, because they assume they must compromise to get agreement. Imagine that a company wants to increase employee training to improve job flexibility, while employees want to be better trained to solidify their job security. While the two groups may have the same goal, the fixed-pie assumption could lead them to assume that their interests are incompatible. "Maybe my employees are planning to look for work elsewhere once I've given them this extra training," a manager might wrongly infer. The mythical fixed pie can cause parties to fall prey to what Thompson calls the "incompatibility bias"—the assumption that one's own interests are incompatible with the other party's.

The mythical fixed pie also leads us to "reactively devalue" any concession made simply because it is offered by an adversary. Stillinger, Epelbaum, Keltner, and Ross (1990) divided 137 individuals into two groups and asked how favorable a specific arms reduction proposal was to the United States and to the USSR. In one group, the interviewer correctly ascribed the proposal to Communist Party General Secretary Mikhail Gorbachev. In the other group, the interviewer implied that President Ronald Reagan (the study was conducted during his presidency) had made the proposal. Fifty-six percent of those who believed the proposal originated with Gorbachev thought that the provisions dramatically favored the Soviet Union; only 16 percent felt it favored the United States, while the remaining 28 percent thought it favored both sides equally. When participants were led to believe that President Reagan had initiated the proposal, 45 percent thought it benefited both sides equally, 27 percent thought it favored the Soviet Union, and 27 percent thought that it favored the United States. Thus, terms that appear mutually beneficial when advanced by one's own side may seem disadvantageous when proposed by the other party, even if the terms of the proposal are equal. As soon as the other party concedes on an issue, negotiators may devalue the issue's worth: "If they are willing to make this concession, the issue must not be very important."

When individuals make such assumptions about the other party's interests, they inhibit the search for mutually beneficial tradeoffs. The fact is, tradeoffs can be quite easy to find when negotiators actively look for them. But when we ask managerial students why they failed to make a tradeoff in a simulated negotiation, they commonly tell us that they did not know that the tradeoff was possible. Why not? The fixed-pie assumption prevented them from initiating the search.

Executives often ask me, "What issue should we discuss first in a negotiation?" Some believe it is critical to get the most important issue resolved in the beginning, arguing that "any other strategy is simply procrastinating." By contrast, in the context of labor relations, many experienced negotiators recommend that it is important to "start with the easy issues first." In my opinion, both perspectives offer bad advice. Leading off with the easy issues may make the initial stages of the negotiation smoother, but it will increase the likelihood of impasse. However, starting with the toughest issue often leads to a breakdown at the beginning of a negotiation. Both strategies eliminate possible tradeoffs that may create joint benefits. Why? Because the mythical fixed pie encourages actors to think about issues one at a time. Unfortunately, once an issue has been "resolved," it is rarely resurrected to create a tradeoff with an issue raised later. Thinking simultaneously about multiple issues is the best way to break the mythical fixed pie and create value in a negotiation.

THE FRAMING OF NEGOTIATOR JUDGMENT

Consider the following scenario:

> You bought your condo in 2001 for $250,000. You have just put it on the market for $299,000, with a real target of $290,000 (your estimation of the condo's true market value). An offer comes in for $280,000. Does this offer represent a $30,000 gain in comparison with the original purchase price, or a $10,000 loss in comparison with your current target?

The answer to this question is "both." From a rational perspective, and based on our intuition, we can easily determine that the difference in the two points of view is irrelevant. However, as described in Chapter 3, Kahneman and Tversky (1982) have demonstrated that important differences arise from individuals' responses to questions framed in terms of losses versus gains. This difference is critical to describing negotiator behavior.

To understand the importance of "framing" in negotiations, consider the following labor–management situation. A trade union insists that management must increase the pay of union members from $12 to $14 an hour and that anything less, given current inflation, represents a loss. Management argues that any raise above $12 an hour imposes an unacceptable expense. What if each side had the choice of settling for $13 an hour (a certain settlement) or going to binding arbitration (a risky settlement)? Since each side views the conflict in terms of what it has to lose, following Tversky and Kahneman's (1981) findings, we can predict that each side will be risk seeking and therefore unwilling to accept the certain settlement. Changing the negotiators' framing from positive to negative, however, results in a very different predicted outcome. If the union views any raise above $12 an hour as a gain, and management views any raise under $14 an hour as a gain, then both sides will be risk averse, and a negotiated settlement will be likely. Neale and Bazerman (1985) found that negotiators with positive frames are significantly more likely to make concessions and to reach mutually beneficial outcomes than their negatively framed counterparts.

Bazerman, Magliozzi, and Neale (1985) found that the frame of buyers and sellers systematically affects their negotiation behavior. Negotiators were led to view transactions in terms of either (1) net profit (gains) or (2) expenses (losses) away from the gross profit of the transactions. While both frames yielded the same objective profit result, positively (gain) framed negotiators experienced the risk aversion necessary to motivate them to compromise. This incentive to compromise led negotiators with a positive frame to complete a larger number of transactions and obtain greater overall profits than negotiators with a negative frame.

What determines whether a negotiator will have a positive or negative frame? The answer lies in the selection of a perceptual anchor. Consider the anchors available to a union leader negotiating a wage with management: (1) last year's wage, (2) management's initial offer, (3) the union's estimate of management's reservation point, (4) the union's reservation point, or (5) the bargaining position that the union publicly announced to its constituency. As the anchor moves from (1) to (5), a modest gain in comparison to last year's wage becomes a loss when compared to the higher goals touted publicly, thus moving the union negotiator from a positive to a negative frame. Specifically, for workers who are currently making $12 per hour and demanding an increase of $2 per hour, a proposed increase of $1 per hour can be viewed as a $1 per hour gain over last year's wage (anchor 1) or a $1 per hour loss when compared to the goals of the union's constituency (anchor 5).

It is easy to see that the frames of negotiators can result in the difference between an important agreement and impasse. Both sides in negotiations typically talk in terms of a certain wage or price they "must" get—setting a high reference point against which gains and losses are measured. When this happens, any compromise away from the reference point will be viewed as a loss. This perceived loss leads negotiators to adopt a negative frame to all compromise proposals, to exhibit risk-seeking behavior, and to be less likely to reach settlement. In order to avoid these adverse effects of framing, negotiators should always be aware of their frames and consider the possibility of adopting alternative frames.

Framing has important implications for the tactics used by negotiators. Framing effects suggest that to induce concessionary behavior in an opponent, a negotiator should always create anchors that lead the opposition toward a positive frame. This means you will be negotiating in terms of what the other side has to gain, thereby increasing opportunities for tradeoffs and compromise. In addition, when you recognize that your opposition has a negative frame, you should encourage them to recognize that they have adopted a risky strategy in a situation where a sure gain is possible.

Finally, the impact of framing has important implications for mediators. When the proposed goal is a compromise, the mediator should strive to convince both parties to view the negotiation in a positive frame. This is tricky, however, since the anchor that will lead to a positive frame for one negotiator is likely to lead to a negative frame for the other. This suggests that when mediators meet with each party separately, they need to present different anchors to create risk aversion in each party. Again, to affect the frame, mediators also must emphasize the realistic risk of the situation, thus calling attention to its uncertainty and leading both sides to prefer a sure settlement.

NONRATIONAL ESCALATION OF CONFLICT

Following decades of animosity, on March 18, 1990, baseball team owners and players reached a four-year agreement to avert a strike that threatened to cancel the 1990 baseball season. The agreement expired on December 31, 1993, and the 1994 baseball season began without a new contract in place. The first offer came from the owners on June 14, 1994, but it was well outside the bargaining range. Dysfunctional bargaining ensued, and on August 12, the players went on strike.[1]

The strike effectively ended the 1994 baseball season and destroyed approximately $1 billion worth of financial opportunity for the owners and players. Food vendors, retailers, baseball card companies, and fans also suffered in various ways during the strike. The strike's inefficiency was highlighted when the courts required the team owners to accept the preexisting structure for the 1995 season while negotiations for the future continued.

From 1986 to 1993, Major League Baseball operated at a profit; by 1993, annual profits had risen to $36 million. The strike changed that picture. The owners lost $375 million in 1994, $326 million in 1995, and between $100 million and $200 million in 1996 (Grabiner, 1996). Meanwhile, players lost money, status, and bargaining power. For at least several years, baseball's position as America's national pastime was tarnished. The strike was an extremely costly and vivid example of a conflict that entered an escalatory spiral.

In the midst of the controversy, Sebenius and Wheeler (1994) offered a potentially advantageous strategy for resolving the disagreement: Continue the baseball season, but do not allow the teams to receive revenue or the players to receive their pay. Rather, revenues and forgone pay would go into a pool until a resolution was reached. In the meantime, watching the funds pile up would be an impetus for both sides to agree on a settlement. Sebenius and Wheeler further argued that the parties could set aside a portion of the fund for charity (such as the Special Olympics) if they failed to reach agreement in a timely fashion—again encouraging compromise, while creating positive rather than negative public relations. Overall, Sebenius and Wheeler outlined a very wise strategy that would have been far more efficient than the strike.

So, why didn't the parties follow this advice? My answer is that because each party was focused almost exclusively on beating the other side, they were primed to escalate their commitment to their initial course of action. One sign that the parties were

---

1. Many observations about the 1994 baseball strike in this section were prompted by the analysis of Chris Maxcy, Lisa Mroz, Keith Rakow, and Cynthia Safford in a course assignment for the MBA negotiations class at the Kellogg Graduate School of Management of Northwestern University.

absorbed by inappropriate objectives was the team owners' gleeful reaction to the cancellation of the 1994 World Series. Too busy congratulating themselves on sticking together, they failed to notice that they were bonding over their destruction of $1 billion in profits. Just four years later, it became apparent that National Basketball Association team owners had learned nothing from baseball's mistakes. Repeating this escalatory pattern, the NBA entered a 202-day lockout that cost the owners over $1 billion and the players more than $500 million in lost salaries.

Nonrational escalation of commitment unfolds in a wide variety of real-world situations, from custody battles to labor strikes to international disputes over land. Escalation begins when both parties enter a negotiation with extreme demands. The escalation literature predicts that if negotiators become committed to their initial public statements, they will nonrationally refuse to even consider concessions. To the extent that negotiators believe they have "too much invested to quit," inappropriate stubbornness is likely. Furthermore, if both sides incur losses as a result of a lack of agreement (such as lost wages and profits in the case of a strike), their commitment to their positions is likely to increase, while their willingness to change to a different course of action (that is, compromise) decreases.

One important finding of the escalation literature is that the public announcement of one's position increases one's tendency to escalate nonrationally (Staw, 1981). Once the general public (or one's constituency) becomes aware of the commitment, it will be much more difficult to retreat from the previously announced position. This suggests that escalation can be reduced if negotiators and third parties avoid setting firm public positions. However, implementation of this recommendation runs contrary to everything known about how negotiators (such as labor leaders, political leaders, and management representatives) behave when they represent constituencies. A firmly set public position is typically perceived as necessary to build constituency support and allegiance. Thus it may be that what is best for the constituency is not necessarily what the constituency rewards.

Diekmann, Tenbrunsel, Shah, Schroth, and Bazerman (1996) explicitly studied escalation in the context of negotiation. They found both sellers and buyers of real estate to be affected by the price that the seller had earlier paid for the property. This "sunk cost" did not affect either party's assessment of the property's value, but it did affect its expectations, reservation prices, and final negotiated outcomes, showing that the seller's sunk costs are transmitted across the negotiation context. An understanding of escalation can be very helpful to a negotiator in anticipating an opponent's behavior. When will the other party really hold out, and when will it give in? The escalation literature predicts that the other side will hold out when it has "too much invested" in its position to quit. Strategically, this suggests that a negotiator should avoid inducing bold, firm statements from an opponent, lest one's adversary later feels trapped in a corner.

NEGOTIATOR OVERCONFIDENCE

In 2004, Matt Harrington, a 6-foot-4-inch, 210-pound, twenty-two-year-old right-hander, was being paid $800 per month to pitch for the Fort Worth Cats in the Central Baseball League (*New York Times*, 7/18/04). During the off-season, Harrington stocked shelves at Target. So far, Harrington sounds like the typical independent leaguer. But in 2000, at age eighteen, Harrington was pictured on the covers of *USA Today* and *Baseball America* and described in the press as a hard-working, modest young man who was probably the best pitcher available in the major-league draft.

That year, Harrington and his family hired Tommy Tanzer, a well-known player's agent, to represent him. To scare away teams with limited budgets, Tanzer told teams with high draft choices that they would need to offer at least a $4.95 million first-year bonus to sign Harrington to a contract. The Colorado Rockies selected Harrington as the seventh pick in the draft but insisted they would not pay the price demanded by Tanzer. After the draft, the Rockies offered Harrington $4.9 million for eight years, then $5.3 million over eight years, and finally $4 million over only two years. Claiming to be insulted by the offers, Harrington, his parents, and Tanzer rejected each one—despite the fact that these figures were typical for a seventh-pick player. The tough negotiations extended for months before breaking down. Harrington could not play for a major-league team that year, or for any of the high-level minor-league teams. He headed for the independent-league St. Paul Saints and hoped for a more successful negotiation the following year.

Harrington had a disappointing season with the Saints, but secured a new agent, Scott Boras, for the 2001 major-league draft. The San Diego Padres chose him as the fifty-eighth overall selection. This time, Harrington turned down an offer of $1.25 million over four years with a $300,000 signing bonus. The next year, 2002, Harrington was the 374th pick. He was offered (and refused) less than $100,000 from the Tampa Bay Devil Rays; in 2003, the Cincinnati Reds drafted him in the twenty-fourth round at number 711, but again talks fell through. Harrington had become the longest holdout in baseball history.

In their four years of failed negotiations, Harrington, his parents, and his agents made a simple but critical mistake: they forgot to say yes. It is certainly useful to know when to hold out for more a better outcome. But at some point, a good negotiator must know when it's time to say yes. Harrington's BATNA was risky at best, terrible at worst. Yet even with professional negotiators representing him, his overconfidence destroyed a tremendous amount of potential.

Overconfidence that the other side will give you what you want can be a devastating negotiation error. This story is extreme, but all kinds of jobseekers overestimate what the other side will pay. More broadly, negotiators who fall victim to overconfidence, and failing to reach agreement as a result, waste tremendous opportunities across negotiation realms.

Research demonstrates that negotiators tend to be overconfident that their positions will prevail if they do not "give in." Similarly, negotiators in final-offer arbitration consistently overestimate the probability that their final offer will be accepted (Bazerman and Neale, 1982). In laboratory studies where there was, on average, only a 50 percent chance of a final offer being accepted, the average individual nonetheless estimated that there was a much higher probability (68 percent) that his or her offer would be accepted. Overconfidence may inhibit a variety of settlements, despite the existence of a positive bargaining zone. If we consider a final offer as a judgment of how much compromise is necessary to win the arbitration, it is easy to argue that when negotiators are overconfident that a particular position will be accepted, their reservation point becomes more extreme and their incentive to compromise is reduced. If a more accurate assessment is made, the negotiator is likely to be more uncertain and uncomfortable about the probability of success and is more likely to accept a compromise. Based on the biasing impact of this overconfidence, Neale and Bazerman (1985) found "appropriately" confident negotiators to exhibit more concessionary behavior and to be more successful than overly confident negotiators.

Overconfidence is most likely to occur when a party's knowledge is limited. As we learned in Chapter 2, most of us follow the intuitive cognitive rule, "When in doubt, be overconfident." This suggests that negotiators should seek objective value assessments from a neutral party, realizing that this neutral assessment is likely to be closer to the other party's position than the negotiator might have intuitively predicted.

SELF-SERVING BIASES IN NEGOTIATIONS

A concept closely related to negotiator overconfidence is the concept of self-serving biases. As we discussed in Chapter 4, while negotiator overconfidence refers to the tendency of negotiators to place too much confidence in their own assessments, self-serving biases refer to the tendency for people to define what is fair in ways that favors themselves. As a result, even when two parties both sincerely claim to want an outcome that is "fair" to both sides, their very different notions of fairness can lead to impasse.

Thompson and Loewenstein (1992) found that self-serving, biased attention to available information in a conflict affected the parties' perceptions of what constituted a fair settlement; in a simulated labor dispute, the magnitude of this bias affected the length of a strike. Babcock, Loewenstein, Issacharoff, and Camerer (1995) presented participants with diverse materials (depositions, medical and police reports, etc.) from a lawsuit resulting from a collision between an automobile and a motorcycle. Participants were assigned the role of plaintiff or defendant and were instructed to attempt to negotiate a settlement. If they were unable to do so, they would pay substantial penalties; in addition, they were told that the amount paid by the defendant to the plaintiff would be determined by an impartial judge who had already made his decision based on exactly the same case materials. Before negotiating, the participants were asked to predict the judge's ruling. They were told that this estimate would not be communicated to the other party and would not affect the judge's decision (which had already been made). Nevertheless, plaintiffs' predictions of the judge's award amount were substantially higher than those of defendants, and the degree of discrepancy between plaintiff and defendant was a strong predictor of whether they settled the case (as opposed to relying on the judge's decision). The participants' fairness assessments were biased according to their assigned role.

A number of follow-up experiments attempted to reduce the magnitude of the bias. Babcock and Loewenstein (1997) rewarded participants who accurately predicted the judge's ruling with cash and had them write an essay arguing the other side's point of view. Neither of these interventions had a measurable effect; participants consistently believed that the judge's own perception of fair judgments would match their own. Other findings from the same series of experiments point to a likely psychological mechanism underlying self-serving biases in negotiation. Participants were presented with eight arguments favoring the side to which they had been assigned (plaintiff or defendant) and eight arguments favoring the other side. They were asked to rate the importance of these arguments as perceived "by a neutral third party." There was a strong tendency to view arguments supporting one's own position as more convincing than those supporting the other side, suggesting that the bias operates by distorting one's interpretation of evidence. Consistent with this finding, when the parties were presented with their roles (plaintiff or defendant) only after reading the case materials, the magnitude of the bias was substantially reduced and almost all of the pairs reached rapid agreement on damages.

Self-serving biases are just as pervasive and detrimental to negotiated settlements in disputes involving more than two parties. Much of the findings regarding self-serving biases and multiparty negotiations concern the decisions of individuals involved in "social dilemmas." In a vivid illustration of a social dilemma, Hardin (1968) offered a parable about a group of herdsmen grazing their cattle in a common pasture. Each herdsman knows that it is to his advantage to increase the size of his herd because each additional animal represents personal profit. However, the cost of grazing, measured by the damage done to the pasture, is shared by all of the herdsmen. If the total number of animals becomes too large, the pasture will be overpopulated and will eventually be destroyed. Thus, the herdsmen have a collective interest in setting individual limits to the number of cattle grazing in the pasture to a degree that matches the rate of pasture replenishment. At the same time, it is in each herdsman's interest to marginally expand his grazing cattle beyond his allotment.

Many of the natural-resource scarcity and pollution issues that we face in contemporary society resemble Hardin's "tragedy of the commons." Wade-Benzoni, Tenbrunsel, and Bazerman (1996) created a social-dilemma simulation in which a group shares a common, scarce resource—in this case, ocean shark—from which individual members can harvest. This simulation is based on the real-life fishery crisis in the northeastern United States, where species of principal groundfish have been depleted, resulting in considerable uncertainty as to when and how they will be brought back to a sustainable level. The two most critical issues facing fishery management are (1) who will pay the cost of reversing the crisis, and (2) who will receive the subsequent benefits. Thus, the northeastern fishery captures the range of issues inherent in managing any commonly held resource. As in any social dilemma, individuals must choose between personal and group concerns. The group's best interest lies in limited harvesting, but personal interests may induce individual members to harvest excessively.

In our shark simulation, participants were assigned roles as representatives of organizations that relied on shark fishing for income. The representatives were gathering for a conference aimed at finding a solution to their common problem, the depletion of large coastal shark. All participants were told that they had two goals: (1) to maximize current profit without depleting the harvest pool to a level that would be too low to provide future harvests, and (2) to maximize the net present value of the profit that their associations would receive. This profit would be broken up into two components: profit received from the current harvest and profit expected from future harvests. Participants were told that a given total harvest level was sustainable, enabling the species to reproduce itself at its current population level; if the total harvest rose above the given level, the species would suffer further depletion. Harvesting above the sustainable level decreased opportunities for future harvesting, resulting in a net decrease in total profit.

A characteristic of virtually all real-world social dilemmas is asymmetry in the parties' contribution to the problem and their willingness to cooperate with proposed solutions. When asymmetry exists, negotiators are likely to exhibit self-serving biases in their judgments about the fairness of resource distribution. To capture this asymmetry in the simulation, participants were told that their organizations placed different weights on the importance of future shark harvests. Specifically, those participants who represented commercial fishing groups harvested relatively large numbers of shark and had a relatively low interest in the future health of the resource. By contrast, the representatives of recreational fishing groups harvested fewer shark and had a very strong interest in the resource's future. Consistent with the real-world situation, participants were told that the commercial groups were better equipped than recreational groups to switch to a different kind of fish should the shark resource be depleted.

After receiving the information just described, but before their simulated conference, the participants recorded what they personally believed to be a fair solution to the crisis. During the thirty-minute conference that followed, participants discussed the issues and potential solutions, but did not make binding commitments. Participants were again asked to make individual fairness judgments following the conference. Self-serving interpretations of fairness were the common pattern in this asymmetric resource dilemma. In addition, we found that the amount of harvesting carried out by each group was positively related to the strength of the level of self-serving biases. Discussion of the issues reduced the magnitude of self-serving biases, thereby increasing cooperation. This research strongly suggests that asymmetry is a key driver of self-serving biases and overharvesting. Real-world resource dilemmas represent a critical area where ambiguity enables individuals to justify what they want to do (take a larger share of a limited resource) instead of what they should do (practice self-restraint). The source of the problem is not our desire to be unfair, but our difficulty interpreting information in an unbiased manner (Messick and Sentis, 1983). Communication-building strategies, including asking questions, seeking tradeoffs, and making concessions, are the key to reducing self-serving biases and creating negotiated solutions that benefit not only the interested parties, but society as a whole.

ANCHORING IN NEGOTIATIONS

From Chapter 2, we know that people tend to be overly affected by an initial anchor, without realizing this effect. Northcraft and Neale (1987) surveyed real estate brokers who claimed they could assess the value of a property to within 5 percent of the true or appraised value. They were unanimous in stating that, when looking at an actual house on the market, they did not factor the listing price of the property into their personal estimate of its "true" value. Northcraft and Neale then asked the brokers, and separately a group of undergraduate students, to estimate the value of an actual house. Both brokers and students were randomly assigned to one of four experimental groups. In each group, all participants were given a ten-page information packet about the house being sold, which included considerable information about the house, as well as data on prices and characteristics of recently sold homes in the area. The only difference in the information given to the four groups was the house's listing price, which was listed as +11 percent, +4 percent, −4 percent, or −11 percent of the actual appraised value of the property. After reading the material, all participants toured the house and the surrounding neighborhood. Participants were then asked to estimate the house's true value. The values estimated by both the brokers and the students suggest that both groups were significantly and strongly affected by the listing price (the anchor). While the students readily admitted the role that the listing price played in their decision-making process, the brokers flatly denied their use of the listing price as an anchor—despite the evidence to the contrary.

Ritov (1996) finds that even very subtle shifts in how negotiations are anchored can create big differences in final outcomes. In her study, she varied whether buyers and sellers in a simulation are looking at possible agreements in an order that moves from best-for-the-buyer to best-for-the-seller, or in an order that moves from the best-for-the-seller to best-for-the-buyer. She finds surprisingly big effects, such that negotiators end up closer to the end of the bargaining zone that corresponds with the starting point (the price listed at the top of the page). As a simplified example, Ritov's research suggests that if possible prices are listed as $1,000, $800, $600, $400, $200, and $0, a higher price will result, on average, than if possible prices are listed as $0, $200, $400, $600, $800, and $1,000. In addition, Ritov found that the first offer is positively correlated with the final outcome, a phenomenon that I will explore further below.

In negotiation, one party must make the first offer. Should it be the buyer or the seller? Should it be you or the other side? Oesch and Galinsky (2003) show that negotiators with good alternatives are more likely to make the first offer than are those with poor alternatives. Similarly, low-power negotiators are less likely to make the first offer than high-power negotiators. Oesch and Galinsky (2003) also find that more extreme offers lead to better deals for those making such offers, but that this benefit comes at the expense of increasing the likelihood of an impasse. While first offers have the power to anchor the negotiation, unreasonable first offers can scare away the other side. Ideally, an effective first offer is reasonable, but also close to your preferred end of the bargaining zone.

Galinsky and Mussweiler (2001) show that first offers have a strong anchoring effect when great ambiguity exists. If your opponent has a good sense of the bargaining zone, or knows what the item is worth to them, your first offer will have little value. However, when your opponent lacks information, he or she may actually make inferences about the value of the object based on your first offer.

How can you protect yourself from first offers that benefit your opponent at your expense? Galinsky and Mussweiler (2001) show that your opponent's first offer will have little effect on you if you focus on your own alternatives and your own objectives. While we learn a great deal in the process of negotiation, we should avoid learning from the potential manipulative effect of the other side's first offer.

VIVIDNESS IN NEGOTIATIONS

To negotiate effectively, you need to know what you want, know where you are going, and pick the best route to get there. These statements may seem obvious. Yet, far too often, negotiators do not know their own preferences. Perhaps the most common failure in assessing one's own preferences is the tendency to overweight vivid concerns and underweight more important, nonvivid concerns. I have often observed this error in the decisions of MBA students.

Business schools typically have a gathering place, such as a lounge or a cafeteria, where students meet between classes to relax and chat. For second-year MBA students, no topic is of greater interest than the job search. Students gather in the lounge to share news about their offers; during good years, a bit of bragging might occur as well. Consider the following statements that might be heard in the lounge during recruiting season:

The company is located within eight miles of where I grew up.

People seemed very happy during my visit to corporate headquarters.

The starting salary is $120,000.

The offer is from McKinsey.

As you learned in Chapter 2, the vividness of data strongly affects our decisions. Which of these statements are most vivid? My assessment is that the high ($120,000) salary and high-prestige (McKinsey) employer will be more vivid than the comments about the company's location and employee contentment. Why? Because others will find facts that convey prestige especially vivid. The students who have received such offers can't help but notice the impressed response of their classmates. Now consider that many MBA graduates switch jobs soon after graduation. Why is the turnover rate so high? One possibility is that, when weighing job offers, students overweight vivid or prestigious attributes and underweight the issues that will more strongly affect their professional and personal satisfaction (Bazerman, 2004; Hall and Staats, 2004). MBAs are not the only group susceptible to vividness attributes in negotiation. Within social clubs, churches, and families, people overweight vivid or prestigious attributes and underweight more important nonvivid attributes of a negotiation.

Wilson, Northcraft, and Neale (1989) showed that vividness affects the negotiations of juries. Study participants were shown videotaped closing arguments from a civil trial. One party (Party A) had sued the other (Party B), and Party B countersued Party A. Each party presented two categories of arguments, such that each side made a claim against the other side and also offered a defense to the opposing party's claim. In the closing arguments, the researchers manipulated vividness. In one condition, Party A's position was supported by ten vivid statements; in the other condition, Party A's position was supported by ten dull statements. The vivid/dull manipulation was made to all ten arguments, but the content of the arguments remained the same. For example, one argument in the vivid condition read, "the slab was jagged and had to be sanded"; in the dull condition, the argument read, "the slab was rough and had to be planed." Participants were then asked to pass judgment on both the claim and the counterclaim and award appropriate damages. Party A prevailed against Party B almost twice as often (82 percent versus 46 percent) when Party A's arguments were vivid, and the study participants made larger awards for vivid arguments. Finally, participants who had witnessed the vivid videotape could list more facts about the case than could those who had seen the dull presentation.

The effects of vivid information extend beyond juries. Imagine a group of executives that is discussing where to allocate research and development dollars. Each executive offers an opinion, and to no one's surprise, they each provide arguments that would direct more dollars to their own division. Which executive prevails? The answer will depend partially on the merits of the case. But it will also depend in part on which executive provides the most vivid arguments for his or her case.

In a simulated labor negotiation, Neale (1984) found that the vividness of costs systematically anchored and influenced the outcomes the negotiators were willing to accept. When the costs of reaching a poor settlement were vivid, such as a negative evaluation by the negotiator's constituency, negotiators were less concessionary and less willing to reach an agreement. As a result, they were much more likely to invoke arbitration, a tactic that transferred the blame for the outcome to the arbitrator (the dispute mechanism in place in case of impasse). By contrast, when the costs of using arbitration (such as the dollar cost, time commitment, and loss of control over the outcome) were vivid, negotiators were significantly more concessionary and more likely to settle. This result occurred despite no change in the objective information offered in the two versions. Negotiators were twice as likely to reach an agreement when arbitration costs were vivid as they were when negotiation-related costs were vivid.

Finally, consider the common negotiation involving buying a new car. During the negotiation, you can expect the salesperson to provide lots of evidence on the reliability of the specific model. Once you have agreed to a specific price, the salesperson will attempt to sell you a service contract, typically in the $400 to $800 range. "Imagine needing to pay $1,200 for a new engine," he says. Notice that this is the same car whose virtue was reliability just minutes earlier. Yet, almost half of new car buyers buy extended warranties—one of the worst consumer purchases available. As recounted in Chapter 3, in one lawsuit against Nissan, evidence was presented that the typical extended warranty contract costing $795 was primarily profit for the dealer. Actual repairs cost $131 of this amount, $109 went to Nissan for administrative costs, and the remaining $555 was dealer profit. The message is clear: Part of the job of the negotiator is to know what he or she wants and to negotiate for it—without being manipulated by vivid data.

CONCLUSIONS

Chapters 9 and 10 have offered an overview of what is commonly known as the decision perspective to negotiation, which can be traced to Raiffa's "asymmetrically prescriptive/descriptive" approach to negotiation. In his groundbreaking 1982 book *The Art and Science of Negotiation*, Raiffa focused on providing the best advice to a focal negotiator (prescriptive) based on the best possible description of the likely behavior of the opponent (descriptive). Raiffa's work represented a turning point in negotiation research for a number of reasons. First, by departing from game theoretic perspectives that assumed full rationality by all parties, Raiffa explicitly acknowledged the importance of developing accurate descriptions of opponents. In addition, his realization that negotiators need advice implicitly acknowledged the fact that we do not intuitively follow purely rational strategies. Finally, Raiffa initiated the groundwork for a dialogue between prescriptive and descriptive researchers, which we have overviewed in these last two chapters.

Chapter 9 provided the basic analytic structure for Raiffa's prescriptive analysis, while Chapter 10 dealt with questions that Raiffa's work left unexamined. For example, if the negotiator and his or her opponent do not act rationally, what systematic departures from rationality can be predicted? I have argued that a successful negotiator will use descriptive models to anticipate the likely behavior of the opponent and to identify errors to avoid in his or her own negotiation behavior.

CHAPTER ELEVEN

Bounded Awareness[1]

Before reading this chapter, please respond to the problems presented in Table 11.1.

TABLE 11.1 Chapter Problems

Respond to the following problems before reading the rest of the chapter.

Problem 1. MBA students from a prestigious university read the following problem and played one of the six roles—A, B, C, D, E, and F:

In this exercise, six people will be randomly assigned to the roles A, B, C, D, E, and F. A will be randomly selected, and given $60 to allot among A, B, C, D, E, and F. The amounts given to B, C, D, E, and F must be equal, but this amount may be different from the amount that A allocates to A (herself/himself). B, C, D, E, and F will be asked to specify the minimum amount that they would accept. If the amount offered by A to each of B, C, D, E, and F is equal to or greater than the largest amount specified by B, C, D, E, or F, the $60 will be divided as specified by A. If, however, any of the amounts specified by B, C, D, E, and F are larger than the amount offered by A, all six parties will receive $0.

Please specify the allocation from A that would maximize A's average dollar payoff:

(Use whole numbers, not decimals/fractions)

   A: $____   B: $____   C: $____   D: $____   E: $____   F: $____

Problem 2. In a recent study, college students were given the following question:

In this problem, you will be given a choice of boxes X, Y, or Z. One of these three boxes has a valuable prize in it. The other two boxes are empty. After you pick one of the boxes, the computer will open one of the other two boxes, show you that this unchosen box does not have the prize, and offer you to trade your chosen box for the unopened, unchosen box. For example, if you were to choose box X, the computer would open one of the two other boxes (e.g., Y) and show you it's empty. The computer would then offer you the opportunity to switch your choice from X to Z.

(Continues)

---

1. The term bounded awareness was first suggested by my colleague Dolly Chugh and first written about in Bazerman and Chugh (2005).

TABLE 11.1 Chapter Problems *(Continued)*

A student who participated in the study picked box Y. The computer then opened box Z, showed the student it was empty, and offered the student to trade box Y (which the student originally chose) for box X (the remaining unopened, unchosen box).

Please state whether the student should have traded box Y for box X or not, in order to have the best chance of winning the prize.

Answer: Yes   No

Problem 3. In this exercise you represent Company A (the acquirer), which is currently considering acquiring Company T (the target) by means of a tender offer. You plan to tender in cash for 100 percent of Company T's shares but are unsure how high a price to offer. The main complication is this: The value of Company T depends directly on the outcome of a major oil exploration project it is currently undertaking. Indeed, the very viability of Company T depends on the exploration's outcome. If the project fails, the company under current management will be worth nothing—$0 per share. But if the project succeeds, the value of the company under current management could be as high as $100 per share. All share values between $0 and $100 are considered equally likely.

By all estimates, the company will be worth considerably more in the hands of Company A than under current management. In fact, whatever the ultimate value under current management, *the company will be worth 50 percent more under the management of A than under Company T*. If the project fails, the company is worth $0 per share under either management. If the exploration project generates a $50 per share value under current management, the value under Company A is $75 per share. Similarly, a $100 per share value under Company T implies a $150 per share value under Company A, and so on.

The board of directors of Company A has asked you to determine the price they should offer for Company T's shares. This offer must be made now, before the outcome of the drilling project is known. From all indications, Company T would be happy to be acquired by Company A, provided the price is profitable. Moreover, Company T wishes to avoid, at all cost, the potential of a takeover bid by any other firm. You expect Company T to delay a decision on your bid until the results of the project are in, then accept or reject your offer before the news of the drilling results reaches the press. Thus, you (Company A) will not know the results of the exploration project when submitting your price offer, but Company T will know the results when deciding whether or not to accept your offer. In addition, Company T is expected to accept any offer by Company A that is greater than the (per share) value of the company under current management.

As the representative of Company A, you are deliberating over price offers ranging from $0 per share (this is tantamount to making no offer at all) to $150 per share. What price offer per share would you tender for Company T's stock?

My tender price is $_____ per share.

(Continues)

TABLE 11.1 Chapter Problems *(Continued)*

Problem 4. MBA students from a prestigious university read the following problem and played one of the six roles—A, B, C, D, E, and F:

In this exercise, six people will be randomly assigned to the roles A, B, C, D, E, and F. A will be randomly selected, and given $60 to allot among A, B, C, D, E, and F. The amounts given to B, C, D, E, and F must be equal, but this amount may be different from the amount that A allocates to A (herself/himself). B, C, D, E, and F will be asked to specify the minimum amount that they would accept. If the amount offered by A to each of B, C, D, E, and F is equal to or greater than the smallest amount specified by B, C, D, E, or F, the $60 will be divided as specified by A. If, however, all of the amounts specified by B, C, D, E, and F are larger than the amount offered by A, all six parties will receive $0.

Please specify the allocation from A that would maximize A's average dollar payoff:

(Use whole numbers, not decimals/fractions)

  A: $_____   B: $_____   C: $_____   D: $_____   E: $_____   F: $_____

Problem 5. In a recent study, college students were given the following question:

In this problem, you will be given a choice of boxes X, Y, or Z. One of these three boxes has a valuable prize in it. The other two boxes are empty. After you pick one of the boxes, the computer may open one of the other two boxes, show you that this unchosen box does not have the prize, and offer you to trade your chosen box for the unopened unchosen box. The computer will make its decision whether to open a box and offer you a switch with the goal of minimizing the likelihood that you get the prize. For example, if you were to choose box X, the computer might decide to open one of the two other boxes (e.g. Y), show you it's empty, and offer you the opportunity to switch your choice from X to Z.

A student who participated in the study picked box Y. The computer then opened box Z, showed the student it was empty, and offered the student to trade box Y (which the student originally chose) for box X (the remaining unopened, unchosen box).

Please state whether the student should have traded box Y for box X or not, in order to have the best chance of winning the prize.

  Answer: Yes   No

Problem 6. Without lifting your pencil (or pen) from the paper, draw four (and only four) straight lines that connect all nine dots shown here:

       •   •   •

       •   •   •

       •   •   •

Chapter 1 introduced the concept of bounded rationality, which describes the fact that our thinking is limited and biased in systematic, predictable ways. In Chapter 4, we explored ideas connected to bounded willpower—when the temporary motivation to pursue a short-term goal or affective state is in conflict with our long-term interests. Chapter 6 focused on bounded self-interest, specifically the way our fairness judgments are influenced by our desires. And in Chapter 8, we introduced the idea of bounded ethicality, which asserts that cognitive biases can lead honorable people to unintentionally engage in unethical behavior. All of these concepts are consistent with Simon's advocacy of a realistic model of human behavior that accounts for our limited rationality. So far, all of these bounds, or limitations, have focused on how people process and make decisions about the information that is part of their cognitive set.

In this chapter, I argue that people have a *bounded awareness* that prevents them from noticing or focusing on observable and relevant data. Bounded awareness exists when individuals do not attend to predictable, accessible, perceivable, and important information, while attending to other equally accessible and perceivable information. The availability heuristic, discussed in Chapters 1 and 2, offers some evidence for this idea. But bounded awareness is distinct from this heuristic. Within specific domains, we can identify information that is systematically outside the awareness of most decision makers. Because of this bounded awareness, useful information remains out of focus for the decision maker. The misalignment between the information needed for a good decision and the information included in awareness results in a focusing failure.

Perhaps the best-known problem that illustrates the concept of bounded awareness is Problem 6 from Table 11.1. Were you able to solve the problem? Most intelligent people fail to solve it, even those who remember seeing the problem before. Most people attempt to apply their logical decision-making skills to the problem that is in focus: connecting all nine dots without going outside the bounds imposed by the nine dots. Common attempts look like the following:

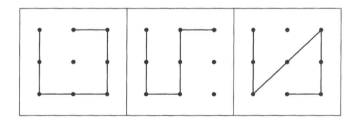

People cognitively create a boundary that frames the problem and constrains them from finding a solution. But note that the problem does not tell you to keep your pencil within the bounds imposed by the nine dots. Once people become aware of the space outside the area bounded by the nine dots, the following solution is fairly easy to achieve:

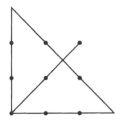

As you can see, the solution is simple. However, very bright people can look at this problem for hours and not solve it. Why? Because bounds created by our minds eliminate the solution. Creativity problems frequently make people feel tricked. A common "trick" of such problems is to misdirect our attention by causing us to psychologically see bounds on the problem. These bounds prevent discovery of the solution. After the teacher breaks the psychological bound, the solution seems obvious. The most critical barriers to creative decisions are our assumptions, or the information we allow into the defined problem space. To fit problems into our previously established decision-making processes, we make false assumptions about them. Creativity problems may not seem to be representative of common real-world decisions, but the tendency to place false perceived bounds is a very common aspect of decision making.

The phenomenon of bounded awareness is captured by the familiar exclamation, "How could I have missed that?" Many of us have this response after seeing important information that we previously overlooked. Offering an intriguing approach to idea innovation, Nalebuff and Ayres (2003) encourage us to ask "Why not?" For example, they argue that the "anticipation" problem posed by a bottle of ketchup was solved by a new design that allows the bottle to be stored upside down, a design later extended to a broad array of products. Nalebuff and Ayres encourage product developers to imagine the products they would want to create if resources were not a constraint. Once you know what you want in an unbounded world, these researchers suggest, you can explore whether it is viable in our real, constrained world.

This chapter examines the prevalence of bounded awareness in a variety of realms: (1) inattentional blindness to obvious information, (2) the failure to notice obvious changes in one's environment, (3) the tendency to focus on only a part of the problem at hand, as well as the bounded awareness of (4) groups, (5) negotiators, and (6) bidders in auctions.

INATTENTIONAL BLINDNESS

Over twenty-five years ago, Neisser (1979) asked people to watch a video of two visually superimposed groups of players passing basketballs. One group wore white shirts and the other group wore dark shirts. Participants were instructed to count the number of passes made between members of one of the two groups. The superimposed video made the task moderately difficult, and participants had to give it their full attention. The interesting result is that only 21 percent of Neisser's participants reported seeing a woman who clearly and unexpectedly walked through the basketball court carrying an open umbrella. My repeated experience, using this video in the classroom, is that far fewer than 21 percent of my students notice the woman.

After showing the video the first time, I ask my students whether anyone saw anything unusual. In a large room, it is common for just a few people to mention seeing a woman with an umbrella. When they offer this observation, the others in the room scoff at it. Yet, when I show the video again to demonstrate what most of the class missed, everyone sees the woman. By focusing on one task—in this case, counting passes—people miss very obvious information in their visual world.

Using a video in which a person in a gorilla costume walks through a basketball game, thumping his chest, and is clearly and comically visible for more than five seconds, Simons and Chabris (1999) have repeatedly replicated Neisser's finding. Simons provides a series of such demonstrations on a video that can be purchased at www.viscog.com.

I find the failure to see the obvious (including my own failure the first time I saw the video) amazing, exceeding common assumptions about our visual awareness. While Neisser (1979) first observed this phenomenon, it has recently become of significant interest to cognitive and perceptual psychologists, and has become known as *inattentional blindness* (Simons and Levin, 2003). Mack and Rock (1998) provide broader evidence in perceptual experiments that people have a broad tendency not to see what they are looking at directly when focused on a different issue. Mack (2003) points out that inattentional blindness might cause an airplane pilot who is attending to his controls to overlook the presence of another airplane in his runway. Similarly, many car accidents undoubtedly result from drivers focusing on matters other than driving, such as talking on their cell phones. I believe that research on inattentional blindness provides ample evidence against the use of cell phones while driving, and even provides the empirical basis for laws to prevent such use.

Recent work connects inattentional blindness to neural regions in the brain (Moore and Egeth, 1997), and identifies many key independent variables that affect the probability of not seeing the obvious (Mack, 2003). Beyond my own fascination with this basic research, I am interested in making an analogy from this work in the visual realm to the inattentional blindness that leads most decision makers to overlook a broad array of information that is readily available in the environment. For instance, I am struck by the many times my spouse has claimed to have told me something of which I have absolutely no recollection. Like many people would, I tend to conclude that my spouse imagined the interaction. But if I could miss seeing the woman with the umbrella in Neisser's video, I must accept the possibility that my spouse did indeed provide the information that she claimed and that my mind was focused elsewhere.

Many years ago, when I was a student, I was also a very good tournament bridge player. One of my assets was the ability to concentrate. Once, in the finals of a tournament, I focused intently on the actions of the other three players, the fifty-two cards, and nothing else. When the final hand was played, and I finally relaxed my attention to the cards and the other players, I noticed that dozens of people were watching the game—the area around the table was very crowded. Yet during the game, these people were not part of my awareness! I was so focused on information relevant to the game that I saved no energy for observing irrelevant data—the people around the table watching. This skill was probably very adaptive to the bridge tournament. But, because I think this tendency to focus generalizes to other aspects of behavior, I now wonder what crucial information I may have missed that might have helped me in important situations. The tough task for future research is to identify how to balance the benefits of intense focus against the potential costs of unintentional blindness.

CHANGE BLINDNESS

Imagine that you are an accountant who is in charge of the audit of a large, well-respected corporation. You have an excellent relationship with your client, which pays your firm tens of millions of dollars in fees each year. For three years, you view and approve the client's high-quality, highly ethical financial statements. All of a sudden, the corporation begins stretching, and even breaking, the law in many areas. First, do you notice these transgressions, and second, do you refuse to sign a statement certifying that the financial statements are acceptable according to government regulations? My guess is that virtually all auditors would notice, and most would refuse to sign.

Now let's revise the story. After you have seen and approved of high-quality, highly ethical financial statements for one year, the corporation begins stretching the law in a few places, but commits no clearly unethical behaviors. The third year, the firm stretches the ethicality of its returns a bit further; some of the company's accounting decisions may in fact violate federal accounting standards. By the fourth year, the corporation is stretching the law in many areas and occasionally breaking them. In this revised story, do you ever notice the unethical aspects of the reporting? And if so, at what point, if any, do you refuse to sign a statement affirming that the financial records are acceptable according to government regulations?

I would predict, along with Cain, Loewenstein, and Moore (2005), that you are much more likely to notice and refuse to sign the statements in the first version than in the second version, even if the unethical behavior is the same in year four of both stories. This prediction is based on the notion of a "slippery slope" of unethical behavior (Cain et al., 2005) and also as "boiling frog syndrome" (Gino, 2004). According to the slippery slope theory, we are far more likely to become unethical one step at a time than in one big step. When our behavior becomes unethical one step at a time, we are less likely to notice that it is unethical and more likely to be able to justify the behavior than if we became unethical all at once (Tenbrunsel and Messick, 2004). Similarly, the boiling frog syndrome is based on the folk wisdom that if you throw a frog in boiling water, it will jump out. But if you put a frog in cold water and slowly raise the temperature, the gradual warming will relax the frog, and it will slowly cook to death due to its inability to notice the gradual temperature change.

The psychological science behind these observations lies in the perceptual area of change detection. Change detection researchers have provided amazing evidence that, in a surprisingly large number of cases, people fail to notice changes in the information that is visually available to them (Simons, 2000). Interestingly, people often cannot describe the change that has taken place, but do have traces of memory of the scene before the change took place. For example, Simons, Chabris, Schnur, and Levin (2002) had an experimenter, who was holding a basketball, stop a pedestrian and ask for directions. While the pedestrian was giving directions, a group of people walked between the experimenter and the pedestrian, and one member of the group surreptitiously took the basketball from the experimenter. After the pedestrian finished providing directions, he or she was asked if he or she noticed anything unexpected or noticed a change. Most of the pedestrians did not report noticing the removal of the basketball. Yet when pushed further with leading questions, many of these same people could recall the presence of the basketball, and even reported features of the ball. Thus, at some level, we do perceive information pre- and post-change, but fail to make the connection that a change has taken place.

In a parallel study, Angelone, Levin, and Simons (2003) showed people a videotape of an interaction in which clearly visible clothing or objects were changed during a cut in the camera position. Many did not notice the change, yet were able to select the pre-change information from a photographic lineup. In a series of studies, Mitroff, Simons, and Franconeri (2002) confirmed this pattern of failing to explicitly notice a change, while having some implicit representation in one's mind of the information pre- and post-change.

Finally, moving closer to the realm of decision making, Johansson, Hall, and Olsson (2004) had people observe two human faces on a computer and choose the more attractive person by moving a cursor. As participants made a cognitive choice between the two pictures and began to move the cursor, an attention-grabbing flash distracted them, and the two pictures were reversed. Most subjects continued to move the cursor in the same direction (now to the picture that they had not chosen). They failed to notice the switch and gave elaborate reasons to support their unintended choice.

To date, the scientific evidence for change blindness has been associated with perceptional changes, not decision making. Yet I find the comparison between obliviousness to changing visual information and other types of changing information to be compelling, and believe we will soon have clear evidence documenting the slippery slope phenomenon and the boiling frog syndrome in contexts relevant to important managerial decisions.

FOCALISM AND THE FOCUSING ILLUSION

Gilbert, Wilson, and their colleagues (Gilbert and Wilson, 2000; Wilson, Wheatly, Meyers, Gilbert, and Axsom, 2000) coined the term *focalism* to describe the common tendency to focus too much on a particular event (the "focal event") and too little on other events that are likely to occur concurrently (Wilson et al., 2000). As a consequence, people tend to overestimate both the degree to which their future thoughts will be occupied by the focal event and the duration of their emotional response to the event. For example, we tend to overestimate the impact of positive and negative events, such as the wins and losses of our preferred sports team or political candidate, on our overall happiness. We even dramatically overestimate the effects on our happiness of being afflicted by a major medical condition.

In a similar vein, Schkade and Kahneman (1998) define the *focusing illusion* as the tendency of people to make judgments based on their attention to only a subset of available information, to overweight that information, and to underweight unattended information. Using logic similar to Gilbert, Wilson, and colleagues, Schkade and Kahneman (1998) asked college students in the Midwest and in Southern California about their own life satisfaction and the perceived life satisfaction of others. Californians and Midwesterners reported a similar level of life satisfaction, yet both groups rated Californians as having greater life satisfaction than Midwesterners. Essentially, differences between California and the Midwest, such as climate, strongly influenced non-residents' judgments of residents' life satisfaction. However, these factors did not predict the experienced life satisfaction of citizens of the two locales. Schkade and Kahneman argue that when students imagined how a move to the other location would affect them, the obvious difference of weather became a salient factor, and all other life events affecting satisfaction were out of focus.

Imagine that eight teams in any game or sport are engaged in a single elimination tournament. Now imagine that eight people are each assigned to each team and asked the probability that "their" team will win the tournament. Of course, some teams would be better, and some would be worse, but the probabilities of the eight teams winning should roughly add up to 100 percent.

Now let's see what really happens in such a situation. When the 1995 National Basketball Association championship was down to eight teams, Fox and Tversky (1998) recruited basketball fans as subjects. Participants were asked either (1) the probability that each team (Chicago, Indiana, Orlando, New York, Los Angeles, Phoenix, San Antonio, and Houston) would win the championship, (2) the probability that the winning team would come from each of the four divisions (Central [Chicago and Indiana], Atlantic [Orlando and New York], Pacific [Los Angeles and Phoenix], and Midwestern [San Antonio and Houston]), or (3) the probability that the winning team would come from either the Eastern conference (comprising the Central and Atlantic divisions) or the Western conference (comprising the Pacific and Midwestern divisions). If the participants were well calibrated, the sum of the probabilities for the eight teams, the sum of the probabilities for the four divisions, and the sum of the probabilities for the two conferences should each add up to 100 percent.

The combined probabilities for the two conferences were close to the expected 100 percent; the sum added up to 102 percent. However, the sum of the probabilities of the four divisions was 144 percent, and the sum of the probabilities of the eight teams was 218 percent. Fox and Tversky argue that when participants focus on an individual team, they can find reasons to support that team winning the tournament; meanwhile, the data that supports other teams winning is out of focus. Similarly, Tversky and Koehler (1994) found that medical doctors, when asked to assess the probabilities of four mutually exclusive prognoses for a patient, gave probabilities for the four prognoses that totaled far in excess of 100 percent. The specific team or prognosis was in focus, and the others teams and other prognoses were out of focus.

Finally, perhaps the most important application of focalism has been to the *Challenger* space shuttle disaster (see Vaughn [1996] for an excellent overall analysis of this disaster). As many readers know, the *Challenger* blew up after being launched at the lowest temperature in its history, due to the failure of O-rings at low temperatures. When the potential problem of low temperatures was brought up in a pre-launch meeting, the decision makers examined the temperatures and magnitude of O-ring problems in the seven prior launches that had had some O-ring failure. Looking at the seven temperatures in these seven launches showed no clear pattern regarding the O-rings, and the decision was made to go ahead with the launch. Unfortunately, no one in the meeting decided to consider seventeen past launches in which no O-ring failure had occurred. This was a critical oversight: an examination of all twenty-four launches shows a clear connection between temperature and O-ring failure. Indeed, a logistic regression of past data suggests that the *Challenger* had a greater than 99 percent chance of malfunction. The failure of NASA engineers to look outside the boundaries of the data at the table caused seven astronauts to lose their lives and perhaps the worst setback in the agency's history. More broadly, I argue that many decision makers and groups err by limiting their analysis to the data in the room, rather than asking what data would best answer the question being asked.

BOUNDED AWARENESS IN GROUPS

As we moving from considering the role of bounded awareness in individual decision making to its effects on groups, consider the fact that the information discussed by a group has a key influence on any final decision (Wegner, 1986). Conversely, information mentally considered by individual members, but not mentioned, will have little influence on the eventual decision. Thus, while individuals' awareness is bounded by the information they mentally consider, the awareness of groups is bounded by the information that becomes part of the discussion.

One of the advantages of groups over individuals is that they collectively possess more information than does any individual member. In fact, in organizations, one of the reasons to create groups is to pool information from different divisions. Thus, sharing unique information is a critical source of group potential, both in an absolute sense and in comparison to individual decision making. Yet Stasser and colleagues (Stasser and Titus, 1985; Stasser, 1988; Stasser and Stewart, 1992) and others (e.g., Gruenfeld, Mannix, Williams, and Neale, 1996) show a consistent tendency of groups to focus much more on shared information (information previously known to all group members) than on unique or unshared information (information previously known by only one group member).

In an early example of this pattern, Stasser and Titus (1985) asked college students to choose between three candidates running for student council president. Data on the candidates was created with the intention of making Candidate A the preferred choice when individuals or groups had access to all of the information about all of the candidates. Accordingly, Candidate A was the preferred option, at 67 percent, by individuals when they had all of the information available. When these fully informed individuals were combined into groups, 83 percent chose Candidate A.

In an alternative version of the exercise intended to simulate the nature of information in most real-world groups, some of the information about the candidates was shared by all group members and some of it was unshared, including much of the positive information about Candidate A. Thus, before interacting in their groups, individuals had little reason to support Candidate A, since they were missing most of the positive information about Candidate A. In this instance, only 23 percent of the individuals in the unshared condition chose Candidate A. Now consider the decisions made by these individuals with unshared information when they were put into groups. Collectively, the group had access to the same information as the shared groups, but the information was diffused among various members. Interestingly, in this case, only 18 percent of the groups with unshared information chose Candidate A.

Why didn't the groups capture the unshared information and make the same decision as the groups in which all members had all of the information? Stasser and Titus (1985) have shown consistently that groups discuss more shared information than unshared information. This is true despite the fact that groups are brought together for the very purpose of pooling information. An interesting paradox exists: groups are created to share information, yet they end up spending their time discussing shared knowledge. My conclusion from this literature is that groups have bounded awareness regarding their unique or unshared information.

To help groups overcome their bounded awareness, Stasser, Vaughn, and Stewart (2000) propose a number of strategies based on encouraging members to share information, particularly unique information. These strategies include forewarning the group in advance of the unique knowledge of different members and identifying expertise in the group before the discussion begins. The overall goal is to recognize the tendency of groups to have bounded awareness of unshared information and to create structures to overcome this tendency.

In an interesting parallel, Slovic and McPhillamy (1974) and Kivetz and Simonson (2000) looked at how individuals choose among products about which they have information on different attributes. People tend to ignore very positive or very negative information about one product if they lack comparative information on that attribute for the other products. At the same time, when they have information about all products on a certain attribute, they dramatically overweight that attribute. Changing our focus from products to people, some critics of college admissions practices argue that too much weight is placed on SAT scores and grades. The research of Slovic and McPhillamy (1974) and Kivetz and Simonson (2000) suggests that this overweighting is a natural result of having this data available for all applicants—for better and for worse. Thus, both individuals and groups appear to drift toward focusing on shared information, whether that sharing occurs across attributes or across members of a group.

BOUNDED AWARENESS IN NEGOTIATIONS

Chapters 9 and 10 presented a systematic framework for thinking about negotiations and a set of common cognitive errors made by negotiators. Because negotiators often fail to consider the critical ingredients of an effective negotiation analysis, Chapter 9 closed with a list of questions for you to consider when preparing for a negotiation. In this section, I will discuss two types of information that are critical for any effective negotiator: the decisions of others and the rules of the game, both of which are often out of focus for negotiators.

This section explores the five problems from Table 11.1 that I have not previously reviewed. As you probably noticed, Problems 1 and 4 were similar, and Problems 2 and 5 were similar. In fact, Problems 1 and 4 are two variations of what is known as the "multiparty ultimatum game," and Problems 2 and 5 are two variations of the "Monty Hall problem." For each problem, I will provide evidence that minor changes in the decisions of others and the rules of the game can create huge differences in the optimal strategy for a negotiator. Due to bounded awareness, however, most people ignore this information. Problem 3 is the "Acquiring a Company" problem; again, the common failure to optimally answer this question results from the failure to think appropriately about the decisions of others and the rules of the game. I will analyze these three problems and discuss related negotiation problems. Then I will offer behavioral evidence of our boundedness regarding the decisions of others and the rules of the game.

Multiparty Ultimatum Games

Chapter 6 discussed ultimatum games in some detail. As a quick review, suppose that Player 1 divides a known, fixed sum of money any way he chooses by filling out a form stating, "I demand X." Player 2 either accepts the offer and receives her portion of the money as allocated by Player 1 or rejects the offer, leaving both parties with nothing. We saw in Chapter 6 that concerns for fairness lead Player 1s to be more generous and Player 2s to demand more than economic models suggest. In this section, we examine multiple-party ultimatum games, typified by Problems 1 and 4 (Messick, Moore, and

Bazerman, 1997). In the multiparty version of the ultimatum game, six participants are assigned to the roles of A, B, C, D, E, and F. Player A is given $60 dollars to allocate to the six parties. The offers to B, C, D, E, and F must be equal and must be an integer. B, C, D, E, and F each record the minimum amount that they would accept.

Problems 1 and 4 differ only in the decision rule for the game. In Problem 1, also known as the "dividing the pie—largest" condition, if the amount that A offers to B–F is equal to or greater than the largest amount requested by B, C, D, E, or F, then A's allocation is distributed. If it is not, all parties receive $0. By contrast, in problem 4, the "dividing the pie—smallest" condition, if the amount that A offers to B–F is equal to or greater than the smallest amount requested by B, C, D, E, or F, then A's allocation offer is distributed; if it is not, all parties receive $0. Consistent with the two-party ultimatum game, a bimodal response pattern emerges from the demands of players B–F. While many B–F players will take $1, since $1 is better than the $0 they would receive from turning the offer down, another large group of players B–F demand $10—they want their "fair" share. As we know from Chapter 2, individuals underestimate disjunctive events (those that can occur independently) and overestimate conjunctive events (those that must occur in conjunction with one another). In the present context, this implies that player As will underestimate the likelihood of how easy it is to get at least one out of five people to accept $1, but will overestimate the likelihood of all five individuals accepting anything less than $10. But you, the reader, were asked to estimate the profit-maximizing strategies for the two different problems. Let's see how you did.

Messick et al. (1997) had MBA students at Northwestern University's Kellogg Graduate School of Management play this game, and calculated which strategy did best on average across all of the trials of each game. The researchers found that the profit-maximizing strategy for player A would be to divide the money 55-1-1-1-1-1 in Problem 4 and to divide it 10-10-10-10-10-10 in Problem 1. In fact, in Problem 1, any allocation less than 10 invariably led to player A receiving $0. To help you evaluate your own decisions, note that players that offered anything less than 10-10-10-10-10-10 in Problem 1 were bound to get $0 themselves (because the probability of getting even 15-9-9-9-9-9 was amazingly small). In addition, players that offered anything more than $1–2 to the other players in Problem 4 were doing so because they wanted to be "fair" or because they made a bad decision; the expected payoff by player As falls dramatically as they increase their offers to B–F.

To players who do not attend to the nuances of the rules of the game and the likely heterogeneity of the other actors, Problems 1 and 4 would look very similar. Bounded awareness keeps negotiators from failing to differentiate the problems. But those who note the important difference between these two versions of the multiparty ultimatum game are likely to do much better. Negotiators often overgeneralize from one situation to another, even when the generalization is inappropriate. They often assume that what worked in one context will work in another. But the rational negotiator is attuned to the important differences that exist, particularly regarding the rules of the game and the likely decisions of other parties.

The Monty Hall Game

For those too young to have seen him, or for those with limited exposure to American television, Monty Hall was a television game-show host who would regularly ask contestants to pick one of three doors, knowing that one of the doors led to the grand prize and that the other two doors were "zonks" leading to small prizes or gag gifts. Once a contestant picked a door, Monty would often open one of the other two doors to reveal a zonk, then offer the contestant the chance to trade their chosen door for the remaining unchosen and unopened door. A common but false analysis is that with only two doors remaining following the opening of one door by the host, the odds are 50–50. Most contestants on the actual show preferred to stick with the door they originally chose.

Many years after the show, *Let's Make a Deal*, went out of production, statisticians, economists, and journalists (Selvin, 1975; Nalebuff, 1987; vos Savant, 1990a, 1990b, 1991) argued that contestants erred by not switching to the remaining unchosen door. Their logic, assuming that Monty always opened an unchosen door (known as the "Monty always opens" condition) and then offered a switch, is simple: when they first chose their door, the contestants had a one-in-three chance of winning the prize. When Monty opened one door to reveal a zonk, which he could always do, this probability did not change. Thus, there was still a one-in-three chance that the contestant had the winner to start with and a two-in-three chance that the big prize was behind one of the other two doors. With one bad door revealed, the two-in-three chance was now carried by the unopened, unchosen door. The contestant should therefore always have switched doors, to increase the odds of winning from one in three to two in three.

Assuming that Monty always opened an unchosen door that did not contain the grand prize is, of course, a critical element in this analysis. Yet one could make a very different assumption regarding Monty's behavior. Assume a "Mean Monty"—one who knew where the grand prize was located and who wanted to minimize the contestant's chances of winning. So, after the contestant picked a door, "Mean Monty" could either declare the game over or open one door and offer a switch. If Monty wanted to minimize the contestant's chances of winning the grand prize, the contestant should never have accepted an offer from Monty to switch. In fact, since Monty wanted the contestant to lose, the fact that Monty makes the offer indicated that the contestant had already picked the winning door.[2]

Thus, you should always switch doors in the "Monty always opens" condition (Problem 2), but never switch in the "Mean Monty" condition (Problem 5). But if people's awareness of the rules of the game and of Monty's decision processes is bounded, they are likely to fail to differentiate the two problems. Did you distinguish between the two versions of the multiparty ultimatum game and the two versions of the Monty Hall game?

Acquiring a Company

In Problem 3, the "Acquiring a Company" problem, one firm (the acquirer) is considering making an offer to buy out another firm (the target). However, the acquirer is uncertain about the ultimate value of the target firm. It knows only that its value under current management is between $0 and $100, with all values equally likely. Since the firm is expected to be worth 50 percent more under the acquirer's management than under the current ownership, it appears to make sense for a transaction to take place. While the acquirer does not know the actual value of the firm, the target knows its current worth exactly. What price should the acquirer offer for the target?

---

2. In a dynamic game-theoretic equilibrium, the contestant would not know that she won, but should still keep her original choice.

The problem is analytically quite simple, yet intuitively perplexing. Consider the logical process that a rational response would generate in deciding whether to make an offer of $60 per share:

> If I offer $60 per share, the offer will be accepted 60 percent of the time—whenever the firm is worth between $0 and $60 to the target. Since all values between $0 and $60 are equally likely, the firm will, on average, be worth $30 per share to the acquirer, resulting in a loss of $15 per share ($45 to $60). Consequently, a $60 per share offer is unwise.

It is easy to see that similar reasoning applies to any positive offer. On average, the acquirer obtains a company worth 25 percent less than the price it pays when its offer is accepted. If the acquirer offers $X and the target accepts, the current value of the company is worth anywhere between $0 and $X. As the problem is formulated, any value in that range is equally likely, and the expected value of the offer is therefore equal to $X/2. Since the company is worth 50 percent more to the acquirer, the acquirer's expected value is 1.5($X/2) = 0.75($X), only 75 percent of its offer price. Thus, for any value of $X, the best the acquirer can do is not make an offer ($0 per share). The paradox of the situation is that even though in all circumstances the firm is worth more to the acquirer than to the target, any offer above $0 generates a negative expected return to the acquirer. The source of this paradox lies in the high likelihood that the target will accept the acquirer's offer when the firm is least valuable to the acquirer—that is, when it is a "lemon" (Akerlof, 1970).

Imagine that while traveling in a foreign country, you meet a merchant who is selling a very attractive gemstone. Although you have purchased a few gems in your life, you are far from an expert. After some discussion, you make the merchant an offer that you believe, but that you are not certain, is on the low side. He quickly accepts, and the transaction is completed. How do you feel? Following this quick acceptance, most people would feel uneasy about the purchase, sensing that they got a rotten deal. This sensation is known as the "winner's curse." But if you were comfortable with your voluntary offer, why would you suddenly wish it had not been accepted?

Groucho Marx understood the tendency to ignore the decisions of others when he famously declared that he didn't want to belong to any club that would have him as a member. If a club's standards were so low as to accept *him*, he didn't want any part of it! In the bargaining context, the key feature of the "winner's curse" is that one side often has much better information than the other side; the party with the better information is usually the seller. Logically, we can conclude that the knowledgeable gem merchant will accept your offer only when the gem is worth less than your estimate.

Similarly, a structural inefficiency is built into the Acquiring a Company exercise: A rational buyer will bid $0 despite the fact that the buyer values the company at a price higher than the seller's valuation. The problem is that the strategic seller will not provide the buyer with information about the company's true value, especially when the company is of low value. As a result, game theory recommends that buyers not make an offer in order to avoid an expected value loss.

What Do People Actually Do?

Across Problems 1 through 5, people make consistent errors due to the failure to think rationally about the game. Specifically, an overly narrow focus on their own thoughts and actions causes negotiators to ignore the rules of the game and the decisions of the opposing party (Tor and Bazerman, 2003). Tor and Bazerman (2003) have shown that these errors existed and led to failure across three seemingly different tasks—the multiparty ultimatum game, the Monty Hall problem, and the Acquiring a Company problem.

In the multiparty ultimatum game, the best strategy for player A diverges dramatically between the two conditions (offers of $1 versus $10). Yet, in studies, the actual behavior of player As has been much closer across the two conditions. On average, Player As allocated $8.15 to the other players in the "dividing the pie—smallest" condition (Problem 4), while allocating $8.47 to the other players in the "dividing the pie—largest condition" (Problem 1). Many player As in Problem 1 miss an easy opportunity to collect $10, while player As in Problem 4 also pass up a significant profit opportunity.

Turning to the Monty Hall problem, in the version in which Monty always opens a door (Problem 2), Friedman (1998) has found substantial failure among study participants to make the correct decision and only limited learning through repeated trials. That is, most people keep the door originally chosen, giving them a one in three chance of winning, rather than trading for a two-in-three chance. Tor and Bazerman (2003) replicated this result, finding specifically that 41 percent of participants traded doors and 59 percent kept the inferior door. In the Mean Monty version (Problem 5), 79 percent made the right decision to keep the existing door, which is consistent with modal intuition in the other version. Finally, most people made the same decision in both versions of the game; only 24 percent answered both versions correctly.

The most extensive evidence on bounded awareness in negotiation comes from "Acquiring a Company," the problem that has been researched for the longest period of time. Substantial research on this problem suggests that bounded awareness leads decision makers to ignore or simplify the cognitions of opposing parties as well as the rules of the game (Carroll, Bazerman, and Maury, 1988). The first group to respond to this problem was comprised of 123 MBA students from Boston University (Samuelson and Bazerman, 1985). Their results are charted in Figure 11.1, which shows that the dominant response fell between $50 and $75. How did students reach this $50–to–$75 decision? One common, but wrong, explanation is that, "On average, the firm will be worth $50 to the target and $75 to the acquirer; consequently, a transaction in this range will, on average, be profitable to both parties."

In fact, the correct answer to the Acquiring a Company problem is so counterintuitive that only nine of 123 participants correctly offered $0 per share. Replications with accounting firm partners, CEOs, investment bankers, and many other skilled groups have produced similar results. Finally, even participants who were paid according to their performance and given many opportunities to learn through experience exhibited the same pattern of responses depicted in Figure 11.1 (Ball, Bazerman and Carroll, 1991; Grosskopf and Bereby-Meyer, 2005).

Most individuals have the analytical ability to follow the logic that the optimal offer is $0 per share. Yet, without assistance, most individuals make a positive offer. Thus, individuals systematically exclude information from their decision-making processes that they have the ability to include. They fail to recognize that their expected return depends on an acceptance by the other party, which in turn is affected by the rules, which state that they get to know the true value before accepting or rejecting the offer. This implies that the acceptance by the target is most likely to occur when it is least desirable to the negotiator making the offer.

FIGURE 11.1 The Distribution of Price Offers

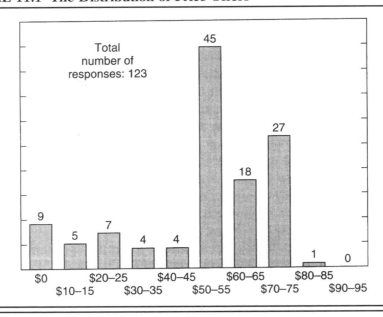

The overwhelming majority of respondents provided solutions that yield a negative expected return. Recently, however, in an adapted version of the Acquiring a Company exercise, Valley, Moag, and Bazerman (1998) found that if the parties talk face-to-face, the common result is a trade at a mutually beneficial value. Thus, social interaction creates a mechanism to overcome the inefficient outcomes predicted by game theory and behavioral decision theory. Valley et al. suggest that communication enhances positive utility for benefits gained by the other party, creates trust, and allows for information exchange not expected by game theoretic models.

These three problems are particularly good examples of instances in which the rules of the game and the decisions of others—two absolutely central and often accessible pieces of information in a negotiation—are out of focus. I believe that these documented focusing failures explain negotiation failures far beyond our five example problems. Ho, Camerer, and Weigelt (1998) examined a game in which each player chooses a number from 0 to 100. The winning number is the one closest to one half of the mean of all of the entries. If the decisions of others and nuances of the rules of the game are out of focus, 50 emerges as a naïve yet common submission. But even the simplest logic should lead people to think that if the average were 50, a better submission would be half the mean, or 25. Of course, this logic requires attention to the rules of the game. Yet when you consider the decisions of other players, it should become clear that others may follow this same logic; therefore, if the mean might be 25, you should submit 12.5. However, if others use this logic, you should submit 6.25, and so on, down to 0—the equilibrium solution. The winning answer is typically greater than 0. Simple numbers such as 50 and 25 are common in this game, and come from not fully focusing on the rules of the game and the thoughts of other players.

Bounded awareness also affects our assessments of competitors. Camerer and Lovallo (1999) show that people are insensitive to the quality of their competition, a phenomenon they label *reference group neglect*. Similarly, Moore and colleagues (Moore and Kim, 2003; Moore and Small, 2004) find that people expect to perform better than average on easy problems, but worse than average on hard problems; they ignore the fact that easy problems are easy for other people as well, and that hard problems are hard for others as well. Moore (2000) also finds bounded awareness in the context of negotiation deadlines. In a negotiation between a buyer and seller in which both parties get zero payoff if no agreement is reached, Moore imposes a publicly known deadline on one of the parties, which intuitively appears to put that party at a disadvantage. Of course, if one party has a deadline, so does the other. Objectively, the deadline affects the two parties symmetrically, but negotiators believed that a deadline put them at an asymmetric disadvantage. In another experiment, Moore imposes time-related costs on one of the two parties. These time-related costs do give the party without time-related costs an advantage. Moore then offers the party with time-related costs the opportunity to impose a firm deadline on the negotiations, thereby eliminating their own asymmetric time-related costs and creating symmetric costs for the failure to reach agreement. Most people pass on this option, despite the strategic benefit it would create. Again, participants fail to think through how the rules of the game would affect the other party, and suboptimize as a result.

Massey and Wu (2001) have examined "system neglect," or the human tendency to undervalue the importance of the general context in which they are making their decision. To me, the most important example of this type of bounded awareness is the widespread failure of U.S. citizens to consider campaign-finance reform as a means of curbing the undue political influence of special-interest groups (Bazerman, Baron, and Shonk, 2001). When people are asked whether they support and care about the issue of campaign-finance reform, they say "yes." Yet, when asked to rank the importance of campaign-finance reform relative to other issues, they rank it very low. Bazerman et al. (2001) argue that voters undervalue campaign-finance reform because their awareness of the indirect impact of campaign finance reform is bounded. Yet, my colleagues and I believe that people should care deeply about such reform, since it affects virtually every other issue (and its effects could be enormous). People do not tend to think through this process. They value issues that are more clearly seen as end states or outcomes (such as tax cuts or education), rather than a using broader awareness that would direct their attention toward a set of outcomes that would have a large, positive effect on many issues (Bazerman et al., 2001).

Finally, bounded awareness can keep negotiators from considering the impact of their decisions on others outside the negotiation. Decision and negotiation scholars often study and teach cooperation in prisoner dilemma games and social dilemmas. A prisoner dilemma game exists when two parties or more would be jointly better off both cooperating with each other than both defecting (betraying each other), yet each party would be better off defecting on the other, regardless of the behavior of the other party. The prisoner dilemma problem has been used a model to understand defection in the nuclear arms race, in the failure of strategic alliance, and in overharvesting and overfishing crises. One of the most common managerial applications of prisoner dilemma games is to price setting. Suppose that two companies that sell the same product would be better off if they both set high prices than if they both set low prices. Because of market share considerations, however, each would be better off charging a low price, regardless of the pricing strategy selected by the other party(s). I agree that both companies clearly would be better off if both charged high prices than if both charged low prices. The interesting aspect of this story is that many negotiation teachers present it as a model example of how managers can create value through cooperation. But, notice that value is created only for the companies involved; the effect of higher prices on consumers remains outside the bounds of the problem. In many situations, parties in a negotiation gain value at the expenses of those out of the bounds of the defined problem.

BOUNDED AWARENESS IN AUCTIONS

Consider the following auctions:

> Your consulting firm is trying to hire a young, highly regarded MBA student from a prestigious university. Many other organizations are also interested in this apparently talented individual. In fact, your firm seems to be competing against these other firms, motivating you to sweeten the deal with a big signing bonus. Finally, the MBA accepts your offer. As she signs on the dotted line, you wonder if her productivity will exceed the high price of hiring her.

> Your company has placed a bid on a firm that has suggested it will gladly be acquired by the highest bidder. The actual value of the target firm is highly uncertain; even the firm itself does not know its real worth. With at least a half-dozen firms pursuing the target, your bid turns out to be the highest. Your offer is accepted and you obtain the acquisition. Should you break out the champagne?

> You just purchased the most beautiful rug you have ever seen in an eBay auction. There were a lot of bids on the rug, showing that you were not alone in recognizing its value. As you anxiously await delivery of the rug, you start to wonder: Did you get a good deal?

In each of these scenarios, a naïve analysis would suggest that you should be glad to have won the competitive situation. However, Bazerman and Samuelson (1983) argue that you may have just become the most recent victim of the "winner's curse" in competitive bidding. In a two-party negotiation between buyer and seller, the winner's curse usually occurs when the buyer fails to consider the perspective of the seller. In auctions, the winner's curse typically results from the winning bidder's failure to consider the implications of bidding higher than his or her competitors—all of whom are at the same information disadvantage relative to the seller.

Bazerman and Samuelson (1983) argue that as the highest bidder, you may have significantly overestimated the actual value of the commodity being sold. Figure 11.2 provides a graphic depiction of what may have occurred. Curve E shows the distribution of bidder estimates for the true value of the commodity, and curve B depicts the distribution of bids. The depiction assumes that (1) the mean of the distribution is equal to the true value of the commodity—that is, no aggregate under- or overestimation is

FIGURE 11.2 Graphic Illustration of the Winner's Curse

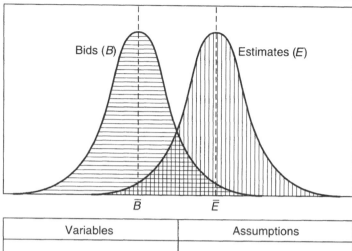

Variables	Assumptions
E = Estimates B = Bid	1. True value $\propto \bar{E}$ 2. True value will be equal for all bidders

SOURCE: M. H. Bazerman and W. F. Samuelson, 1983, "I Won the Auction But Don't Want the Prize." *Journal of Conflict Resolution* 27, pp. 618–634. Copyright © by Sage Publications, Inc. Reprinted by permission of Sage Publications, Inc.

expected; and (2) bidders discount their estimates a fixed amount in making bids, which explains the leftward shift of the estimate distribution. The figure suggests that a winning bid—that is, one from the right tail of the distribution—is likely to exceed the actual value of the commodity. The highest bidder is likely to have been one of the highest estimators, and unless they had reason to believe that they had better information than the other bidders, overpayment is likely. In fact, our research found that the winning bidder in auctions of highly uncertain commodities with a large number of bidders commonly pays more than the commodity is worth.

Why does the winning bidder fall prey to the winner's curse? Because of the information that is excluded from his or her thought processes—in other words, because of bounded awareness. If a particular bidder or bidding group assumes that their bid will win the auction, their assumption should tell them that they are likely to have overestimated the value of the commodity in comparison to other bidders. Based on this reasoning, bidders on highly uncertain commodities who are competing against a large number of other bidders should adjust their estimates of the true value of the commodity downward and lower their bids accordingly. Thus, if they do win, they are less likely to have overbid, or at least not by the same margin. Yet, most people ignore the effects of uncertainty, even falsely viewing the presence of lots of bidders as a signal that they should be confident of the commodity's value and quality.

Corporate takeovers in the 1980s have provided ample evidence that acquiring companies often compete destructively against each other and pay too much for what they get. As many as one-third of all acquisitions proved to be failures, and an additional one-third failed to live up to expectations. In addition, any financial synergy created by mergers usually goes to the target, not the acquirer. On average, any financial benefit achieved by the acquirer goes exclusively to shareholders. Potential acquirers should temper their optimism by recognizing that the winning bidder is likely to acquire a company that is worth far less than the winning bidder's estimate of its value.

As the Internet attracts more and more auction participants each day, the lessons of the winner's curse become more important. The good news is that eBay and other Web-based auction sites have created an excellent means of enabling efficient trades between a seller and a buyer who potentially values a particular item more than the seller. The bad news is that, among these buyers, there will be lots of suckers. Who will they be? They are most likely to be ill-informed buyers in auctions with lots of bidders; these buyers will have failed to consider the auction from the perspective of the seller or the other bidders. So, the next time you place an online bid on a hot commodity, remember to ask what its popularity might tell you about your valuation.

The tendency to ignore the perspective of others also helps to explain the escalation bias described in Chapter 5. Why do bidders enter into the $20-auction exercise? Because they recognize their own potential for profit, but fail to notice that other bidders will be equally optimistic about their chances of success. The central message of this section is obvious: During a negotiation, before you commit to a course of action on behalf of yourself or your organization, consider the decisions of the other party.

DISCUSSION

This chapter, new to this edition of the book, reflects a shift in the field of behavioral decision making. Moving beyond the traditional focus on the mistakes people make when considering available information, new research has begun to demonstrate the ways in which critical information escapes the notice of decision makers.

The concept of bounded awareness overlaps to a degree with the concept of availability (Tversky and Kahneman, 1974) introduced in Chapter 1 and exemplified in Chapter 2. Both concepts confront the fact that important information often remains unavailable to the decision maker. However, the two concepts have different foci. Unlike bounded awareness, availability is a general cognitive heuristic. That is, availability explains the tendency for decision makers to assume that, across contexts, information that is most readily available, such as vivid data, is more common than less available information. In contrast, bounded awareness examines the specific groups of variables that are likely to be in or out of focus in specified domains. We are only beginning to understand what information is bounded in different contexts. However, the evidence in this chapter documents specific findings of bounded awareness in the following contexts:

- **Inattentional blindness:** When people are focusing on one task (such as counting basketball passes), they are likely to be blind to important information that is not associated with the assigned task.

- **Change blindness:** People show a surprising ability to fail to notice changes that occur slowly over time or that occur when the mind is distracted by other tasks.

- **Focalism:** People tend to overfocus on the impact of a particular event and to ignore other events that could affect them just as strongly.

- **Bounded awareness in groups:** Groups tend to focus on shared information and to ignore unique or unshared information

- **Bounded awareness in negotiators:** Negotiators tend to ignore the rules of the game and the decisions of other parties.

- **Bounded awareness in auctions:** Bidders tend to ignore the impact of uncertainty and the number of competing bidders on their decision.

I close this chapter with an acknowledgement that in just a few years it will appear incomplete. More than any other chapter in the book, this one outlines research that is at an early stage in development. I hope that we will soon have a fuller understanding of the types of information that remain outside of the bounds of human awareness in many more contexts, and that we will also have a clearer and broader understanding of the cognitive processes that explain bounded awareness across contexts.

CHAPTER TWELVE

Improving Decision Making

When the first edition of this book was published in the 1980s, most decision researchers were pessimistic about the ability of human beings to improve their decision making. Fischhoff's (1982) classic article showed the amazing robustness of many of the biases described in this book. The good news is that many theories suggesting interventions to improve decision making have emerged in the behavioral decision research literature in recent years, and many of these interventions have been developed and succeeded in the real world.

Perhaps the most well-known story of an effective decision-changing process appears in *Moneyball,* Michael Lewis's (2003) account of how Billy Beane, the general manager of the Oakland Athletics, transformed a baseball team by questioning the intuition of baseball professionals. From 1999, when Beane took over as a general manager of the Oakland Athletics, through 2002, the team achieved a truly amazing record. In the 1999 season, the team ranked eleventh of fourteen in the American League in terms of payroll, yet placed fifth out of fourteen in wins. In both the 2000 and 2001 seasons, the Athletics ranked twelfth in payroll and second in wins in the American League. In 2002, they were twelfth in payroll and first in wins in the league. Over this four-year period, the team had the second-best record in major league baseball with one of the two smallest payrolls. The players earned less than a third of the amount earned by the New York Yankees, yet they won more games than the Yankees.

How did the Athletics achieve this success? The simple answer is that manager Billy Beane, with the help of Paul DePodesta, a recent Harvard economics graduate, realized that the intuition of baseball executives was limited and systematically biased, and that their perceived "wisdom" nonetheless had been incorporated into personnel management in ways that created enormous inefficiencies. For example, Beane found that, on average, players drafted out of high school are much less likely to succeed than are players drafted out of college. High school players were being systematically overvalued, and college players were systemically undervalued. Accordingly, Beane decided to stop drafting players out of high school. Baseball executives also tended to form their judgments by looking at players in snippets (typically by watching them play one game), rather than by looking at the players' overall performance data. Similarly, some players had a dramatically higher tendency than others to be "walked," and walks were inappropriately undervalued by baseball professionals (Thaler and Sunstein, 2003). More broadly, Lewis (2003) argues that baseball executives were consistently guilty of three mistakes. First, they overgeneralized from their personal experiences. Second, they were overly influenced by players' recent performances. Third, they were overly influenced by what they saw, when players' multiyear records provided far better data.

Bill James had been writing about the use of statistics in baseball for decades. James, a quirky self-trained writer-statistician, was a night watchman for a pork-and-beans factory, and spent his spare time writing the early classics of what is emerging as the new wisdom on how to run a baseball team. Even after James developed a following among nerdy baseball fans, the experts who ran baseball teams ignored his evidence in favor of intuition.

Beane and DePodesta were the first baseball insiders to take James's theories seriously. Following his ideas, they ran statistical analyses to determine which measurable data actually predicted runs scored in the major leagues. Beane and DePodesta found that expert intuition in baseball systematically overweighted some variables and underweighted other variables (Thaler and Sunstein, 2003). The results made it clear that, in baseball, statistics have outperformed the experts. After allowing intuition to rule decision making in baseball for over a hundred years, teams are only now replacing their "experts" with nerds who know how to run regression equations. In Lewis's (2003) words, "the market for baseball players was so inefficient, and the general grasp of sound baseball strategy so weak, that superior management could run circles around taller piles of cash." Following Beane's success, many teams tried to hire DePodesta as their general manager, the Boston Red Sox hired James, and other teams have hired some of James's disciples.

The story of the Athletics' success raises some interesting questions. Why did it take so long for rationality to enter into decision making in baseball? To what extent are managers in other industries still relying on false expertise when better strategies exist? As Thaler and Sunstein (2003) note in their insightful review of *Moneyball*, baseball professionals are not stupid, but they are human. Like all of us, they have tended to rely on simple heuristics, traditions, and habits, which in turn created the conventional wisdom that governed baseball for over a century. It takes time, effort, and courage for an organization to move from relying on faulty intuition to carefully assessing data and using appropriate statistical techniques.

Lewis (2003) argues that the mistakes documented in baseball are probably more severe in other industries. After all, the sport of baseball is full of excellent, reliable data. Thaler and Sunstein (2003) compare the tendency of baseball executives to overlook a wealth of statistics to the tendency of personnel managers to base hiring decisions on their "gut" reactions to job interviews rather than on the hard data available on applicants. Executives tend to trust their intuitive reactions to interviews, despite extensive research showing that interviews provide little predictability about future performance. Thaler and Sunstein (2003) argue for personnel selection based on real performance predictors (grades, test scores, past company performance, etc.) rather than on intuition gathered from interviews.

In this chapter, I argue that most organizations have the opportunity to significantly increase the effectiveness of their decision-making processes. I do not argue that executives are lacking in intelligence. Rather, like baseball executives, most professionals make decisions that fall short of objectively rational behavior and do so in specific and systematic ways. The critical question is, what we can do to correct these deficiencies? This concluding chapter examines six concrete and complementary strategies for making better decisions: (1) acquiring experience and expertise, (2) reducing bias in your judgment, (3) analogical reasoning, (4) taking an outsider's view, (5) using linear models, and (6) understanding biases in others.

STRATEGY 1: ACQUIRING EXPERIENCE AND EXPERTISE

Many of the biases examined in this book were identified among student participants who were not rewarded for accurate performance and who were making decisions in task domains unfamiliar to them. Thus, one optimistic possibility is that experts or experienced decision makers facing important real-world decisions might be far less affected by biases than most test subjects. Does this book unfairly distort the prevalence of judgment biases? This is certainly an important question, since experience and expertise might be useful tools for improving decision making.

Some researchers believe that the process of improving judgment will occur naturally as individuals receive feedback about their past decisions. This view is represented by Kagel and Levin (1986, p. 917) in their analysis of the winner's curse in competitive bidding discussed in Chapter 11:

> Given sufficient experience and feedback regarding the outcomes of their decisions, we have no doubt that our experimental participants, as well as most bidders in "real world" settings, would eventually learn to avoid the winner's curse in any particular set of circumstances. The winner's curse is a disequilibrium phenomenon that will correct itself given sufficient time and the right kind of information feedback.

In fact, Kagel and Levin (1986) do show a reduction in the winner's curse in the auction context as the market (but not necessarily specific players) "learns" over time. However, much of this learning can be attributed to the phenomenon in which the most aggressive bidders go broke and drop out of the market. Additional learning occurs by observing the consistent losses being suffered by "winners" in the auction.

Clearly, life experiences help us to improve numerous skills and abandon many bad habits. Unfortunately, our judgmental distortions might not be among them. Tversky and Kahneman (1986) have argued that basic judgmental biases are unlikely to correct themselves over time. Responsive learning requires accurate and immediate feedback, which is rarely available in the real world because

> (i) outcomes are commonly delayed and not easily attributable to a particular action; (ii) variability in the environment degrades the reliability of feedback . . .; (iii) there is often no information about what the outcome would have been if another decision had been taken; and (iv) most important decisions are unique and therefore provide little opportunity for learning (see Einhorn and Hogarth, 1978) . . . any claim that a particular error will be eliminated by experience must be supported by demonstrating that the conditions for effective learning are satisfied. (pp. s274–s275)

Using the "Acquiring a Company" problem described in Chapter 11, Ball, Bazerman, and Carroll (1991) tested the ability of individuals to learn to avoid the winner's curse by incorporating the decisions of others into their decision making. Participants in this experiment played for real money, played in twenty trials, and were given full feedback immediately after each trial based on a random determination of the value of the firm; in addition, they could observe changes in their asset balance (which virtually always went down). Thus, when compared to the limitations cited by Tversky and Kahneman, ideal conditions existed for learning from past mistakes. The only limitation that was not eliminated, namely, the variability of the environment (ii above), is part of the winner's curse phenomenon. Thus, we were able to look at whether or not the ability to consider the cognitions of the other party in a bilateral negotiation problem can be learned in a highly favorable environment.

Remembering that $0 is the correct answer and that $50 to $75 is the answer typically obtained when decision makers ignore the cognitions of others, examine the mean bids across the twenty trials in Figure 12.1. Across the twenty trials, there is no obvious trend indicating that participants learned the correct response. In fact, only five of seventy-two participants from a leading MBA program learned over the course of the trials. Our general conclusion? Individuals are unlikely to overcome the winner's curse simply by experience or feedback.

This evidence paints a very pessimistic picture of the idea that experience will cure the decision biases identified in this book. In fact, Bereby-Meyer and Grosskopf (2002) documented that even hundreds of trials do not lead most study participants to solve the Acquiring a Company problem. This evidence is consistent with the documentation of extensive bias in decision making by actual investors, real estate agents, medical doctors, and numerous other "expert" groups. Neale and Northcraft (1989) proposed that biased decision-making outcomes could be eliminated or ameliorated through the development of expertise. While we often think of experience and expertise as closely related, Neale and Northcraft defined experience simply as repeated feedback. By contrast, they assert that expertise results when individuals develop a

**FIGURE 12.1 Mean Offers Across Twenty Trials
of the "Acquiring a Company" Problem**

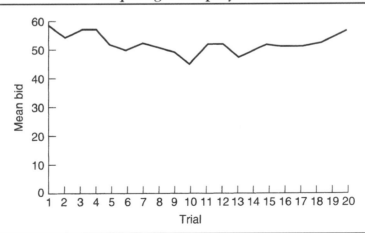

"strategic conceptualization" of what constitutes a rational decision-making process and learn to recognize the biases that limit rationality.

Neale and Northcraft's experience/expertise distinction is highly relevant to the question of whether or not experienced decision makers can benefit from the study of decision making. Northcraft and Neale's (1987) study of anchoring and adjustment among real estate agents suggests that experienced decision makers can be very biased. In addition, while most "effective decision makers" are successful in a specific domain, experience without expertise can be quite dangerous when it is transferred to a different context or when the environment changes. Evidence from Chapter 2 suggests that as the amount of ignorance increases, individuals become more overconfident regarding their fallible judgment.

Stressing the drawbacks of relying on experience for knowledge, Dawes (1988) notes that Benjamin Franklin's famous quote "experience is a dear teacher" is often misinterpreted to mean "experience is the best teacher," when in fact Franklin was using "dear" as a synonym for expensive. After all, the quote continues, "yet fools will learn in no other [school]." Dawes writes,

> Learning from an experience of failure . . . is indeed "dear," and it can even be fatal. . . . moreover, experiences of success may have negative as well as positive results when people mindlessly learn from them . . . . People who are extraordinarily successful—or lucky—in general may conclude from their "experience" that they are invulnerable and consequently court disaster by failing to monitor their behavior and its implications.

This view of experience reiterates the comparative value of gaining a conceptual understanding of how to make a rational decision, rather than simply depending upon the relatively mindless, passive learning obtained via experience. Expertise requires much more than the unclear feedback of uncertain, uncontrollable, and often delayed results; it necessitates constant monitoring and awareness of our decision-making processes.

The final benefit of developing a strategic conceptualization of decision-making concerns transferability. If you were to ask experienced decision makers for the secrets of their success, they will probably insist that their skills have developed over years of observation and experience that cannot be taught. This obviously reduces their ability to pass on their knowledge to others. Thus, experience without expertise limits the ability to transfer knowledge to future generations.

A key element of developing a strategic conceptualization of decision making is learning to avoid the many biases in individual and group contexts that we have discussed in Chapters 1 through 11. However, awareness is just one step in the process. Another strategy, debiasing, is the topic of the next section.

STRATEGY 2: DEBIASING JUDGMENT

Debiasing refers to a procedure for reducing or eliminating biases from the cognitive strategies of the decision maker. Fischhoff (1982) proposed four steps that decision-making teachers or trainers can follow to encourage their students to make wiser judgments: (1) offer warnings about the possibility of bias, (2) describe the direction of the bias, (3) provide a dose of feedback, and finally, (4) offer an extended program of training with feedback, coaching, and whatever else it takes to improve judgment.

Fischhoff also argues that debiasing is an extremely difficult process that must be closely monitored and guided by a psychological framework for change. For example, research on the hindsight bias (Fischhoff, 1977), described in Chapter 2, has shown that even when the bias is explicitly described to participants and they are instructed to avoid it, the bias remains.

In contrast, a recent review by Larrick (2004) paints a rosier picture of our ability to overcome bias through training. Yet Larrick (2004) also notes that most successful debiasing strategies tend to be context- and bias-specific; training and testing must be closely linked and must occur in close time proximity. For example, research on the overconfidence bias has found that intensive, personalized feedback is moderately effective in improving judgment (Lichtenstein and Fischhoff, 1980), but only in the short term. Occasionally, a broader effect of training has been documented. For example, Soll and Klayman (2004) demonstrate that the simple prompt of encouraging people to "consider the opposite" of whatever they are deciding reduces overconfidence, hindsight, and anchoring effects. Larrick (2004) also highlights the partial debiasing success of using groups instead of individuals, training in statistical reasoning, and making people accountable for their decisions (Lerner and Tetlock, 1999).

Based on Lewin's framework outlined in Chapter 1, Fischhoff's debiasing research, Larrick's recent review, and my own judgment-training programs with MBA and executive students, this section makes specific suggestions for debiasing judgment.

Unfreezing

Chapter 1 noted that many behaviors at the individual, group, and organizational levels are ingrained, or part of a standard repertoire, and are therefore quite difficult to change. Factors that inhibit individuals from changing their behavior include satisfaction with the status quo, risk aversion, and a preference for the certain outcomes of known behavior to the uncertain outcomes of innovative behavior. For improved decision making to occur and continue over time, an explicit "unfreezing" process of ingrained thinking and behaviors must take place. For at least three key reasons, unfreezing old strategies is crucial to changing the decision-making processes of individuals.

First, individuals will have typically relied on their current intuitive strategy for many years. To want to change would be to admit that past strategies were flawed, and this realization is likely to be psychologically disturbing. Thus, individuals may be motivated to avoid the disconcerting truth about their judgmental deficiencies.

Second, individuals who have achieved a certain level of professional success (such as students in MBA and executive education programs) are likely to have received positive reinforcement for many of their past decisions. According to the basics of reinforcement theory, individuals tend to continue behaviors that are positively rewarded. For example, because many successful executives rise to the top using intuitive strategies, they tend to resist information indicating that their judgment is systematically deficient in some demonstrable manner.

A third, related point has to do with balance theory (Heider, 1958), which suggests that individuals try to manage their cognitions into a consistent order. For successful managers, the cognition that "there is something fundamentally wrong with my decision-making processes" clashes with their awareness of their success. The cognition

"I am currently an excellent decision maker" is much more harmonious with the notion of success; therefore, according to balance theory, that cognition is more likely to dominate.

Overall, a pattern emerges of an intelligent manager who has multiple reasons for believing in the high quality of his or her decision-making processes and resisting any change in his or her intuitive strategies. Most successful people will be motivated to view their intuition as a talent rather than a handicap. In fact, this book has provided substantial evidence that there is significant room for improvement in the intuitive strategies of even the brightest, most successful managers. Thus, we conclude that improving on intuition is an important activity for successful managers to attempt, but that cognitive resistance to change is a predictable pattern.

This book has sought to create changes in your judgment by exposing you to concrete evidence that leads you to question your current strategies. The quiz-and-feedback format was designed specifically to unfreeze your decision-making processes. Most readers make a substantial number of mistakes on these items and are then ready to learn where they went wrong and how they could have performed better. This format unfreezes the notion that your decision-making processes do not require improvement; as you begin to question your current strategies, you become receptive to alternatives. In other cases (such as the dollar auction), vivid examples were intended to unfreeze your thinking by leading you to identify with individuals who fell victim to judgmental deficiencies.

Change

Once an individual has unfrozen past behaviors, he or she becomes willing to consider alternatives. The next stage consists of making the change itself. However, change is far from guaranteed; internal resistance is likely, causing the individual to continually reassess the desirability of change. There are three critical steps to changing one's decision-making process: (1) clarification of the existence of specific judgmental deficiencies, (2) explanation of the roots of these deficiencies, and (3) reassurance that these deficiencies should not be taken as a threat to the individual's self-esteem.

The first step consists of abstracting from the concrete example that was used for unfreezing to identify the more general bias that exists. In addition, for the bias to have face validity to the individual, an explanation of why the bias exists is necessary; this often consists of clarifying the heuristic or phenomenon that underlies the bias. Finally, this information may be threatening enough to increase the resistance that was partially overcome in the unfreezing stage. Thus, it is critical that the individual understand that virtually everyone is subject to judgment biases and that having them does not imply that one is a poor decision maker, but simply that one is human.

Refreezing

Once the change takes place, it is still easy for the individual to revert back to past practices and bad habits. The old biases still exist and can be easily and even accidentally used. Meanwhile, the new procedures are foreign and must develop into intuitive strategies, a process that takes place with practice over time. As the individual consciously uses new strategies in multiple applications, they will slowly become second nature, taking the place of old patterns. However, frequent application and overviews of past training are necessary if the change is to last.

For refreezing to occur, you must continue to examine your decisions for bias long after you have finished this book. You should schedule routine checkups to evaluate your recent important decisions, those made individually and as a negotiator or group member, while remaining aware of the limits of your judgment.

STRATEGY 3: ANALOGICAL REASONING

One recent direction that has shown tremendous promise for debiasing efforts is the analogical reasoning research of Thompson, Gentner, and Loewenstein (2000; Loewenstein, Thompson, and Gentner, 1999, 2003). These researchers show that people learn far more from cases, simulations, and real-world experiences when they are able to take away an abstract form of the learning message. In the context of learning to negotiate through simulations, much greater debiasing occurred among participants when they took part in two exercises that had the same lesson and were asked how the two simulations were related than when they assessed the same two exercises and were asked to explain the lesson of each one. When people learn from one episode at a time, they too often focus on surface-level characteristics of the situation and assume that the message applies only to the specific context of the decision (such as learning how to buy a house). By contrast, the process of abstracting similar lessons from two episodes (such as learning to overcome the mythical fixed pie of negotiation following a house purchase and a workplace negotiation) creates more generalizable insight.

By assessing performance on a third task, Gentner, Loewenstein, and Thompson (2003) have demonstrated remarkable evidence of debiasing decision-making and negotiation behavior through analogical reasoning. They have replicated this research conclusion across a number of studies, many involving executives and consultants. Thompson et al. claim that making a comparison triggers a focus on the similarities between examples, making their common structure more transparent. Identifying the common structure—the principle shared by both examples—helps the learner form a schema that is less sensitive to the irrelevant surface or context features of the particular examples. Such an abstract principle is more likely to be transferred to new situations with different contexts than a principle that is not abstracted from its original context. These impressive findings on the effectiveness of analogical reasoning open up important new directions for debiasing research, as well as offering important guidance on how to use cases and simulations to maximize generalizable learning.

Building off of Thompson et al.'s analogical reasoning work, Idson, Chugh, Bereby-Meyer, Moran, Grosskopf, and Bazerman (2004) suggest that understanding differences, as well as similarities, across problems may also be a very useful means of transferring knowledge. Idson et al. (2004) show that training based on differences can reduce bias in the Acquiring a Company problem, which, as discussed earlier, had proven resistant to many other debiasing techniques. Using the five problems from Tor and Bazerman (2004, see Chapter 11), Idson et al. (2004) had study participants either (1) examine the two versions of the Monty Hall problem and the two versions of the Dividing a Pie problem as four separate problems, or (2) presented the problems in pairs. All participants were then given multiple trials to solve the Acquiring a Company problem, with pay based on performance. They also gave the same Acquiring a Company problem to other study participants who were not trained on the Monty Hall problem and the Dividing a Pie problem. Idson et al. (2004) found that allowing study participants to view the Monty Hall and Dividing a Pie problems in pairs helped them understand the differences between the two versions of each problem and generalized the importance of focusing on the decisions of other parties and the rules of the game. These lessons, the keys to solving the Acquiring a Company problem, indeed enabled participants to perform with dramatic effectiveness in the Acquiring a Company problem. This research offers evidence that examining differences between seemingly related problems may be a successful direction for improving decision making.

What is the optimal level of abstraction that should occur to help people form analogies across problems? Moran, Bereby-Meyer, and Bazerman (2005) argue that teaching people more *general* negotiation principles (such as, "Value can be created," or, "It is important to understand how parties' interests interrelate") enables successful transfer to a broader range of new negotiation tasks than the focused analogies of Loewenstein et al. (2003). Moran et al. (2005) argue that learning general principles will improve not only the ability to positively transfer specifically learned principles, but also the ability to discriminate their appropriateness—i.e., to determine when a principle should and should not be applied.

Moran et al. (2005) found that learners who previously received analogical training for one specific negotiation strategy (namely, logrolling issues to create value) did not perform well when confronted with a diverse face-to-face negotiation with a very different structure. Thus, logrolling may have limited generalizability to other value-creating processes. To test this idea, Moran et al. adapted Thompson et al.'s analogical reasoning training to teach negotiators broad thought processes for creating value in negotiations. Moran et al. (2005) compared *specific training,* wherein learners compare two cases that illustrate the same specific strategy instances (e.g., logrolling), with *diverse training,* wherein they compare two cases that illustrate different value-creating strategies (e.g., one illustrates logrolling and the other compatibility). Training effectiveness was assessed by looking at performance and outcomes in a negotiation simulation that contains potential for using various value-creating strategies, some of which were previously learned and others which were not.

Moran et al. (2005) found that more diverse analogical training, wherein negotiators learn and compare several different value-creating strategies, fostered greater learning of underlying value-creating negotiation principles than more specific analogical training. This method facilitated transfer to a very distinctive task and improved performance on a variety of value-creating strategies, including some that participants had never previously encountered. The improved performance was also accompanied by a deeper understanding of the potential to create value. Thus, more diverse analogical training can be effective for attaining a higher level of expertise, which enables an understanding of which particular strategies might be effective in different situations and why. At the same time, when training becomes too diverse, the applicability of the message may be lost. The optimal level of abstraction remains an interesting question for future research, as does the question of how analogical reasoning can be applied to improve individual decision making.

STRATEGY 4: TAKING AN OUTSIDER'S VIEW

In Chapter 2, I asked you to estimate ten obscure quantities and to place 98 percent confidence intervals around your estimates. As reported, most people answer only three to seven of the ten items correctly, despite being 98 percent confident of their intervals. This study bolsters the widespread finding that people are overconfident in their decisions. Interestingly, after people make these ten assessments and are asked to estimate the number of questions for which the correct answer will be within their confidence interval, these more global estimates are fairly accurate (Gigerenzer, Hoffrage, and Kleinbolting, 1991; Kahneman and Lovallo, 1993). That is, participants generally understand that only three to seven of their 98 percent confidence intervals will actually contain the true estimate!

Kahneman and Lovallo (1993) explain this apparent contradiction by theorizing that we all have two perspectives on decision making: an *insider* view and an *outsider* view. The insider is the biased decision maker who looks at each situation as unique. The outsider, on the other hand, is more capable of generalizing across situations and identifying similarities. Because these two viewpoints exist simultaneously, a member of a consulting team might be well aware that most projects take longer to complete than initial estimates (outsider view), while also believing that her own estimate of an upcoming project's duration is somehow accurate and unbiased (insider view). Similarly, people who undertake a new home construction or major home renovation know from their friends that such projects typically end up being 20–50 percent over budget and overdue (outsider view). Nevertheless, most people who initiate such a building project believe that theirs will be different—that their home will be completed on time and near the projected costs (insider view).

Kahneman identified a classic situation of insider optimism within a group of colleagues he was working with to define a new curriculum (Kahneman and Lovallo, 1993). The group estimated that the book project would take eighteen to thirty months to complete. Kahneman asked a member of the team, who was a distinguished expert in curriculum design, "We are surely not the only team to have tried to develop a curriculum where none existed before. Please try to recall as many cases as you can. Think of them as they were in a stage comparable to ours at present. How long did it take them, from that point, to complete their project?" The team member answered that 40 percent of the projects were never completed, and none were completed in less than seven years. He also mentioned that he thought their book was "below average, but not by much" in comparison to the other projects he had worked on. As it turned out, the team took *eight years* to finish its book. This pattern resonates well with writers. Most of us understand that books take a long time to write; nonetheless, we are optimistic about meeting our own unrealistic deadlines when we sit down to write the first chapter. We may never complete the book, but we will probably believe that the next project will be different. Similarly, Cooper, Woo, and Dunkelberg (1988) found that over 80 percent of entrepreneurs perceived their chances of success to be 70 percent or better, and one-third of them described their success as certain. In contrast, they estimated the mean success rates of businesses similar to their business to be 59 percent. Meanwhile, the five-year survival rate for new businesses is only about 33 percent (Kahneman and Lovallo, 1993).

Kahneman and Lovallo provide convincing evidence that the outsider makes better estimates and decisions than the insider. The outsider view incorporates more relevant data from previous decisions—yet we tend to believe and act on the insider view. Why? Certainly, optimism and overconfidence are factors. In addition, Kahneman and Lovallo also document the human tendency to consider all of a decision's various details into our judgment process and, as a consequence, to view each decision as unique. This focus on the here-and-now leads us to overlook historic data and to let our biases run wild. As a result, we follow the insider view, despite the readily available insights of the outsider view.

The insider-outsider distinction suggests another strategy to reduce bias: When making an important decision, invite an outsider to share his or her insight. This may mean conferring with a trusted friend or colleague who has experience with similar decisions. Interestingly, when a friend is building a house, we often expect that construction will cost more and take longer than expected. Our friend is the only one who doesn't know this! So, for decisions that really matter, ask friends you trust for their estimate of what will happen, and understand that their outsider perspective may be more accurate than your biased insider view. Alternatively, ask yourself what your outsider self thinks of the situation. To assess this, imagine that the decision was a friend's, and ask yourself what advice would you give them. The key is to figure out how to give the outsider a stronger voice in the decision-making process.

STRATEGY 5: USING LINEAR MODELS AND OTHER STATISTICAL TECHNIQUES

The four judgment-improvement strategies I have just described respond directly to the biases discussed in this book. Debiasing is the book's central strategy for improving your decisions. However, for a number of reasons, we should examine alternative approaches. First, because we are human, we will never be entirely debiased. Second, even if we could always make the "rational" choice, the amount of time that it would take to perfect our decisions might not be worth the effort. In addition, we are often faced with the problem of creating a decision-making environment under which others, who may not be debiased, will be making decisions. Certain strategies respond to the limitations of human judgment in specific contexts by creating alternative mechanisms for debiasing intuition.

One alternative mechanism for debiasing consists of using the knowledge of an expert to build linear models that will analyze and judge future decisions. Can a computer model adequately replace human judgment? Many experts are not optimistic or even friendly to this possibility. When I asked a well-known arbitrator to make a number of decisions as part of a study on arbitrator decision-making processes, he responded:

> You are on an illusory quest! Other arbitrators may respond to your questionnaire; but in the end you will have nothing but trumpery and a collation of responses which will leave you still asking how arbitrators decide cases. Telling you how I would decide in the scenarios provided would really tell you nothing of any value in respect of what moves arbitrators to decide as they do. As well ask a youth why he is infatuated with that particular girl when her sterling virtues are not that apparent. As well ask my grandmother how and why she picked a particular "mushmelon" from a stall of

"mushmelons." Judgment, taste, experience, and a lot of other things too numerous to mention are factors in the decisions. (Bazerman, 1985, p. 563)

In contrast with this arbitrator's denial of the value of computer models, research in this area actually shows dramatic success. In repeatable decision-making situations, experts *can* be replaced by models based on their judgments, and these models can make better predictions than the experts! This section examines a strategy that is capable of capturing the arbitrator's decision-making model (or his grandmother's choice of mushmelon).

The statistical technique that is typically used is regression analysis. (Our purpose is not to examine the technical properties of such procedures, but to describe the essence of using a linear model to capture an expert's decision-making processes. Slovic and Lichtenstein, 1971, review the technical use of regression analysis to capture decision processes.) This approach necessitates that an expert make decisions based on a large number of cases, each of which is defined by the same set of factors. A regression equation that describes the expert's idiosyncratic model for making decisions is then developed.

One compelling example of the success of linear models is provided by Dawes's (1971) work on graduate-school admissions decisions. Dawes modeled the average judgment of a four-person committee, using three predictors: (1) Graduate Record Examination scores, (2) undergraduate grade point average, and (3) the quality of the undergraduate school. Dawes used the model to predict the average rating of 384 applicants. He found that the model could be used to reject 55 percent of the applicant pool without ever rejecting an applicant that the selection committee had in fact accepted. In addition, the three predictors of the committee's behavior were better than the committee itself in predicting future ratings of the accepted and matriculated applicants by faculty! In 1971, Dawes estimated that the use of a linear model as a screening device by the nation's graduate schools (not to mention the larger domains of undergraduate admissions, corporate recruiting, and so on) could result in an annual savings of about $18 million in professional time. Adjusted for today's dollars and the current number of graduate-school applications, that number would easily exceed $500 million.

Researchers have found that linear policy-capturing models produce superior predictions across an impressive array of domains. In addition, research has found that more complex models produce only marginal improvements above a simple linear framework. Why do linear models work so well? Dawes (1979) argues that the underlying reason is that people are much better at selecting and coding information (such as what variables to put in the model) than they are at integrating the information (using the data to make a prediction). Einhorn (1972) illustrates this point in a study of physicians who coded biopsies of patients with Hodgkin's disease and then made an overall rating of severity. The individual ratings had no predictive power of the survival time of the patients, all of whom died of the disease. The variables that the physicians selected to code did, however, predict survival time when optimal weights were determined with a multiple regression model. The point is that the doctors knew what information to consider, but they did not know how to integrate this information consistently into valid predictions.

In addition to having difficulty integrating information, we are also unreliable. Given the same data, we will not always make the same decision. Our judgment is affected by mood, subjective interpretations, environment, deadlines, random fluctuations, and many others nonstable characteristics. In contrast, a linear model will always make the same decisions with the same inputs. Thus, the model captures the underlying policy that the expert uses while avoiding the expert's random error. Furthermore, the expert is likely to be affected by certain biases triggered by specific cases. In contrast, the model includes only the actual data that are empirically known to have predictive power, not the salience or representativeness of that or any other available data.

This point was brought home to me by the case of a graduate student, whom I will call Mark Sonet, enrolled in the department of one of my early faculty positions. Sonet was extremely bright, and his acceptance to the department was based on excellent standardized test scores, good grades, and his experience in a number of graduate programs (from which he had not graduated). In our department, Sonet was viewed as a disappointment, never seeming to make much progress toward completing his doctorate and failing to live up to his initial promise. While looking over some recent admissions decisions, I noticed an applicant who had excellent grades, strong test scores, and previous experience in graduate school. The applicant seemed to have identified his real interests, and yet my department had rejected him. It seemed apparent to me that the applicant was well above the standards of the department and would have been easily accepted by a Dawes-type admissions procedure. When I asked the decision committee why the applicant had been rejected, I was told that he reminded them too much of Mark Sonet!

Similar examples of arbitrary bias are common in financial decisions, corporate personnel decisions, bank loan decisions, and routine purchasing decisions. The common aspect of these domains is that each requires the decision maker to make multiple routine decisions based on the same set of variables. These characteristics lend themselves well to the linear policy-capturing methodology, and ample evidence suggests that the linear models of experts will outperform the experts themselves. In addition, such models allow the organization to identify the factors that are important in the decisions of its experts. Thus, independent of their superior predictive powers, the feedback and training opportunities provided by linear models make them a valuable managerial tool.

While evidence amply supports the power of policy capturing, such models have not been widely used. Why not? Resistance to them is strong. Early in the development of the methodology, some scientists criticized their predictive ability on technical grounds (Dawes, 1979). These arguments have generally been addressed, and the literature continues to provide compelling arguments in favor of the models. Others have raised ethical concerns, such as this one described by Dawes:

> When I was at the Los Angeles Renaissance Fair last summer, I overheard a young woman complain that it was "horribly unfair" that she had been rejected by the Psychology Department at the University of California, Santa Barbara, on the basis of mere numbers, without even an interview. "How could they possibly tell what I'm like?" The answer is they can't. Nor could they with an interview. (1979, p. 580)

Dawes argues that decision makers demonstrate unethical conceit in believing that a half-hour interview leads to better predictions than the information contained in a transcript covering three-and-a-half years of work and the carefully devised aptitude assessment of graduate board exams.

The other main argument against the use of linear models is that they have not been used in the past. Change is threatening. What will bank loan officers or college admissions officers do when computers make the decisions? Such concerns are common and express the fear that people are not central to the use of linear models. In fact, people play a crucial role in models. People make the initial decisions that are the ingredients of the model, and people determine the variables to put into the model. People also monitor the model's performance and determine when it needs to be updated. Nevertheless, resistance to change is natural, and resistance to the use of linear decision models is clearly no exception. Overcoming a bias against expert-based, computer-formulated judgments is yet another step you can take toward improving your decision-making abilities.

Rather than simply offering a narrow endorsement of linear models, the goal of this section has been to emphasize the potential of statistical techniques in general as decision-making tools. In addition, this section highlights the common resistance to replacing intuition with empirically validated statistical techniques. The chapter's opening story about Billy Beane offered a very different example in which human judgment was successfully replaced by statistics; many more opportunities exist across applied domains.

STRATEGY 6: UNDERSTANDING BIASES IN OTHERS

The nature of managerial life requires that one work closely with the decisions of others, reviewing recommendations, transforming recommendations into decisions, and adjusting decisions made by others in the past. The task of evaluating the decisions of others is fundamentally different from the task of auditing one's own decisions. Nonetheless, from reading this book, you have learned that everyone's decisions are influenced to some degree by a shared set of biases. How can you systematically detect bias in your own decisions and those of others? Consider the following managerial situation:

> You are the director of marketing for a retail chain that has forty stores in fourteen cities. Annual sales in these stores average between $2 million and $4 million with mean sales of $3 million. Twenty-five of the stores have opened in the last three years, and the company plans to open thirty new stores in the next four years. Because of this growth, you have hired a site location analyst to predict the sales in each potential site. Unfortunately, predicting sales in new markets is very difficult, and even the best analyst faces a great deal of uncertainty. As the marketing director, you are evaluated in part by the accuracy of the forecasts coming out of your department. The site location analyst has just given you her latest forecast, $3.8 million in annual sales for a potential site. Demographic data backs up the analyst's claim that this area should make the store one of the top producers in the chain. What is your reaction to the forecast?

At a naïve level, there is reason to have confidence in the analyst's forecast. After all, she knows more than you about the details of the data that underlie the prediction. In addition, your overview of the area also predicts that the store will do well in comparison to existing stores; this evaluation is based on matching the representativeness of this site to other existing sites. The prediction begins to lose force, however, when we consider the prediction in light of a basic but counterintuitive statistical concept: regression to the mean. In Chapter 2, we saw that the extremeness of our predictions should be moderated toward the mean by the degree of uncertainty in the prediction (Kahneman and Tversky, 1982).

With this rule in mind, let's imagine that the site location analyst was known for her extreme accuracy. In fact, there was a perfect (1.0) correlation between her predictions and actual sales. If this were true, it would be appropriate to rely on the $3.8 million prediction. Now let's consider the case in which there is a correlation of zero between the analyst's predictions (based on demographic data) and actual sales. If this is true, her forecast is meaningless, and the only pertinent information is that the average store has sales of $3 million. Therefore, this figure becomes your best estimate. It is most likely, in fact, that the analyst has achieved neither total success nor total failure, but an intermediate level of predictability over the course of her career. The forecast should then fall between sales of the mean store and the analyst's estimate, becoming progressively closer to the analyst's estimate as her ability to predict sales increases (Kahneman and Tversky, 1982). This analysis suggests that, as the director, you will want to reduce the forecast to somewhere between $3 million and $3.8 million, depending on your assessment of the correlation between the analyst's forecasts and actual sales. In essence, the understanding of human judgment taught by this book should help you to systematically adjust the analyst's initial decision.

The preceding analysis offers a rough guide to adjusting the decisions of others. Kahneman and Tversky (1982) have formalized this process into a five-step procedure whose steps are outlined here, using the site location problem as an example. In reviewing each step, you should think about how you might convert this systematic training into an intuitive, natural response. This will allow you, as a manager, to recognize the existence and direction of a wide range of biases across a wide range of decisions and make adjustments accordingly.

1. **Select a comparison group.** This first step consists of selecting the set of past observations to which the current decision or forecast is to be compared. In the site location problem, comparing the new store to the population of all company stores is an obvious group. However, other comparison groups often exist. For example, you might decide that only stores that have opened in the last three years are appropriate for comparison, particularly if recent stores are closer in description to the future store than established stores. A more inclusive group allows for a larger base for comparison, but its heterogeneity may reduce its comparability to the targeted forecast.

2. **Assess the distribution of the comparison group.** The next step involves assessing the characteristics of the past observations to which the current decision is being compared. If the comparison group consists of all stores, we know the range and mean from the data presented. If we limit the group to recent stores, these data would need to be recalculated. In addition, we might want to get additional data about the shape of the distribution around the mean.

3. **Incorporate intuitive estimation.** This step calls for identification of the decision or forecast of the expert. In this case, the site location analyst's

assessment, $3.8 million, is the intuitive estimate that needs to be adjusted. The next two steps attempt to improve this forecast.

4.   **Assess the predicted results of the decision.** This is the most difficult step in the corrective procedure, as it requires us to determine the correlation between the decision or forecast and the comparison group data. It may be possible to assess this correlation by comparing past estimates to actual sales. In the absence of these data, you must determine some subjective procedure for this assessment. Kahneman and Tversky (1982) discuss this process in more detail. For our purposes, the key point is that the analyst's estimate assumes a correlation of 1.0 between her prediction and actual sales. In virtually all cases, we must adjust away from this biased estimate.

5.   **Adjust the intuitive estimate.** In this step we must calculate the adjustment that reduces the bias error of the initial decision or forecast. For example, this procedure should produce an estimate of $3.8 million when the correlation in Step 4 is 1.0, an estimate of $3 million when the correlation is zero, and estimates proportionally in between when the correlation falls between zero and one. This adjustment can be formalized as follows:

adjusted estimate = group mean + correlation (initial estimate – group mean)

In our example, it is easy to see that this leads to a prediction of $3.4 million when the correlation is 0.5, $3.6 million when the correlation is 0.75, and so on. The person making the adjustment should fully understand the logic of the procedure and evaluate its relevance to the decision at hand. When arguing for this adjustment, you must recognize that you are likely to face resistance to change.

These five steps provide a clearly delineated process for debiasing an individual's intuition by adjusting for the regression-to-the-mean bias. The formal procedure will typically improve the forecast. More important, a manager who understands the process will become capable of intuitively assessing the degree to which an initial estimate should be regressed to the mean.

We now have a model for adjusting a wide range of biased decisions in both individual and multiparty contexts. Broadly, it involves three phases. First, we need to accurately perceive and analyze the context within which the decision is being made. Next, we need to distinguish the potential bias(es) surrounding the decision and the decision makers. Finally, we need to identify and make the appropriate logical adjustments for that decision. This judgment-improvement technique can be used to evaluate and adjust our own, as well as others', intuitive judgments in a variety of situations.

This section shows that we can use an understanding of biases to understand systematic error in the decisions of others. Adjusting for regression to the mean is simply one example of how such a technique can be systematized. When I consult with organizations, I find that my knowledge of the various biases documented in this book allows me to identify biases across a variety of problem types.

You can also use your new knowledge of the biases of others to identify optimal moves in a competitive environment. Richard Thaler, whose ideas I have cited often in this book, teamed up with Russell Fuller to create the Fuller-Thaler mutual funds (www.fullerthaler.com). These funds buy securities by taking advantage of the predictable biases of key market participants. Fuller and Thaler argue that these biases result in mispricing of securities. For example, they argue that most analysts underreact to new, positive information about firms. By identifying how decision biases create under- and overvalued firms, Fuller and Thaler have created funds that significantly outperform the market.

CONCLUSION

In this final chapter, I have introduced six strategies for correcting the deficiencies in our decision making. The first three strategies seek to create broad change in our intuitive responses to decision-making situations. In general, they strive to heighten our awareness of our cognitive limitations and our susceptibility to bias. The last three strategies provide techniques for improving specific decisions in specific contexts. They offer concrete methods for testing and adjusting actual decisions. Together, these six strategies provide tools for changing and "refreezing" your intuitive decision-making processes in the future.

An optimistic, but naïve, view of this book is that its readers are now immediately capable of improving their decision making. Why naïve? Because it is premature to expect readers to have fully integrated the process of changing their judgment for the better. If unfreezing did not take place, then the book failed. If you were not provided with sufficient information for change, the book again failed. However, the responsibility for refreezing new processes and using the decision-improvement strategies suggested in this last chapter lies with you. Refreezing requires a period in which you constantly review your decision-making processes for the errors identified in this book. Refreezing also requires that you be vigilant in your search for biases in the more complex world of decisions that you face. Creating lasting internal improvement in decision making is a complex task that occurs gradually over time through persistent monitoring. It is far easier to identify a bias while you are reading a book about decision making than when you are in the midst of an organizational crisis. Raiffa (1984) has found that his students are likely to use appropriate decision-making strategies in an exam when he is the teacher, but fail to generalize the relevance of these strategies to similar problems in courses taught by other instructors. Thus, making adjustments to your decision-making processes requires constant attention.

In addition to improving your own decisions, the ideas in this book should be very useful for informing you about the decisions of others. We are often faced with situations in which we are suspicious of another party's decision making, but we lack the vocabulary to articulate the flaws in their logic. This book offers systematic clues for understanding and explaining the biases of others. You can practice spotting others' biases while reading the newspaper or watching a sporting event on television. Reporters, sportscasters, politicians, and other information providers and public servants constantly make statements that exemplify the biased decision-making processes outlined in this book.

I hope that this book has broken some of your assumptions about decision making. I also hope that this book has raised your awareness of the importance of the decision-making process itself, rather than just the results of this process. I am disturbed by the fact that most managers reward results rather than good decisions. As we have seen, many decisions are made under conditions of uncertainty or for the wrong reasons. Thus, many good decisions turn out badly, and many bad decisions turn out well. To the extent that a manager rewards results, and not sound decision making, the manager is likely to be rewarding behaviors that may not work in the future.

Davis (1971) argues that "interesting" writing leads readers to question issues that they never thought about before. Thus, identifying new issues may be more important than providing new answers to old questions. In this sense, I hope this book has succeeded at being "interesting" by making you aware of aspects of your decision-making process that inspire new questions and problems.

References

Ainslie, G. (1975). Specious reward: A behavioral theory of impulsiveness and impulse control. *Psychological Bulletin* 82, 463–509.

Akerlof, G. (1970). The market for lemons. *Quarterly Journal of Economics* 89, 488–500.

Akerlof, G. A., and Yellen, J. L. (1990). The fair wage-effort hypothesis and unemployment. *Quarterly Journal of Economics* 105, 255–283.

Allison, S. T., Messick, D. M., and Goethals, G. R. (1989). On being better but not smarter than others: The Mohammed Ali effect. *Social Cognition* 7, 275–296.

Alloy, L. B., and Abramson, L. Y. (1979). Judgment of contingency in depressed and nondepressed students: Sadder but wiser? *Journal of Experimental Psychology: General* 108(4), 441–485.

Alpert, M., and Raiffa, H. (1969). A progress report on the training of probability assessors. Later published in D. Kahneman, P. Slovic, and A. Tversky (Eds.), *Judgment under uncertainty: Heuristics and biases.* Cambridge: Cambridge University Press, 1982.

Angelone, B. L., Levin, D. T., and Simons, D. J. (2003). The relationship between change detection and recognition of centrally attended objects in motion pictures. *Perception* 32(8), 947–962.

Asendorpf, J. B., Banse, R., and Muecke, D. (2002). Double dissociation between implicit and explicit personality self-concept: The case of shy behavior. *Journal of Personality & Social Psychology* 83(2), 380–393.

Babcock, L., and Loewenstein, G. (1997). Explaining bargaining impasse: The role of self-serving biases. *Journal of Economic Perspectives* 11(1), 109–126.

Babcock, L., Loewenstein, G., Issacharoff, S., and Camerer, C. (1995). Biased judgments of fairness in bargaining. *American Economic Review* 85(5), 1337–1343.

Badaracco, Joseph L., Jr., and A. P. Webb. (1995). Business ethics: The view from the trenches. *California Management Review* (winter).

Ball, S. B., Bazerman, M. H., and Carroll, J. S. (1991). An evaluation of learning in the bilateral winner's curse. *Organizational Behavior and Human Decision Processes* 48, 1–22.

Banaji, M. R. (2001). Ordinary prejudice. *Psychological Science Agenda, American Psychological Association* 14(Jan–Feb), 8–11.

Banaji, M. R. (2004). The opposite of a great truth is also true: Homage of Koan #7. In J. T. Jost and M. R. Banaji (Eds.), *Perspectivism in social psychology: The yin and yang of scientific progress.* Washington, DC: American Psychological Association.

Banaji, M. R., Bazerman, M. H., and Chugh, D. (2003). How (un)ethical are you? *Harvard Business Review.*

Banaji, M. R., and Bhaskar, R. (2000). Implicit stereotypes and memory: The bounded rationality of social beliefs. In D. L. Schacter and E. Scarry (Eds.), *Memory, brain, and belief.* Cambridge, MA: Harvard University Press.

Barber, B. M., and Odean, T. (2000a). Trading is hazardous to your wealth: The common stock investment performance of individual investors. *Journal of Finance* 55, 773–806.

Barber, B. M., and Odean, T. (2000b). Too many cooks spoil the profits: The performance of investment clubs. *Financial Analysts Journal,* January/February 2000, 17–25.

Barber, B. M., and Odean, T. (2001). Boys will be boys: Gender, overconfidence, and common stock investment. *Quarterly Journal of Economics* 116(1), 261–292.

Barber, B. M., and Odean, T. (2002). Online investors: Do the slow die first? *Review of Financial Studies* 15(2), 455–487.

Barber, B. M., Odean, T., and Zheng, L. (2000). Are mutual fund investors rational? Working paper.

Bar-Hillel, M. (1973). On the subjective probability of compound events. *Organizational Behavior and Human Performance* 9, 396–406.

Baron, J., and Ritov, I. (1993). Intuitions about penalties and compensation in the context of tort law. *Journal of Risk and Uncertainty* 7, 17–33.

Bazerman, M. H. (1985). Norms of distributive justice in interest arbitration. *Industrial and Labor Relations Review* 38, 558–570.

Bazerman, M. H. (1999). *Smart money decisions.* New York: Wiley.

Bazerman, M. H. (2004). What's really relevant? The role of vivid data in negotiation. *Negotiation* 7(5), 9–11.

Bazerman, M. H., Baron, J., and Shonk, K. (2001). *"You can't enlarge the pie": Six barriers to effective government.* New York: Basic Books.

Bazerman, M. H., and Brett, J. M. (1991). *El-Tek Simulation.* Dispute Resolution Research Center, Northwestern University.

Bazerman, M. H., and Chugh, D. (2005). Focusing in negotiation. In L. Thompson (Ed.), *Frontiers of Social Psychology: Negotiations.* London: Psychology Press.

Bazerman, M. H., Curhan, J. R., and Moore, D. A. (2000). The death and rebirth of the social psychology of negotiation. In M. Clark and G. Fletcher (Eds.), *Blackwell Handbook of Social Psychology.* Cambridge, MA: Blackwell.

Bazerman, M. H., Curhan, J. R., Moore, D. A., and Valley, K. L. (2000). Negotiation. *Annual Review of Psychology* 51, 279–314.

Bazerman, M. H., and Gillespie, J. J. (1999). Betting on the future: The virtues of contingent contracts. *Harvard Business Review.*

Bazerman, M. H., Giuliano, T., and Appelman, A. (1984). Escalation in individual and group decision making. *Organizational Behavior and Human Performance* 33, 141–152.

Bazerman, M. H., Loewenstein, G., and Moore, D. (2002). Why good accountants do bad audits. *Harvard Business Review,* November.

Bazerman, M. H., Loewenstein, G. F., and White, S. B. (1992). Psychological determinants of utility in competitive contexts: The impact of elicitation procedure. *Administrative Science Quarterly* 37, 220–240.

Bazerman, M. H., Magliozzi, T., and Neale, M. A. (1985). The acquisition of an integrative response in a competitive market. *Organizational Behavior and Human Performance* 34, 294–313.

Bazerman, M. H., Moore, D., Tenbrunsel, A. E., Wade-Benzoni, K. A., and Blount, S. (1999). Explaining how preferences change across joint versus separate evaluation. *Journal of Economic Behavior and Organization* 39, 41–58.

Bazerman, M. H., Morgan, K. P., and Loewenstein, G. F. (1997). The impossibility of auditor independence. *Sloan Management Review,* Summer, 89–94.

Bazerman, M. H., and Neale, M. A. (1982). Improving negotiation effectiveness under final offer arbitration: The role of selection and training. *Journal of Applied Psychology* 67, 543–548.

Bazerman, M. H., and Neale, M. A. (1992). *Negotiating rationally.* New York: Free Press.

Bazerman, M. H., Russ, L. E., and Yakura, E. (1987). Post-settlement settlements in dyadic negotiations: The need for renegotiation in complex environments. *Negotiation Journal* 3, 283–297.

Bazerman, M. H., and Samuelson, W. F. (1983). I won the auction but don't want the prize. *Journal of Conflict Resolution* 27, 618–634.

Bazerman, M. H., Schroth, H., Pradhan, P., Diekmann, K., and Tenbrunsel, A. (1994). The inconsistent role of comparison of others and procedural justice in reactions to hypothetical job descriptions: Implications for job acceptance decisions. *Organizational Behavior and Human Decision Processes* 60(3), 326–352.

Bazerman, M. H., Tenbrunsel, A. E., and Wade-Benzoni, K. (1998). Negotiating with yourself and losing: Understanding and managing conflicting internal preferences. *Academy of Management Review* 23, 225–241.

Bazerman, M. H., Wade-Benzoni, K. A., and Benzoni, F. (1996). A behavioral decision theory perspective to environmental decision making. In D. M. Messick and A. Tenbrunsel (Eds.), *Ethical Issues in Managerial Decision Making,* New-York: Russell Sage.

Bazerman, M. H., and Watkins, M. (2004). *Predictable surprises.* Cambridge, MA: Harvard Business School Press.

Belsky, G., and Gilovich, T. (1999). *Why smart people make big money mistakes.* New York: Simon and Schuster.

Benartzi, S., and Thaler, R. (1999). Naïve diversification strategies in retirement savings plans. Working paper, UCLA.

Benartzi, S. and Thaler, R., (2004), Save more tomorrow: using behavioral economics to increase employee savings. *Journal of Political Economy,* 112(1), 164–187.

Bereby-Meyer, Y., and Grosskopf, B., (2002). Overcoming the winner's curse: An adaptive learning perspective. AoM Conflict Management Division 2002 Mtgs., No. 13496.

Bernoulli, D. (1954). Exposition of a new theory on the measurement of risk. *Econometrica* 22, 23–36 (original work published 1738).

Blount, S., and Bazerman, M. H. (1996). The inconsistent evaluation of comparative payoffs in labor supply and bargaining. *Journal of Economic Behavior and Organizations* 891, 1–14.

Bodenhausen, G. V., Gabriel, S., and Lineberger, M. (2000). Sadness and susceptibility to judgmental bias: The case of anchoring. *Psychological Science* 11(4), 320–323.

Bogle, J. C. (1994). *Bogle on mutual funds.* New York: Irwin.

Boles, T. L., and Messick, D. M. (1990). Accepting unfairness: Temporal influence on choice. In K. Borcherding, O. Larichev, and D. M. Messick (Eds.), *Contemporary issues in decision making,* pp. 375–390. Amsterdam: North Holland.

Brawley, L. R. (1984). Unintentional egocentric biases in attributions. *Journal of Sport Psychology* 6, 264–278.

Brewer, M. B. (1986). Ethnocentrism and its role in intergroup conflict. In S. Worchel and W. G. Austin (Eds.), *Psychology of intergroup relations.* Chicago: Nelson-Hall.

Brewer, M. B., and Kramer, R. M. (1985). The psychology of intergroup attitudes and behaviors. In M. R. Rosenzweig and L. W. Porter (Eds.), *Annual review of psychology* 36, 219–243. Palo Alto, CA: Annual Reviews.

Brief, A. P., Dietz, J., Cohen, R. R., Pugh, S., and Vaslow, J. B. (2000). Just doing business: Modern racism and obedience to authority as explanations for employment discrimination. *Organizational Behavior & Human Decision Processes* 81(1), 72–97.

Brinthaupt, T. M., Moreland, R. L., and Levine, J. M. (1991). Sources of optimism among prospective group members. *Personality and Social Psychology Bulletin* 17, 36–43.

Brodt, S. E. (1990). Cognitive illusions and personnel management decisions. In C. L. Cooper and I. T. Robertson (Eds.), *International Review of Industrial and Organizational Psychology* 5, 229–279. New York: Wiley.

Brown, J. D. (1986). Evaluations of self and others: Self-enhancement biases in social judgments. *Social Cognition* 4, 353–376.

Cain, D. M., Loewenstein, G., and Moore, D. A.(2005). The dirt on coming clean: Perverse effects of disclosing conflicts of interest. *Journal of Legal Studies.*

Caldwell, D. F., and O'Reilly, C. A. (1982). Responses to failures: The effects of choices and responsibility on impression management. *Academy of Management Journal* 25, 121–136.

Camerer, C. F. (2000). Prospect theory in the wild: Evidence from the field. In D. Kahneman and A. Tversky (Eds.), *Choices, values, and frames.* Cambridge, New York, and Melbourne: Cambridge University Press; New York: Russell Sage Foundation.

Camerer, C., Babcock, L., Loewenstein, G., and Thaler, R. (1997). Labor supply of New York City taxi drivers: One day at a time. *Quarterly Journal of Economics* 112, 407–441.

Camerer, C., and Lovallo, D. (1999). Overconfidence and excess entry: An experimental approach. *American Economic Review* 306–318.

Camerer, C. F., Lowenstein, G. F., and Weber, M. (1989). The curse of knowledge in economic settings: An experimental analysis. *Journal of Political Economy* 97, 1232–1254.

Carhart, M. M. (1997). On persistence in mutual fund performance. *Journal of Finance* 52, 57–82.

Carroll, J. S., Bazerman, M. H., and Maury, R. (1988). Negotiator cognitions: A descriptive approach to negotiators' understanding of their opponents. *Organizational Behavior & Human Decision Processes* 41(3), 352–370.

Caruso, E. M., Epley, N., and Bazerman, M. H. (2005a). Leader of the packed: Unpacking, egocentrism, and the costs and benefits of perspective taking in groups. *Manuscript under review.*

Caruso, E. M., Epley, N., and Bazerman, M. H. (2005b). The good, the bad, and the ugly of perspective taking in groups. In E. A. Mannix, M. A. Neale, and A. E. Tenbrunsel (Eds.), *Research on Managing Groups and Teams: Ethics and Groups* 8. New York: Elsevier/JAI, forthcoming.

Chapman, L. J., and Chapman, J. P. (1967). Genesis of popular but erroneous diagnostic observations. *Journal of Abnormal Psychology* 72, 193–204.

Choi, J., Laibson, D., Madrian, B., and Metrick, A. (2003). For better or for worse: Default effects and 401(k) savings behavior. In David Wise, editor, *Perspectives on the Economics of Aging.* Chicago: University of Chicago Press, 397–421.

Chugh, D. (2004). Societal and managerial implications of implicit social cognition: Why milliseconds matter. *Social Justice Research* 17(2).

Chugh, D., Bazerman, M. H., and Banaji, M. R. (2005). Bounded ethicality as a psychological barrier to recognizing conflicts of interest. In D. A. Moore, D. M. Cain, G. Loewenstein, and M. H. Bazerman (Eds.), *Conflicts of Interest: Problems and Solutions from Law, Medicine and Organizational Settings.* London: Cambridge University Press.

Cooper, A., Woo, C., and Dunkelberg, W. (1988). Entrepreneurs' perceived chances for success. *Journal of Business Venturing* 3, 97–108.

Cowherd, D. M., and Levine, D. I. (1992). Product quality and pay equity between lower-level employees and top management: An investigation of distributive justice theory. *Administrative Science Quarterly* 37(2) Special Issue: Process and Outcome: Perspectives on the Distribution of Rewards in Organizations, 302–320.

Cox, A. D., and Summers, J. O. (1987). Heuristics and biases in the intuitive projection of retail sales. *Journal of Marketing Research* 24, 290–297.

Crocker, J. (1982). Biased questions in judgment of covariation studies. *Personality and Social Psychology Bulletin* 8, 214–220.

Damato, K. (1997). Mutual funds quarterly review: Ghosts of dead funds may haunt results. *Wall Street Journal*, R1.

Dasgupta, N. (2004). Implicit ingroup favoritism, outgroup favoritism, and their behavioral manifestations. *Social Justice Research* 17(2), 143–170.

Davis, M. S. (1971). That's interesting! *Philosophy of Social Science*, 309–344.

Dawes, R. M. (1971). A case study of graduate admissions: Applications of three principles of human decision making. *American Psychologist* 26, 180–188.

Dawes, R. M. (1979). The robust beauty of improper linear models in decision-making. *American Psychologist* 34, 571–582.

Dawes, R. M. (1988). *Rational choice in an uncertain world.* New York: Harcourt Brace Jovanovich.

Dawson, E., Gilovich, T., Regan, D. T. (2002). Motivated reasoning and performance on the Wason Selection Task. *Personality & Social Psychology Bulletin* 28(10), 1379–1387.

DeBondt, W. F. M., and Thaler, R. (1985). Does the stock market overreact? *Journal of Finance* 53, 1839–1885.

Depken, C. A. (2000). Wage disparity and team productivity: Evidence from major league baseball. *Economic Letters* 67, 87–92.

Diekmann, K. A. (1997). "Implicit justifications" and self-serving group allocations. *Journal of Organizational Behavior* 18(1), 3–16.

Diekmann, K. A., Samuels, S. M., Ross, L., and Bazerman, M. H. (1997). Self-interest and fairness in problems of resource allocation. *Journal of Personality and Social Psychology* 72, 1061–1074.

Diekmann, K. A., Tenbrunsel, A. E., Shah, P. P., Schroth, H. A., and Bazerman, M. H. (1996). The descriptive and prescriptive use of previous purchase price in negotiation. *Organizational Behavior and Human Decision Processes* 66(2), 179–191.

Einhorn, H. J. (1972). Expert measurement and mechanical combination. *Organizational Behavior and Human Performance* 7, 86–106.

Elster, J. (1979). *Ulysses and the Sirens: Studies in rationality and irrationality.* Cambridge: Cambridge University Press.

Epley, N. (2004). A tale of Tuned Decks? Anchoring as accessibility and anchoring as adjustment. In D. J. Koehler and N. Harvey (Eds.), *Blackwell Handbook of Judgment and Decision Making*. Oxford, England: Blackwell.

Epley, N., and Dunning, D. (2000). Feeling "holier than thou": Are self-serving assessments produced by errors in self or social prediction? *Journal of Personality and Social Psychology* 79, 861–875.

Epley, N., and Gilovich, T. (2001). Putting adjustment back in the anchoring and adjustment heuristic. *Psychological Science* 12, 391–396.

Epley, N., Idson, L., and Mak, D. (2005). Rebate or bonus? The impact of income framing on spending and saving. *Manuscript under review.*

Erev, I., Wallsten, T. S., Budescu, D. V. (1994). Simultaneous over- and underconfidence: The role of error in judgment processes. *Psychological Review* 101(3): 519–527.

Esty, B. (1998). The acquisition of Consolidated Rail Corporation. Harvard Business School Case #9-298-095.

Fischhoff, B. (1975). Hindsight foresight: The effect of outcome knowledge on judgment under uncertainty. *Journal of Experimental Psychology: Human Perception & Performance* 1, 288–299.

Fischhoff, B. (1977). Cognitive liabilities and product liability. *Journal of Products Liability* 1, 207–220.

Fischhoff, B. (1982). Debiasing. In D. Kahneman, P. Slovic, and A. Tversky (Eds.), *Judgment under uncertainty: Heuristics and biases.* Cambridge: Cambridge University Press.

Fischhoff, B., Slovic, P., and Lichtenstein, S. (1977). Knowing with certainty: The appropriateness of extreme confidence. *Journal of Experimental Psychology: Human Perception and Performance* 3, 552–564.

Fisher, R., and Ury, W. (1981). *Getting to Yes.* Boston: Houghton Mifflin.

Fiske, S. T. (2004). Intent and ordinary bias: Unintended thought and social motivation create casual prejudice. *Social Justice Research* 17(2), 117–128.

Forsyth, D. R., and Schlenker, B. R. (1977). Attributional egocentrism following performance of a competitive task. *Journal of Social Psychology* 102, 215–222.

Fox, C. R., and Tversky, A. (1998). A belief-based account of decision under uncertainty. *Management Science* 44(7).

Friedman, A. (1996, October). High-altitude decision making. Paper presented at the Jeffrey Z. Rubin Memorial Conference, Cambridge, Mass.

Friedman, D. (1998). Monty Hall's three doors: Construction and deconstruction of a choice anomaly. *American Economic Review* 88, 933–946.

Galinsky, A. D., and Mussweiler, T. (2001). First offers as anchors: The role of perspective-taking and negotiator focus. *Journal of Personality & Social Psychology* 81(4), 657–669.

Gentner, D., Loewenstein, J., and Thompson, L. (2003). Learning and transfer: A general role for analogical encoding. *Journal of Educational Psychology* 95(2), 393–408.

Gigerenzer, G., Hoffrage, U., and Kleinbolting, H. (1991). Probabilistic mental models: A Brunswikian theory of confidence. *Psychological Review* 98, 506–528.

Gilbert, D. T. (2002). Inferential correction. In T. Gilovich, D. Griffin, and D. Kahneman (Eds.), *Heuristics and Biases: The psychology of intuitive judgment,* 167–184. Cambridge: Cambridge University Press.

Gilbert, D. T., and Wilson, T. D. (2000). Miswanting: Some problems in the forecasting of future affective states. In J. P. Forgas (Ed.), *Feeling and thinking: The role of affect in social cognition.* Studies in emotion and social interaction, second series, 178–197. Cambridge: Cambridge University Press.

Gilovich, T., Vallone, R., and Tversky, A. (1985). The hot hand in basketball: On the misperception of random sequences. *Cognitive Psychology* 17, 295–314.

Gilovich, T., and Medvec, V. H. (1995). The experience of regret: What, when, and why. *Psychological Review* 102(2): 379–395.

Gino, F. (2004). The impact of information on behavior and decision making: Three essays. Unpublished doctoral dissertation, Sant'Anna School of Advanced Studies, Pisa, Italy.

Glassman, J. K., and Hassett, K. A. (1999). *Dow 36,000: The new strategy for profiting from the coming rise in the stock market.* New York: Times Business.

Goetzmann, W. N., and Peles, N. (1997). Cognitive dissonance and mutual fund investors. *Journal of Financial Research* 20, 145–158.

Gore, A. (1992). *Earth in the Balance.* New York: Penguin Books USA.

Gould, C. (2000). A seven-year lesson in investing. *New York Times,* July 9, p. 18.

Grabiner, D. (1996). Frequently asked questions about the 1994 strike. Web site: www.remarque.org/~grabiner/strikefaq.html.

Green, J. (2000). Talk on annuities and retirement planning. Negotiations, Organizations, and Markets seminar, Harvard Business School.

Greenwald, A. G. (1980). The totalitarian ego: Fabrication and revision of personal history. *American Psychologist* 35, 603–618.

Greenwald, A. G., McGhee, D. E., and Schwartz, J. L. K. (1998). Measuring individual differences in implicit cognition: The Implicit Association Test. *Journal of Personality and Social Psychology* 74(6), 1464–1480.

Grosskopf, B., and Bereby-Meyer, Y. (2005). Learning to avoid the winner's curse. Manuscript in preparation, Harvard Business School, Cambridge, MA., Working paper.

Gruenfeld, D., Mannix, E. A., Williams, K. Y., and Neale, M. A. (1996). Group composition and decision making: How member familiarity and information distribution affect process and performance. *Organizational Behavior and Human Decision Processes* 67, 1–15.

Guth, W., Schmittberger, R., and Schwarze, B. (1982). An experimental analysis of ultimatum bargaining. *Journal of Economic Behavior and Organization* 3, 367–388.

Hall, B. J., and Staats, P. T. (2004). Do the numbers get in your way? *Negotiation* 7(10), 4–6.

Hammond, J. S., Keeney, R. L., and Raiffa, H. (1999). *Smart choices.* Boston, MA: Harvard Business School Press.

Hardin, G. (1968). The tragedy of the commons. *Science* 162, 1243–1248.

Harris, S. (1946). *Banting's miracle: The story of the discovery of insulin.* Toronto: J. M. Dent and Sons.

Hastorf, A. H., and Cantril, H. (1954). They say a game: A case study. *Journal of Abnormal and Social Psychology* 49, 129–134.

Heider, F. (1958). *The psychology of interpersonal relations.* New York: Wiley.

Heinrich, J., Boyd, R., Bowles, S., Camerer, C., Fehr, E. Gintis, H., McElreath, R., Alvard, M., Barr, A., Ensminger, J., Hill, K., Gil-White, F., Gurven, M., Patton, J. Q., Smith, N., and Tracer, D. (2001). "Economic Man" in cross-cultural perspective: Behavioral experiments in 15 small-scale societies. Working paper, Santa Fe Institute.

Hershey, J. C., and Schoemaker, P. J. H. (1980). Prospect theory's reflection hypothesis: A critical examination. *Organization Behavior and Human Performance* 3, 395–418.

Ho, T. H., Camerer, C., and Weigelt, K. (1998). Interated dominance and interated best response in experimental 'p-beauty' contests. *American Economic Review* 88, 44–69.

Hoch, S. J. (1988). Who do we know: Predicting the interests and opinions of the American consumer. *Journal of Consumer Research* 15(3), 315–324.

Hsee, C. (1996). The evaluability hypothesis: An explanation for preference reversals between joint and separate evaluations of alternatives. *Organizational Behavior & Human Decision Processes* 67(3): 247–257.

Hsee, C. K. (1998). Less is better: When low-value options are judged more highly than high-value options. *Journal of Behavioral Decision Making* 11, 107–121.

Hsee, C. K, Loewenstein, G. F., Blount, S., and Bazerman, M. H. (1999). Preference reversals between joint and separate evaluation of options: A review and theoretical analysis. *Psychological Bulletin* 125, 576–590.

Hughes, E. J. (1978). The presidency versus Jimmy Carter. *Fortune*, December 4, p. 58.

Idson, L. C., Chugh, D., Bereby-Meyer, Y., Moran, S., Grosskopf, B., and Bazerman, M. H. (2004). Overcoming Focusing Failures in Competitive Environments. *Journal of Behavioral Decision Making*.

Janis, I. L. (1962). Psychological effects of warnings. In G. W. Baker and W. Chapman (Eds.), *Man and society in disaster*. New York: Basic Books.

Jegadeesh, N., and Titman, S. (1993). Returns to buying winners and selling losers: Implications for stock market efficiency. *Journal of Finance* 48, 65–91.

Johansson, P., Hall, L., and Olsson, A. (2004). *From change blindness to choice blindness*. Toward a Science of Consciousness Conference, Tucson, AZ.

Johnson, E. J., and Goldstein, D. (2003). Do defaults save lives? *Science* 302, 1338–1339.

Johnson, E. J., and Tversky, A. (1983). Affect, generalization, and the perception of risk. *Journal of Personality & Social Psychology* 45(1), 20–31.

Jordan, D. J., and Diltz, J. D. (2003). The profitability of day traders. *Financial Analysts Journal* 59(6), 85–94.

Joyce, E. J., and Biddle, G. C. (1981). Anchoring and adjustment in probabilistic inference in auditing. *Journal of Accounting Research* 19, 120–145.

Kagel, J. H., and Levin, D. (1986). The winner's curse and public information in common value auctions. *American Economic Review* 76, 894–920.

Kahneman, D. (2003). A perspective on judgment and choice: Mapping bounded rationality. *American Psychologist* 58, 697–720.

Kahneman, D., and Frederick, S. (2002). Representativeness revisited: Attribute substitution in intuitive judgment. In T. Gilovich, D. Griffin, and D. Kahneman (Eds.), *Heuristics and Biases: The Psychology of Intuitive Judgment*, 49–81. New York: Cambridge University Press.

Kahneman, D., Knetsch, J. L., and Thaler, R. (1986). Fairness as a constraint on profit seeking: Entitlements in the market. *American Economic Review* 76, 728–741.

Kahneman, D., Knetsch, J. L., and Thaler, R. (1990). Experimental tests of the endowment effect and the Coarse theorem. *Journal of Political Economy* 98, 1325–1328.

Kahneman, D., and Lovallo, D. (1993). Timid choices and bold forecasts: A cognitive perspective on risk taking. *Management Science* 39, 17–31.

Kahneman, D., and Miller, D. T. (1986). Norm theory: Comparing reality to its alternatives. *Psychological Review* 93, 136–153.

Kahneman, D., and Ritov, I. (1994). Determinants of stated willingness to pay for public goods: A study in the headline method. *Journal of Risk and Uncertainty* 9, 5–38.

Kahneman, D., Schkade, D., and Sunstein, C. (1998). Shared outrage and erratic awards: The psychology of punitive damages. *Journal of Risk and Uncertainty* 16, 49–86.

Kahneman, D., and Tversky, A. (1972). Subjective probability: A judgment of representativeness. *Cognitive Psychology* 3, 430–454.

Kahneman, D., and Tversky, A. (1973). On the psychology of prediction. *Psychological Review* 80, 237–251.

Kahneman, D., and Tversky, A. (1979). Prospect theory: An analysis of decision under risk. *Econometrica* 47, 263–291.

Kahneman, D., and Tversky, A. (1982). Psychology of preferences. *Scientific American* 246, 161–173.

Keysar, B. (1994). The illusory transparency of intention: Linguistic perspective taking in text. *Cognitive Psychology* 26(2), 165–208.

Kivetz, R., and Simonson, I. (2000). The effect of incomplete information on consumer choice. *Journal of Marketing Research* 37(4), 427–448.

Koriat, A., Lichtenstein, S., Fischhoff, B. (1980). Reasons for confidence. *Journal of Experimental Psychology: Human Learning & Memory* 6(2), 107–118.

Kramer, R. M. (1991). The more the merrier? Social psychological aspects of multiparty negotiations. In M. H. Bazerman, R. J. Lewicki, and B. H. Sheppard (Eds.), *Handbook of negotiation research: Research on negotiation in organizations* 3, 307–332. Greenwich, CT: JAI Press.

Kramer, R. M. (1994). Self-enhancing cognitions and organizational conflict. Working paper.

Kramer, R. M., Newton, E., and Pommerenke, P. L. (1993). Self-enhancement biases and negotiator judgment: Effects of self-esteem and mood. *Organizational Behavior and Human Decision Processes* 56, 113–133.

Kramer, R. M., Shah, P. P., and Woerner, S. L. (1995). Why ultimatums fail: Social identity and moralistic aggression in coercive bargaining. In R. M. Kramer and D. M. Messick (Eds.), *Negotiation as a social process*. Thousand Oaks, CA: Sage.

Kruger, J., and Dunning, D. (1999). Unskilled and unaware of it: How difficulties in recognizing one's own incompetence lead to inflated self-assessments. *Journal of Personality & Social Psychology* 77(6), 1121–1134.

Laibson, D. (1994). Essays in hyperbolic discounting. Unpublished doctoral dissertation, MIT, Cambridge, MA.

Laibson, D. I., Repetto, A., and Tobacman, J. (1998). Self-control and saving for retirement. *Brookings paper on economic activity*, 1, 91–196.

Langer, E. J. (1975). The illusion of control. *Journal of Personality and Social Psychology* 32, 311–328.

Larrick, R. P. (1993). Motivational factors in decision theories: The role of self-protection. *Psychological Bulletin* 113, 440–450.

Larrick, R. P. (2004). Debiasing. In D. J. Koehler and N. Harvey (Eds.), *Blackwell Handbook of Judgment and Decision Making*. Oxford, England: Blackwell.

Larrick, R. P., and Boles, T. L. (1995). Avoiding regret in decisions with feedback: A negotiation example. *Organizational Behavior and Human Decision Processes* 63, 87–97.

Latane, B., and Darley, J. (1969). Bystander "apathy." *American Scientist* 57, 244–268.

Lax, D. A., and Sebenius, J. K. (1986). *The manager as negotiator.* New York: Free Press.

Lax, D. A., and Sebenius, J. K. (2002). Dealcrafting: The substance of three-dimensional negotiations. *Negotiation Journal* 18(1), 5–28.

Lerner, J. S., Goldberg, J. H., and Tetlock, P. E. (1998). Sober second thought: The effects of accountability, anger, and authoritarianism on attributions of responsibility. *Personality & Social Psychology Bulletin* 24(6), 563–574.

Lerner, J. S., and Keltner, D. (2000). Beyond valence: Toward a model of emotion-specific influences on judgment and choice. *Cognition & Emotion* 14 (4, Special Issue: Emotion, cognition, and decision making), 473–493.

Lerner, J. S., Small, D. A., and Loewenstein, G. (2004). Heart strings and purse strings: Carryover effects of emotions on economic transactions. *Psychological Science* 15(5), 337–341.

Lerner, J. S., and Tetlock, P. E. (1999). Accounting for the effects of accountability. *Psychological Bulletin* 125(2), 255–275.

Lewin, K. (1947). Group decision and social change. In T. M. Newcomb and E. L. Hartley (Eds.), *Readings in social psychology.* New York: Holt, Rinehart and Winston.

Lewis, M. (2003). *Moneyball: The art of winning an unfair game.* New York: W. W. Norton.

Lichtenstein, S., and Fischhoff, B. (1980). Training for calibration. *Organizational Behavior and Human Performance* 26, 149–171.

Lichtenstein, S., Fischhoff, B., Phillips, L. D. (1982). Celebration of probabilities: State of the art to 1980. In D. Kahneman, P. Slovic, and A. Tversky (Eds.), *Judgment Under Uncertainty: Heuristics and Biases.* New York: Cambridge University Press.

Lind, E. A., and Tyler, T. R. (1988). *The social psychology of procedural justice.* New York: Plenum.

Loewenstein, G. (1988). Frames of mind in intertemporal choice. *Management Science* 34, 200–214.

Loewenstein, G. (1996). Out of control: Visceral influences on behavior. *Organizational Behavior and Human Decision Processes* 65 (3), 272–292.

Loewenstein, G., and Thaler, R. (1989). Anomalies: Intertemporal choice. *Journal of Economic Perspectives* 3, 181–193.

Loewenstein, G., Thompson, L., and Bazerman, M. H. (1989). Social utility and decision making in interpersonal contexts. *Journal of Personality and Social Psychology* 57, 426–441.

Loewenstein, G., Weber, E., Hsee, C., and Welch, N. (2001). Risk as feelings. *Psychological Bulletin* 127, 267–286.

Loewenstein, J., Thompson, L., and Gentner, D. (1999). Analogical encoding facilitates knowledge transfer in negotiation. *Psychonomic Bulletin & Review* 6(4), 586–597.

Loewenstein, J., Thompson, L., and Gentner, D. (2003). Analogical learning in negotiation teams: Comparing cases promotes learning and transfer. *Academy of Management Learning and Education* 2(2), 119–127.

Lowenthal, D. J. (1996). What voters care about: How electoral context influences issue salience in campaigns. Unpublished doctoral dissertation, Carnegie-Mellon University.

Mack, A. (2003). Inattentional blindness: Looking without seeing. *Current Directions in Psychological Science* 12(5), 180–184.

Mack, A., and Rock, I. (1998). *Inattentional blindness.* Cambridge, MA: Bradford Books.

Madrian, B. C., and Shea, D. F. (2001). The power of suggestion: Inertia in 401(k) participation and savings behavior. *The Quarterly Journal of Economics* 116(4), 1149–1187.

March, J. G., and Simon, H. A. (1958). *Organizations.* New York: Wiley.

Massey, C., and Wu, G. (2001). Detecting regime shifts: A study of over-and under-reaction. Unpublished manuscript, Chicago, IL.

McConnell, A. R., and Leibold, J. M. (2001). Relations among the Implicit Association Test, discriminatory behavior, and explicit measures of racial attitudes. *Journal of Experimental Social Psychology* 37(5), 435–442.

Medvec, V. H., Madey, S. F., and Gilovich, T. (1995). When less is more: Counterfactual thinking and satisfaction among Olympic medalists. *Journal of Personality and Social Psychology* 69, 603–610.

Messick, D. M. (1991). Equality as a decision heuristic. In B. Mellers (Ed.), *Psychological issues in distributive justice.* New York: Cambridge University Press.

Messick, D. M., and Bazerman, M. H. (1996). Ethics for the 21st century: A decision making approach. *Sloan Management Review* 37, 9–22.

Messick, D. M., Bloom, S., Boldizar, J. P., and Samuelson, C. D. (1985). Why we are fairer than others. *Journal of Experimental Social Psychology* 21, 480–500.

Messick, D. M., Moore, D. A., and Bazerman, M. H. (1997). Ultimatum bargaining with a group: Underestimating the importance of the decision rule. *Organizational Behavior & Human Decision Processes* 69(2), 87–101.

Messick, D. M., and Sentis, K. (1983). Fairness, preference, and fairness biases. In D. M. Messick and S. Cook (Eds.), *Equity theory: Psychological and sociological perspectives,* 61–64. New York: Praeger.

Milgram, S. (1963). Behavioral study of obedience. *Journal of Abnormal and Social Psychology* 67, 371–378.

Miller, D. T., and Ross, M. (1975). Self-serving biases in attribution of causality: Fact or fiction? *Psychological Bulletin* 82, 213–225.

Mitroff, S. R., Simons, D. J., and Franconeri, S. L. (2002). The Siren Song of implicit change detection. *Journal of Experimental Psychology: Human Perception and Performance* 28, 798–815.

Mokdad, A. H., Marks, J. S., Stroup, D. F., and Gerberding, J. L. (2004). Actual causes of death in the United States, 2000. *Journal of the American Medical Association* 291, 1239–1245.

Moore, C. M., and Egeth, H. (1997). Perception without attention: Evidence of grouping under conditions of inattention. *Journal of Experimental Psychology: Human Perception & Performance* 23(2), 339–352.

Moore, D. (2000). The unexpected benefits of negotiating under time pressure. Unpublished doctoral dissertation, Northwestern University, Evanston, IL.

Moore, D., Cain, D., Loewenstein, G., and Bazerman, M. H. (2005). *Conflicts of interest: Problems and solutions from law, medicine, and organizational settings.* London: Cambridge University Press.

Moore, D. A., and Kim, T. G. (2003). Myopic social prediction and the solo comparison effect. *Journal of Personality & Social Psychology* 85(6), 1121–1135.

Moore, D. A., Kurtzberg, T. R., Fox, C. R., and Bazerman, M. H. (1999). Positive illusions and biases of prediction in mutual fund investment decisions. *Organizational Behavior and Human Decision Processes* 79, 95–114.

Moore, D. A., Loewenstein, G., Tanlu, L., and Bazerman, M. H. (2004). Psychological dimensions of holding conflicting roles: Is it possible to play advocate and judge at the same time? Tepper Working Paper 2004-E40, Pittsburgh, PA.

Moore, D. A., and Small, D. A. (2004). Error and bias in comparative social judgment: On being both better and worse than we think we are. Tepper working paper 2004-E1, Pittsburgh, PA.

Moran, S., Bereby-Meyer, Y., and Bazerman, M. H. (2005). Getting more out of analogical reasoning in negotiations. HBS working paper.

Murnighan, J., and Pillutla, M. M. (1995). Fairness versus self-interest: Asymmetric moral imperatives in ultimatum bargaining. In R. M. Kramer and D. M. Messick (Eds.), *Negotiation as a social process.* Thousand Oaks, CA: Sage.

Murnighan, K. K., Cantelon, D. A., and Elyashiv, T. (2004). In J. A. Wagner III, J. M. Bartunek, and K. D. Elsbach (Eds.), *Advances in qualitative organizational research,* 3. New York: Elsevier/JAI.

Mussweiler, T., and Strack, F. (1999). Hypothesis-consistent testing and semantic priming in the anchoring paradigm. A selective accessibility model. *Journal of Experimental Social Psychology* 35, 136–164.

Mussweiler, T., and Strack, F. (2000a). The use and category and exemplar knowledge in the solution of anchoring tasks. *Journal of Personality and Social Psychology* 78, 1038–1052.

Mussweiler, T., and Strack, F. (2000b). The semantics of anchoring. *Organizational Behavior and Human Decision Processes* 86, 234–255.

Nalebuff, B. (1987). Puzzles: Choose a Curtain, Duel-ity, Two Point Conversions, and more. *Economic Perspectives* 1(1), 157–163.

Nalebuff, S., and Ayres, I. (2003). *Why not? How to use everyday ingenuity to solve problems big and small.* Boston: Harvard Business School Press.

Neale, M. A. (1984). The effects of negotiation and arbitration cost salience on bargainer behavior: The role of the arbitrator and constituency on negotiator judgment. *Organizational Behavior & Human Decision Processes* 34(1), 97–111.

Neale, M. A., and Bazerman, M. H. (1985). Perspectives for understanding negotiation: Viewing negotiation as a judgmental process. *Journal of Conflict Resolution* 29, 33–55.

Neale, M. A., and Northcraft, G. B. (1989). Experience, expertise, and decision bias in negotiation: The role of strategic conceptualization. In B. Sheppard, M. Bazerman, and R. Lewicki (Eds.), *Research on negotiations in organizations* 2. Greenwich, CT.: JAI Press.

Neisser, U. (1979). The concept of intelligence. *Intelligence* 3(3), 217–227.

New York Stock Exchange (2000). www.nyse.com.

Nisbett, R. E., and Ross, L. (1980). *Human inference: Strategies and shortcomings of social judgment.* Englewood Cliffs, NJ: Prentice Hall.

Northcraft, G. B., and Neale, M. A. (1987). Experts, amateurs and real estate: An anchoring–and–adjustment perspective on property pricing decisions. *Organizational Behavior and Human Decision Processes* 39, 84–97.

Northcraft, G. B., and Neale, M. A. (1993). Negotiating successful research collaboration. In J. K. Murnighan (Ed.), *Social psychology in organizations: Advances in theory and research.* Englewood Cliffs, NJ: Prentice Hall.

Nosek, B. A., Banaji, M., and Greenwald, A. G. (2002). Harvesting implicit group attitudes and beliefs from a demonstration Web site. *Group Dynamics: Theory, Research, & Practice* 6(1), 101–115.

Ochs, J., and Roth, A. E. (1989). An experimental study of sequential bargaining. *American Economic Review* 79, 335–385.

O'Connor, K. M., De Dreu, C. K. W., Schroth, H., Barry, B., Lituchy, T. R., and Bazerman, M. H. (2002). What we want to do versus what we think we should do: An empirical investigation of intrapersonal conflict. *Journal of Behavioral Decision Making* 15(5), 403–418.

Odean, T. (1998). Are investors reluctant to realize their losses? *Journal of Finance* 53, 1775–1798.

Odean, T. (1999). Do investors trade too much? *American Economic Review* 89, 1279–1298.

O'Donoghue, T., and Rabin, M. (1999). Doing it now or later. *American Economic Review* 89(1), 103–124.

Oesch, John M., and Galinsky, Adam D., First offers in negotiations: Determinants and effects. 16th Annual IACM Conference, Melbourne, Australia.

Park, J., and Banaji, M. R. (2000). Mood and heuristics: The influence of happy and sad states on sensitivity and bias in stereotyping. *Journal of Personality & Social Psychology* 78(6), 1005–1023.

Pollan, S. M., and Levine, M. (1997). *Die broke.* New York: Harper Business.

Pruitt, D. G., and Rubin, J. (1985). *Social conflict: Escalation, impasse, and resolution.* Reading, MA: Addison-Wesley.

Rabin, M., and Thaler, R. H. (2001). Anomalies: Risk aversion. *Journal of Economic Perspectives* 15(1), 219–232.

Raiffa, H. (1968). Decision analysis: Introductory lectures on choices under uncertainty. Reading, MA: Addison Wesley; reissued in 1997, New York: McGraw-Hill.

Raiffa, H. (1982). *The Art and Science of Negotiation.* Cambridge, MA: Belknap.

Raiffa, H. (1984). Invited address to the Judgment and Decision Making Society (November), San Antonio.

Raiffa, H. (1985). Post-settlement settlements. *Negotiation Journal* 1, 9–12.

Raiffa, H. (2001). *Collaborative decision making.* Cambridge, MA: Belknap.

Ritov, I. (1996). Anchoring in simulated competitive market negotiation. *Organizational Behavior and Human Decision Processes* 67, 16–25.

Ritov, I., and Baron, J. (1990). Reluctance to vaccinate: Omission bias and ambiguity. *Journal of Behavioral Decision Making* 3(4), 263–277.

Robins, R. W., and Beer, J. S. (2001). Positive illusions about the self: Short-term benefits and long-term costs. *Journal of Personality & Social Psychology* 20(2), 340–352.

Ross, J., and Staw, B. M. (1986). Expo 86: An escalation prototype. *Administrative Science Quarterly* 31, 274–297.

Ross, L., and Stillinger, C. (1991). Barriers to conflict resolution. *Negotiation Journal* 7(4), 389–404.

Ross, M., and Sicoly, F. (1979). Egocentric biases in availability and attribution. *Journal of Personality and Social Psychology* 37, 332–337.

Roth, A. E. (1991). An economic approach to the study of bargaining. In M. H. Bazerman, R. J. Lewicki, and B. H. Sheppard (Eds.), *Handbook of negotiation research: Research in negotiation in organizations,* 3. Greenwich, CT: JAI Press.

Rozin, P., Markwith, M., and Ross, B. (1990). The sympathetic magical law of similarity, nominal realism and neglect of negatives in response to negative labels. *Psychological Science* 1, 383–384.

Rudman, L. A., and Borgida, E. (1995). The afterglow of construct accessibility: The behavioral consequences of priming men to view women as sexual objects. *Journal of Experimental Social Psychology* 31(6), 493–517.

Rudman, L. A., and Glick, P. (2001). Prescriptive gender stereotypes and backlash toward agentic women. *Journal of Social Issues* 57(4), 743–762.

Salovey, P., and Rodin, J. (1984). Some antecedents and consequences of social comparison jealousy. *Journal of Personality and Social Psychology* 47, 780–792.

Samuelson, P. A. (1963). Risk and uncertainty: A fallacy of large numbers. *Scientia* 98, 108–113.

Samuelson, W. F., and Bazerman, M. H. (1985). The winner's curse in bilateral negotiations. In V. Smith (Ed.), *Research in Experimental Economics*, 3. Greenwich, CT: JAI Press.

Samuelson, W., and Zeckhauser, R. (1988). Status quo bias in decision making. *Journal of Risk and Uncertainty* 1, 7–59.

Sanfey, A. G., Rilling, J. K., Aronson, J. A., Nystrom, L. E., and Cohen, J. D. (2003). The neural basis of economic decision-making in the ultimatum game. *Science* 300, 1755–1758.

Schelling, T. C. (1984). *Choice and consequence.* Cambridge, MA: Harvard University Press.

Schkade, D. A., and Kahneman, D. (1998). Does living in California make people happy? A focusing illusion in judgments of life satisfaction. *Psychological Science* 9(5), 340–346.

Schoemaker, P. J. H., and Kunreuther, H. (1979). An experimental study of insurance decisions. *Journal of Risk and Insurance* 46, 603–618.

Schoorman, F. D. (1988). Escalation bias in performance appraisals: An unintended consequence of supervisor participation in hiring decisions. *Journal of Applied Psychology* 7(5), 58–62.

Sebenius, J. K., and Wheeler, M. (1994). Let the game continue. *New York Times,* October 30, sec. 3, 9.

Sebenius, J. K. (2000). *Dealmaking essentials: Creating and claiming value for the long term.* HBS Dealmaking Course Note Series: 800–443.

Seligman, M. E. P. (1991). *Learned optimism.* New York: Knopf.

Selvin, S. (1975). [Letter to the editor]. *American Statistician* 29, 67.

Shafir, E., and Thaler, R. (1998). Buy now, consume later, spend never: Mental accounting through time. Manuscript, The University of Chicago.

Sharpe, W. F. (1991). The arithmetic of active management. *Financial Analysts Journal* 47, 7–9.

Shefrin, H. (2000). *Beyond greed and fear.* Boston: Harvard Business School Press.

Shefrin, H., and Statman, M. (1985). The disposition to sell winners too early and ride losers too long: Theory and evidence. *Journal of Finance* 40, 777–790.

Shefrin, H., and Thaler, R. H. (1988). The behavioral life-cycle hypothesis. *Economic Inquiry* 26, 609–643.

Shepard, R. (1990). *Mind sight: Original visual illusions, ambiguities, and other anomalies.* New York: W. H. Freeman.

Shleifer, A. (2000). *Inefficient markets.* New York: Oxford University Press.

Shubik, M. (1971). The dollar auction game: A paradox in noncooperative behavior and escalation. *Journal of Conflict Resolution* 15, 109–111.

Simon, H. A. (1957). *Models of man.* New York: Wiley.

Simons, D. J. (2000). Current approaches to change blindness. *Visual Cognition* 7(1–3), 1–15.

Simons, D. J., and Chabris, C. F. (1999). Gorillas in our midst: Sustained inattentional blindness for dynamic events. *Perception* 28(9), 1059–1074.

Simons, D. J., Chabris, C. F., Schnur, T., and Levin, D. T. (2002). Evidence for preserved representations in change blindness. *Consciousness & Cognition: An International Journal* 11(1), 78–97.

Simons, D. J., and Levin, D. (2003). What makes change blindness interesting? In D. E. Irwin and B. H. Ross (Eds.), *The psychology of learning and motivation.* San Diego, CA: Adcademic Press.

Slovic, P., Finucane, M., Peters, E., and MacGregor, D. G. (2002). The affect heuristic. In T. Gilovich, D. Griffin, and D. Kahneman (Eds.), *Heuristics and biases: The psychology of intuitive judgment.* Cambridge: Cambridge University Press, 397–420.

Slovic, P., and Fischhoff, B. (1977). On the psychology of experimental surprises. *Journal of Experimental Psychology: Human Perception and Performance* 3, 544–551.

Slovic, P., and Lichtenstein, S. (1971). Comparison of Bayesian and regression approaches in the study of information processing in judgment. *Organizational Behavior and Human Performance* 6, 649–744.

Slovic, P., Lichtenstein, S., and Fischhoff, B. (1982). Characterizing perceived risk.. In R. W. Kataes and C. Hohenemser (Eds.), *Technological hazard management.* Cambridge, MA: Oelgesschlager, Gunn and Hain.

Slovic, P., and McPhillamy, D. J. (1974), Dimensional commensurability and cue utilization in comparative judgment. *Organizational Behavior and Human Performance* 11, 172–194.

Sniezek, J. A., and Henry, R. A. (1989). Accuracy and confidences in group judgment. *Organizational Behavior and Human Decision Processes* 4(3), 1–28.

Soll, J. B., and Klayman, J. (2004). Overconfidence in Interval Estimates. *Journal of Experimental Psychology: Learning, Memory, and Cognition* 30, 299–314.

Sorenson, T. C. (1965). *Kennedy.* New York: Harper and Row.

Spranca, M., Minsk, E., and Baron, J. (1991). Omission and commission in judgment and choice. *Journal of Experimental Social Psychology* 27, 76–105.

Stanovich, K. E., and West, R. F. (2000). Individual differences in reasoning: Implications for the rationality debate. *Behavioral and Brain Sciences* 23, 645–665.

Stasser, G. (1988). Computer simulation as a research tool: The DISCUSS model of group decision making. *Journal of Experimental Social Psychology* 24, 393–422.

Stasser, G., and Stewart, D. (1992). Discovery of hidden profiles by decision-making groups: Solving a problem versus making a judgment. *Journal of Personality & Social Psychology* 63(3), 426–434.

Stasser, G., and Titus, W. (1985). Pooling of unshared information in group decision making: Biased information sampling during discussion. *Journal of Personality & Social Psychology* 48, 1467–1478.

Stasser, G., Vaughn, S. I., and Stewart, D. D. (2000). Pooling unshared information: The benefits of knowing how access to information is distributed among group members. *Organizational Behavior & Human Decision Processes* 82(1), 102–116.

State of Jimmy Carter, The. (1979). *Time.* February 5, 1979, 11.

Staw, B. M. (1976). Knee-deep in the Big Muddy: A study of escalating commitment to a chosen course of action. *Organizational Behavior & Human Decision Processes* 16(1), 27–44.

Staw, B. M. (1980). Rationality and justification in organizational life. In B. M. Staw and L. L. Cummings (Eds.), *Research in organizational behavior,* 2. Greenwich, CT: JAI Press.

Staw, B. M. (1981). The escalation of commitment to a course of action. *Academy of Management Review* 6, 577–587.

Staw, B. M., and Hoang, H. (1995). Sunk costs in the NBA: Why draft order affects playing time and survival in professional basketball. *Administrative Science Quarterly* 40, 474–493.

Staw, B. M., and Ross, J. (1978). Commitment to a policy decision: A multi-theoretical perspective. *Administrative Science Quarterly* 23, 40–64.

Staw, B. M., and Ross, J. (1980). Commitment in an experimenting society: An experiment on the attribution of leadership from administrative scenarios. *Journal of Applied Psychology* 65, 249–260.

Staw, B. M., and Ross, J. (1987). Behavior in escalation situations: Antecedents, prototypes, and solutions. *Research in Organizational Behavior* 9.

Stigler, G., and Becker, G. (1977). De gustibus non est disputandum. *American Economic Review* 67, 76–90.

Stillinger, C., Epelbaum, M., Keltner, D., and Ross, L. (1990). The reactive devaluation barrier to conflict resolution. Unpublished manuscript, Stanford University.

Strotz, R. H. (1956). Myopia and inconsistency in dynamic utility maximization. *Review of Economic Studies* 23, 165–180.

Sunstein, C. R. (2002). Toward behavioral law and economics. In R. Gowda and J. C. Fox (Eds.), *Judgments, decisions, and public policy.* New York: Cambridge University Press.

Sutton, R., and Kramer, R. M. (1990). Transforming failure into success: Impression management, the Reagan Administration, and the Iceland Arms Control Talks. In R. L. Zahn and M. N. Zald (Eds.), *Organizations and nation-states: New perspectives on conflict and co-operation.* San Francisco: Jossey-Bass.

Taylor, S. E. (1989). *Positive illusions.* New York: Basic Books.

Taylor, S. E., and Brown, J. (1988). Illusion and well-being: A social psychological perspective on mental health. *Psychological Bulletin* 103, 193–210.

Taylor, S. E., and Brown, J. D. (1994). Positive illusions and well-being revisited: Separating fact from fiction. *American Psychologist* 49(11), 972–973.

Teger, A. I. (1980). *Too much invested to quit: The psychology of the escalation of conflict.* New York: Pergamon Press.

Tenbrunsel, A. E. (1995). Justifying unethical behavior: The role of expectations of others' behavior and uncertainty. Unpublished doctoral dissertation, Northwestern University.

Tenbrunsel, A. E., and Bazerman, M. H. (1995). Moms.com negotiation simulation. Dispute Resolution Research Center, Northwestern University.

Tenbrunsel, A. E., and Messick, D. M., Ethical fading: (2004). The role of self deception in unethical behavior. *Social Justice Research* 17(2), 223–236.

Thaler, R. (1980). Toward a positive theory of consumer choice. *Journal of Economic Behavior and Organization* 1, 39–80.

Thaler, R. (1985). Using mental accounting in a theory of purchasing behavior. *Marketing Science* 4, 12–13.

Thaler, R. (1999). Mental accounting matters. *Journal of Behavioral Decision Making* 12, 183–206.

Thaler, R. (2000). From homo economicus to homo sapiens. *Journal of Economic Perspectives*, 14, 133–141.

Thaler, R. (2004). Unrestricted teaching files, faculty Web site at University of Chicago School of Business: http://gsb.uchicago.edu/ fac/richard.thaler/.

Thaler, R. H., and Benartzi, S. (2001). Save more tomorrow: Using behavioral economics to increase employee saving.

Thaler, R., and DeBondt, W. F. M. (1992). A mean reverting walk down Wall Street. In R. Thaler (Ed.), *The winner's curse: Paradoxes and anomalies of economic life.* New York: Free Press.

Thaler, R., and Sunstein, C. (2003). Who's on first? *The New Republic,* Sept. 9, 27.

Thaler, R., and Ziemba, W. (1988). Anomalies: Parimutuel betting markets: Racetracks and lotteries. *Journal of Economic Perspectives* 2(2), 161–174.

Thompson, L. (2001). *The mind and the heart of the negotiator.* Upper Saddle River, NJ: Prentice Hall.

Thompson, L., Gentner, D., and Loewenstein, J. (2000). Analogical training more powerful than individual case training. *Organizational Behavior and Human Decision Processes,* 82, 60–75.

Thompson, L., and Loewenstein, G. (1992). Egocentric interpretations of fairness and negotiation. *Organization Behavior and Human Decision Processes* 51, 176–197.

Tor, A., and Bazerman, M. H. (2003). Focusing failures in competitive environments: Explaining decision errors in the Monty Hall game, the acquiring a company problem, and multiparty ultimatums. *Journal of Behavioral Decision Making* 16(5), 353–374.

Tritsch, S. (1998). Bull marketing. [On-line]. Available at www.chicagomag.com/ text/features/beards/beards.ttm. *Chicago Magazine,* March 1998.

Tversky, A., and Kahneman, D. (1971). The belief in the "law of numbers." *Psychological Bulletin* 76, 105–110.

Tversky, A., and Kahneman, D. (1973). Availability: A heuristic for judging frequency and probability. *Cognitive Psychology* 5, 207–232.

Tversky, A., and Kahneman, D. (1974). Judgment under uncertainty: Heuristics and biases. *Science* 185, 1124–1131.

Tversky, A., and Kahneman, D. (1981). The framing of decisions and the psychology of choice. *Science* 211, 453–463.

Tversky, A., and Kahneman, D. (1983). Extensional versus intuitive reasoning: The conjunction fallacy in probability judgment. *Psychological Review* 90, 293–315.

Tversky, A., and Kahneman, D. (1986). Rational choice and the framing of decisions. *Journal of Business* 59, 251–294.

Tversky A., and Koehler D. J. (1994). Support theory: a nonextensional representation of subjective probability. *Psychological Review,* 101, 547–67.

Tyler, T., and Hastie, R. (1991). The social consequences of cognitive illusions. In M. H. Bazerman, R. J. Lewicki, and B. H. Sheppard (Eds.), *Research in negotiation in organizations* 3. Greenwich, CT.: JAI Press.

Valley, K. L., Moag, J. S., and Bazerman, M. H. (1998). A matter of trust: Effects of communication on the efficiency and distribution of outcomes. *Journal of Economic Behavior and Organization* 35.

Vaughn, D. (1996). *The Challenger launch decision: Risky technology, culture, and deviance at NASA.* Chicago: University of Chicago.

vos Savant, M. (1990a). Ask Marilyn. *Parade Magazine.* September 9, 1990. New York.

vos Savant, M. (1990b). Ask Marilyn. *Parade Magazine.* December 2, 1990. New York.

vos Savant, M. (1991). Ask Marilyn. *Parade Magazine.* February 17, 1991. New York.

Wade-Benzoni, K. A., Tenbrunsel, A. E., and Bazerman, M. H. (1996). Egocentric interpretations of fairness in asymmetric environmental social dilemmas: Explaining harvesting behavior and the role of communication. *Organizational Behavior and Human Decision Processes* 67(2), 111–126.

Wade-Benzoni, K. A., Thompson, L., and Bazerman, M. H. (2005). The malleability of environmentalism.

Wason, P. (1960). On the failure to eliminate hypotheses in a conceptual task. *Quarterly Journal of Experimental Psychology A* 12, 129–140; Taylor & Francis/Psychology Press, England.

Wegner, D. M. (1986). *Transactive Memory: A Contemporary Analysis of the Group Mind.* In B. Mullen and G. R. Goethals (Eds.), *Theories of group behavior,* 185–208. New York: Springer-Verlag.

Wegner, D. M. (2002). *The illusion of conscious will.* Cambridge, MA: MIT Press.

Wilson, M. G., Northcraft, G. B., and Neale, M. A. (1989). Information competition and vividness effects in on-line judgments. *Organizational Behavior & Human Decision Processes* 44(1), 132–139.

Wilson, T. D., Wheatley, T., Meyers, J. M., Gilbert, D. T., and Axsom, D. (2000). Focalism: A source of durability bias in affective forecasting. *Journal of Personality & Social Psychology* 78(5), 821–836.

Wohl, M. J. A., and Enzle, M. E. (2002). The deployment of personal luck: Sympathetic magic and illusory control in games of pure chance. *Personality and Social Psychology Bulletin* 28(10), 1388–1397.

Yates, J. F., and Carlson, B. W. (1986). Conjunction errors: Evidence for multiple judgment procedures, including "signed summation." *Organizational Behavior and Human Decision Processes* 37, 230–253.

Zander, A. (1971). *Motives and goals in groups.* New York: Academic Press.

Zweig, J. (2000). Mutual competition. *Money Magazine.* Available at www.money.com/money/depts/investing/fundamentalist/archive/0008/html. Accessed August 1, 2000.

Index

Note: Page numbers followed by f indicate figures; those followed by t indicate tables; and those followed by n indicate notes.